KNARESBOROUGH

THROUGH TIME

Paul Chrystal & Mark Sunderland

AMBERLEY PUBLISHING

Acknowledgements

This book was only made possible through the generosity of the following people and organisations. Their pride in and enthusiasm for Knaresborough is an example to anyone anywhere who wants to preserve their local heritage:
Barbara Asquith; Maurice Bardon, Lavender Rooms; Andy Brown; F. Brown, Furnishers; Nancy Buckle; Janice Chatten; Courthouse Museum; The Crown Hotel, Knaresborough; Sarah Domstead; Dropping Well Inn; David Druett; Gallon House Hotel; Maggie Gell, *Knaresborough Post*; Gerald Hardwick, Harrogate Photographic Society; Ian Hayman; Doris Hayton; Imogene Sky Higham; Rory Hoy; Wendy Kent, Knaresborough Library; Doris Kirkhope; Knaresborough Civic Society; Knaresborough Fire Service; Knaresborough Lions; Knaresborough Town AFC; Marigold Café and Boating; Val Maxwell, Knaresborough Town Council; Mollie Midgley; Bill Midgley; Mark Oglesby, Goldsborough Hall; The Old Royal Oak; Dr Conrad Plowman; Adrian Sayers, Mother Shipton's Cave; Simon Stockdale, St Mary's Catholic Primary School; Carl Sugden, King James's School; Lisa Taylor; Viv Thornes, Chapel of Our Lady of the Crag; Jackie Walton; The Ordnance Survey for kind permission to reproduce the map on p. 74.

This book is dedicated to Dr Arnold Kellett

Royalties from sales of this book are being donated to King James's School Knaresborough to fund an annual prize in Dr Kellett's name.

More of Mark Sunderland's work can be found at www.marksunderland.com
For more books on Knaresborough and Yorkshire go to www.knaresboroughbookshop.com

First published 2010

Amberley Publishing Plc
Cirencester Road, Chalford,
Stroud, Gloucestershire, GL6 8PE

www.amberley-books.com

ISBN 978 1 84868 854 4

British Library Cataloguing in Publication Data.

A catalogue record for this book is available from the British Library.

Typeset in 9.5pt on 12pt Celeste.
Typesetting by Amberley Publishing.
Printed in the UK.

Introduction

Knaresborough is one of those English towns fortunate to have seen more than its fair share of history. It can also boast an impressive number of characters who have left their mark here down the years. Situated as it is at the top of a deep gorge above the River Nidd, it has some breathtaking scenery and elegant architecture which, despite the best efforts of successive planners, endures today and provides locals and visitors alike with one of England's finest townscapes and some truly spectacular scenery.

The aim of this book is not just to show off Knaresborough's rich heritage through a series of old pictures but to demonstrate how that heritage lives on today, how it has changed or how it has disappeared. It does this by juxtaposing contemporary photographs with the older ones so that each page gives a fascinating 'then and now' picture of Knaresborough and its people.

Historically speaking we start with the imposing castle built by Henry I in 1130 and developed by King John in 1205; its story takes in the refuge it provided for Hugh de Morville and the other murderers of Thomas Becket, its destruction by Oliver Cromwell and the 800th anniversary celebrations in 2010 of the very first giving of Maundy money by King John. Thanks largely to research undertaken by Arnold Kellett, we now know this to have taken place in Knaresborough in the castle grounds.

The world famous Chapel of Our Lady of the Crag and the magical Dropping Well, the second of two magnificent railway viaducts (the first fell down), the zoo and the Oldest Chemist Shop in Britain in the medieval market place are all included here. Mother Shipton – soothsayer and witch – Eugene Aram – schoolteacher, fraudster and murderer – and Blind Jack – musician, smuggler and road builder extraordinaire – populate the book along with the ordinary people of the town as they go about their local trade and industry through the years. Then, as now, this would take place largely in the bustling ancient market place and the streets leading off it, in the High Street or

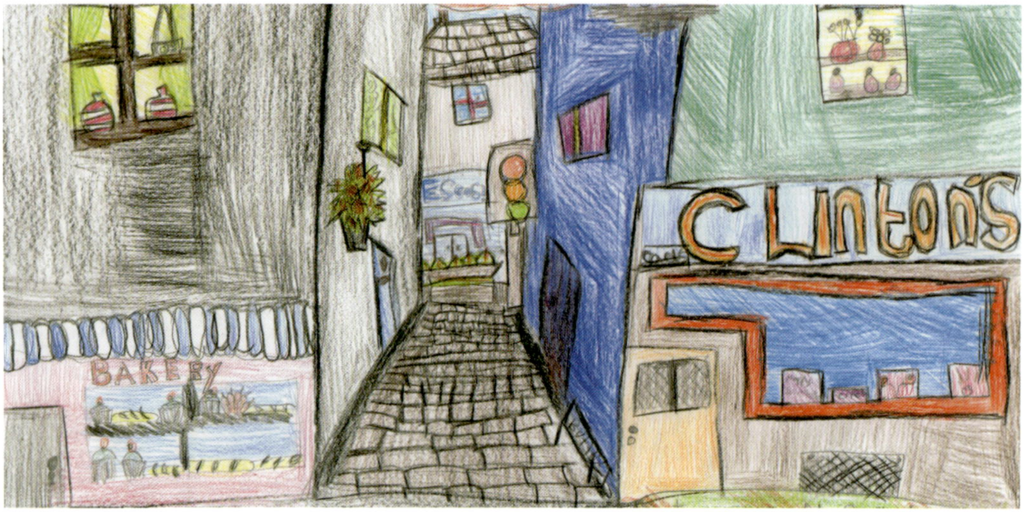

The drawing above is by Imogene Sky Higham, aged 10½ a pupil at St Mary's Catholic Primary School, Knaresborough; it was her entry in the Knaresborough Bookshop World Book Day 2010 competition and shows the view from Market Place looking down Butter Lane to the High Street. Who needs cameras!

on the banks of the Nidd. Football teams and bands still survive today with centuries of tradition and history between them. Schools, pubs and the various places of worship – the bedrock of any town – are all shown in their past and present glory.

In keeping with a town so steeped in history, the Knaresborough calendar is full of events and anniversaries. Apart from the Maundy celebrations in 2010 the annual Festival of Entertainment and Visual Arts (*feva*), the celebrated Great Bed Race, Mediaeval Day, the Edwardian Christmas Market and the River Nidd New Year duck race are all depicted here as modern equivalents of the annual Tradesman's Processions and spectacular Water Carnivals of yesteryear.

So, a book to be dipped into or read straight through as a glimpse of English history through a truly historical town from the early middle ages to the early twenty-first century. It will interest, entertain and inform local resident and visitor alike and indeed anyone who has moved away from the town and needs a nostalgic reminder of what they remember and how far it has changed. If it inspires the reader to pursue Knaresborough's local history further then it will have more than served its purpose.

The modern photography is by Mark Sunderland; he has done a sterling job to show the 'now' – despite the ravages of time, relentless traffic, rampant foliage and so-called street furniture. The book is dedicated to Dr Arnold Kellett who has done more than anyone else to illuminate the history of Knaresborough and make it accessible to a wide audience. He and the people acknowledged above, who helped make the book possible by loaning photographs and postcards and giving information on the 'then', are the true heroes of this book.

Paul Chrystal
May 2010

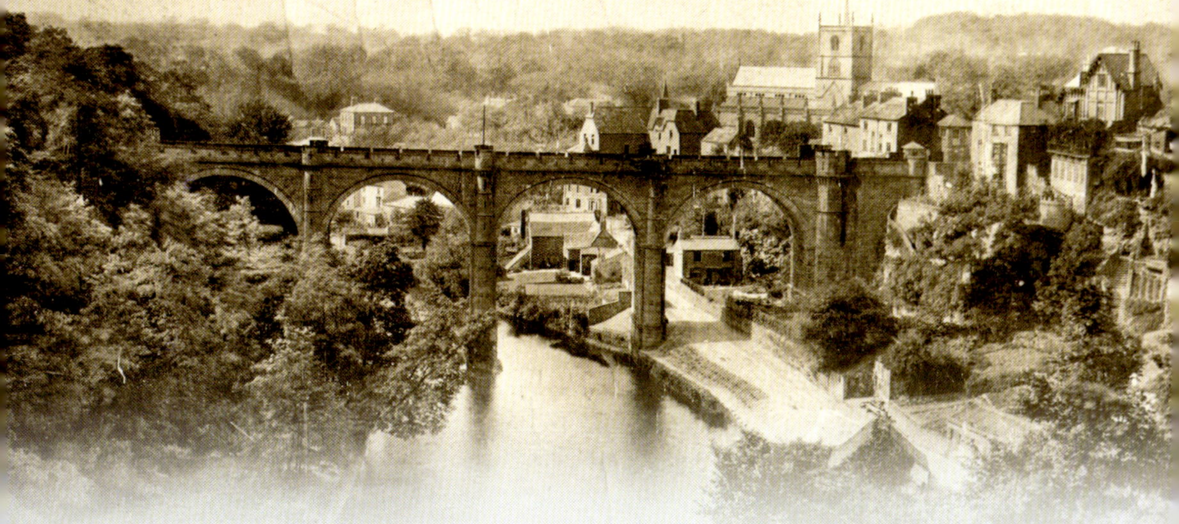

CHAPTER 1

Knaresborough's Tourism and Leisure

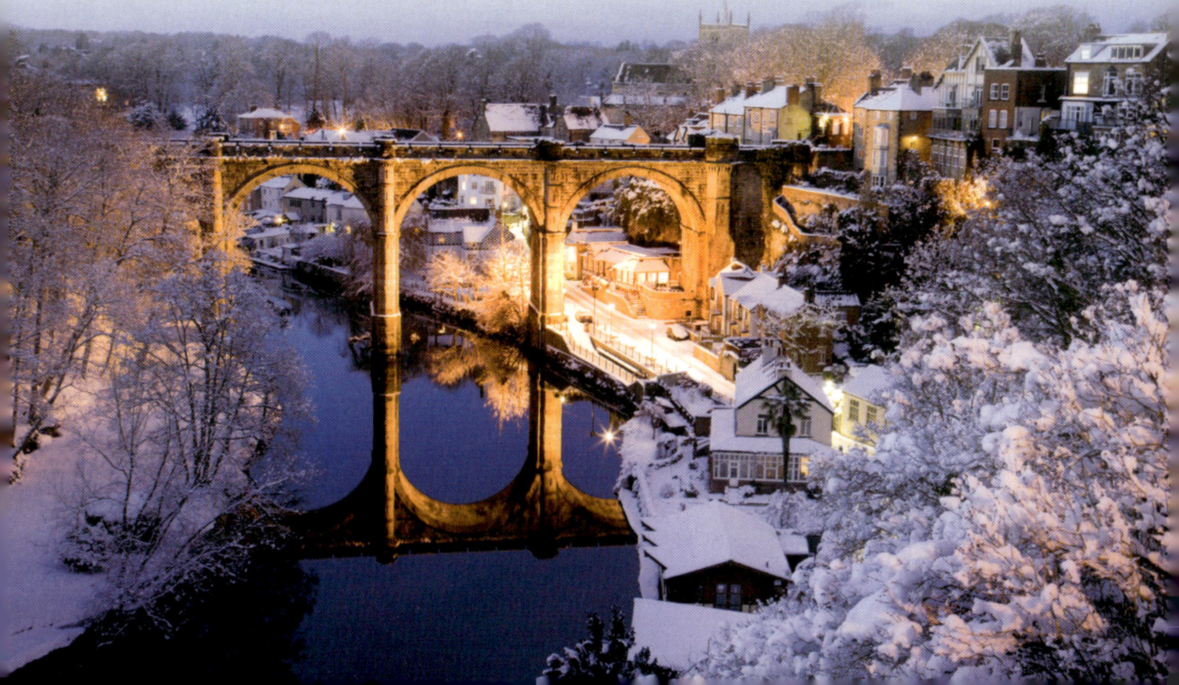

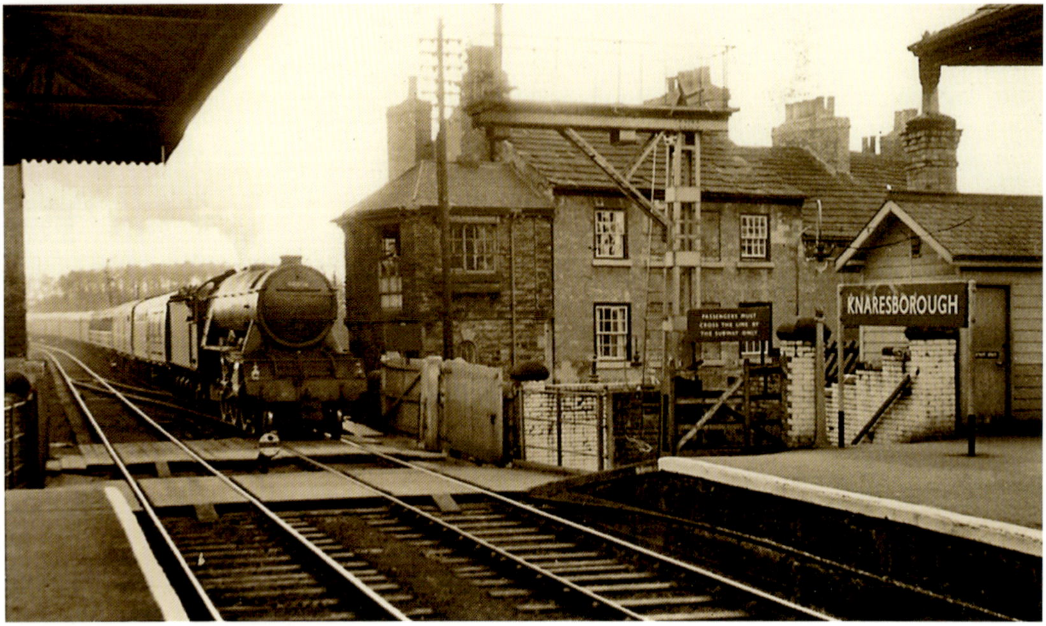

Knaresborough Railway Station

Visitors to Knaresborough have been arriving at the town's Grade II listed station since its opening in 1848 on the Harrogate line 17 miles west of York. The signal box is very unusual in that it was built as an annex onto an existing row of terraced houses at 53 Kirkgate. You can't help feeling that the twenty-first century train here lacks the passion and drama of the steam train as it passes through in the early 1960s.

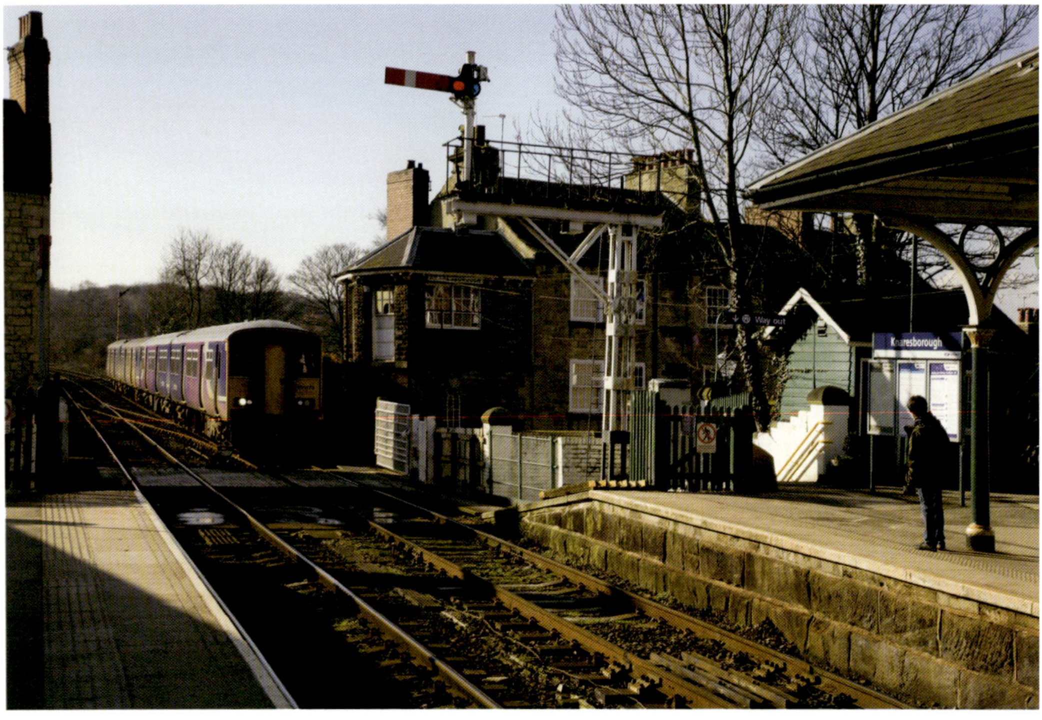

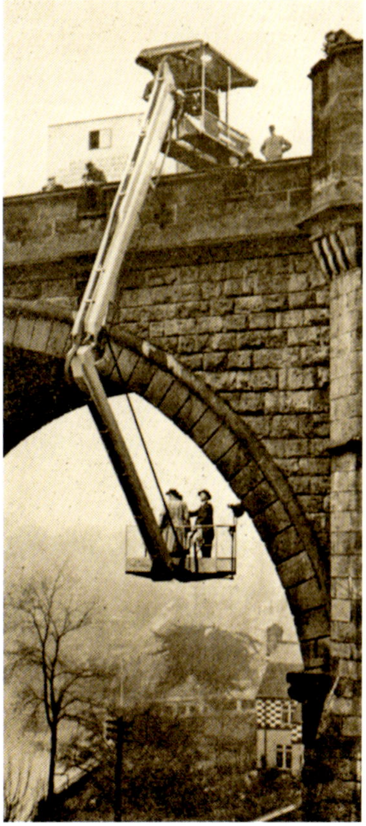

The Viaduct and the 'Gozunda'

To the west of the station is the 300 feet, four span (each 56' 9" wide) viaduct designed by Thomas Grainger Engineering and built by a 270 strong workforce led by George Wilson, railway contractor. It carries the line over the River Nidd 78 feet below. Disaster struck when, nearly complete, it collapsed on March 11 1848. It took three and a half years to rebuild and eventually opened in 1851 at a cost of £9,803. The older picture shows a British Railways inspection taking place in 1960 using the 'Gozunda' (hydraulically-operated rail-mounted viaduct inspection unit to you and me). The newer photograph gives an idea of how the viaduct must have looked to the intrepid inspectors.

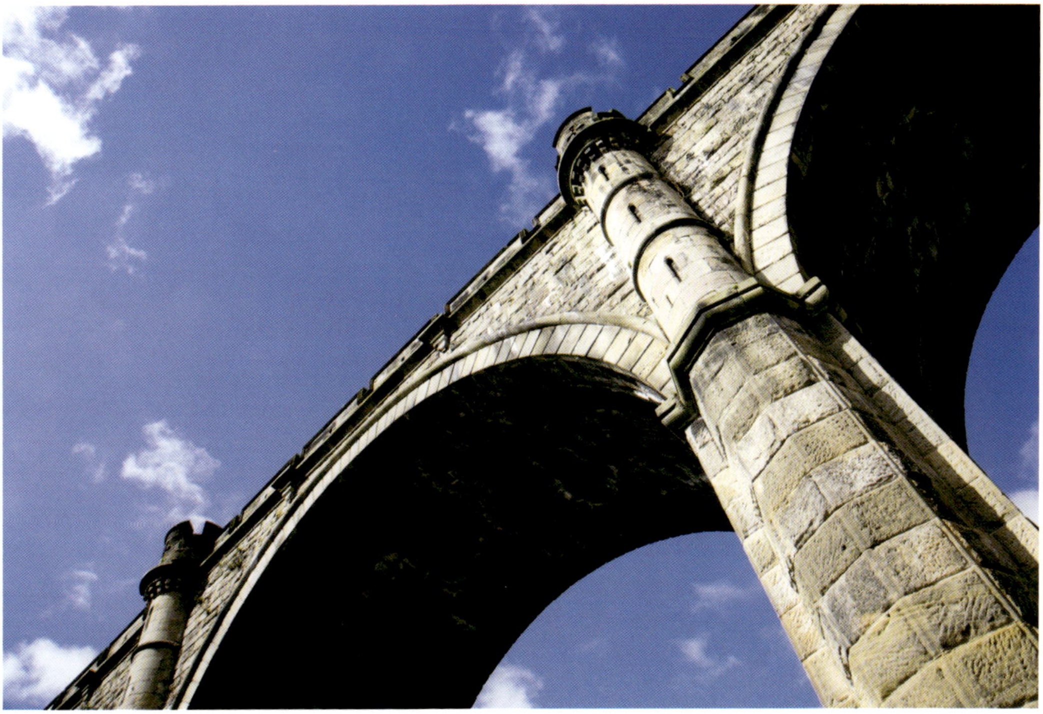

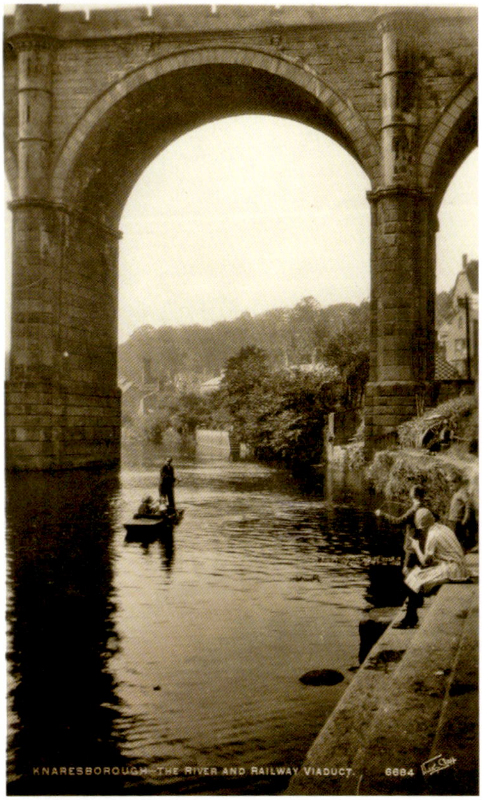

Punting on the Nidd

Punting was popular in Victorian and later times as this 1921 picture of punters under the viaduct shows. You can see the crenellated towers which form the upper part of the piers on the viaduct.

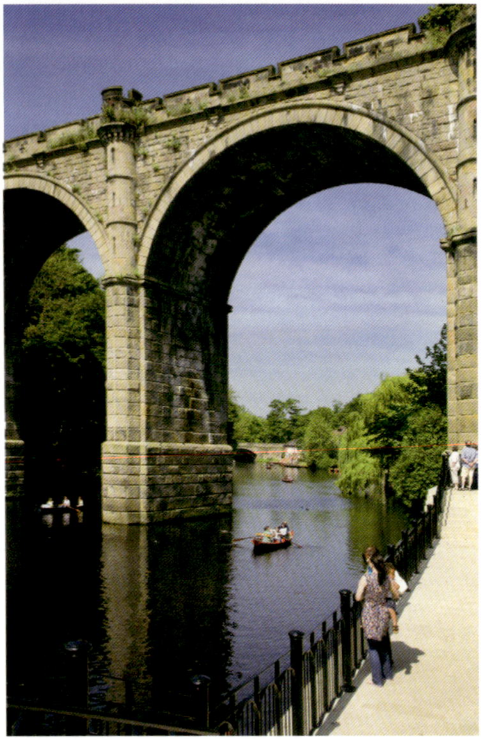

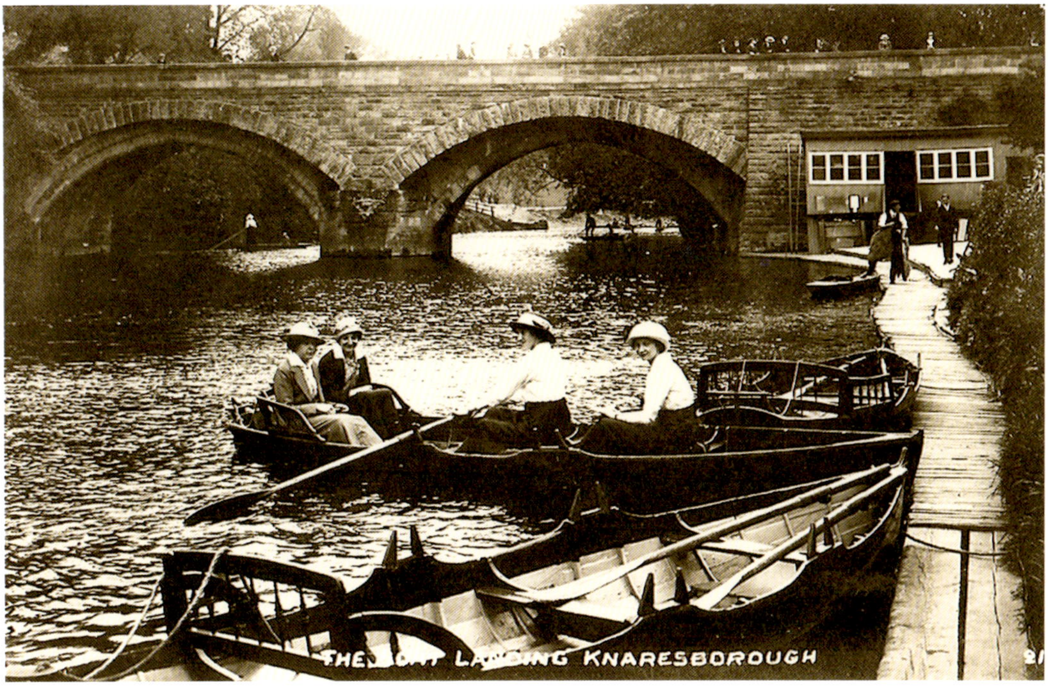

Boating on the Nidd

Just as sedate and even more popular, boating is still a major attraction on the Nidd today. This photograph shows Edwardian boaters near the boat houses at High Bridge. William Bluett was the first to let boats here followed by Richard Sturdy under the castle and, Charles Blenkhorn.

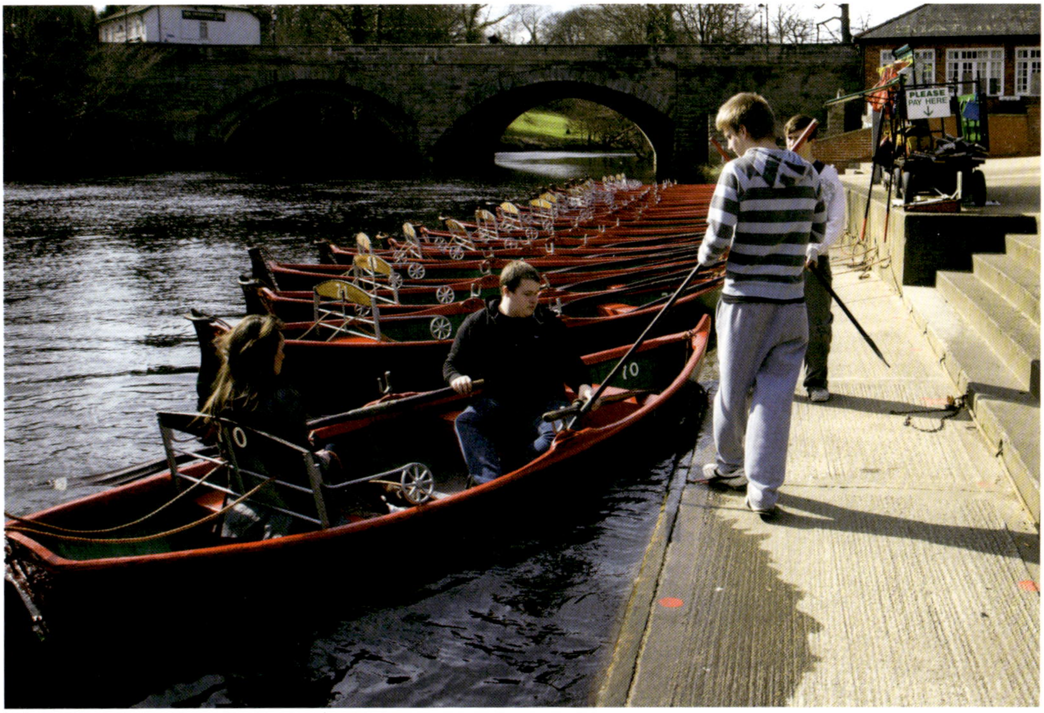

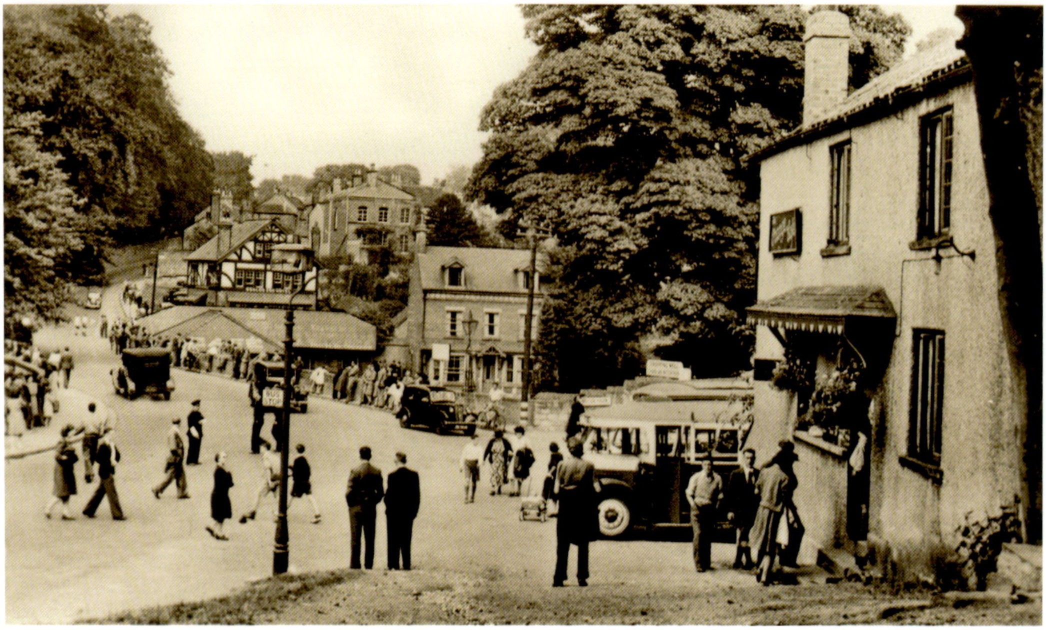

High Bridge

Originally called Danyell Bridge it was widened in 1773 and then again in 1924 in response to the growing traffic on what is now the A59 Harrogate road. This 1938 picture shows an early traffic policeman, the High Bridge Private Hotel (opened 1906), the New Century Dining Rooms (1900) and the timbered World's End pub in the distance. All three establishments were owned by Charles Blenkhorn who also competed with Richard Sturdy in the boating business. The modern picture shows today's entrance to Mother Shipton's cave.

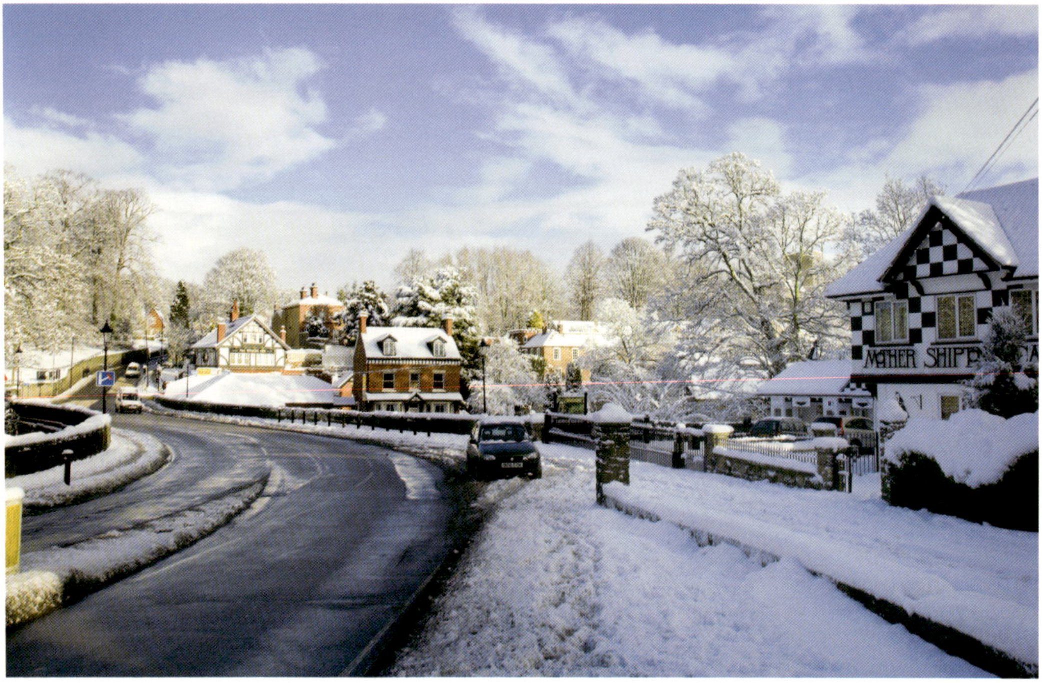

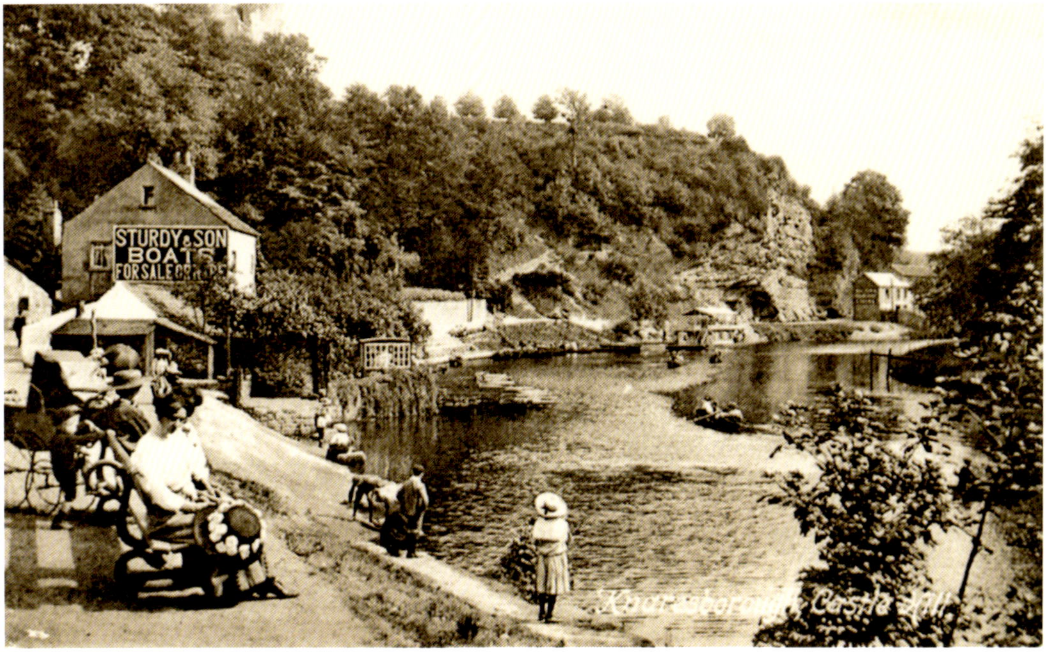

Sturdy & Son Boatbuilders

The River Nidd has always been central to Knaresborough's tourism. This shows more of the boats built and hired out by Sturdy & Son (140 to Blenkhorn's 90). Founded by Richard Sturdy (1837-1913) about 1850 the firm bought and expanded the boat business previously run by a Mr Bluett. Sturdy's was subsequently taken over by Bill Henry and then sold to Harrogate Council in 1965.

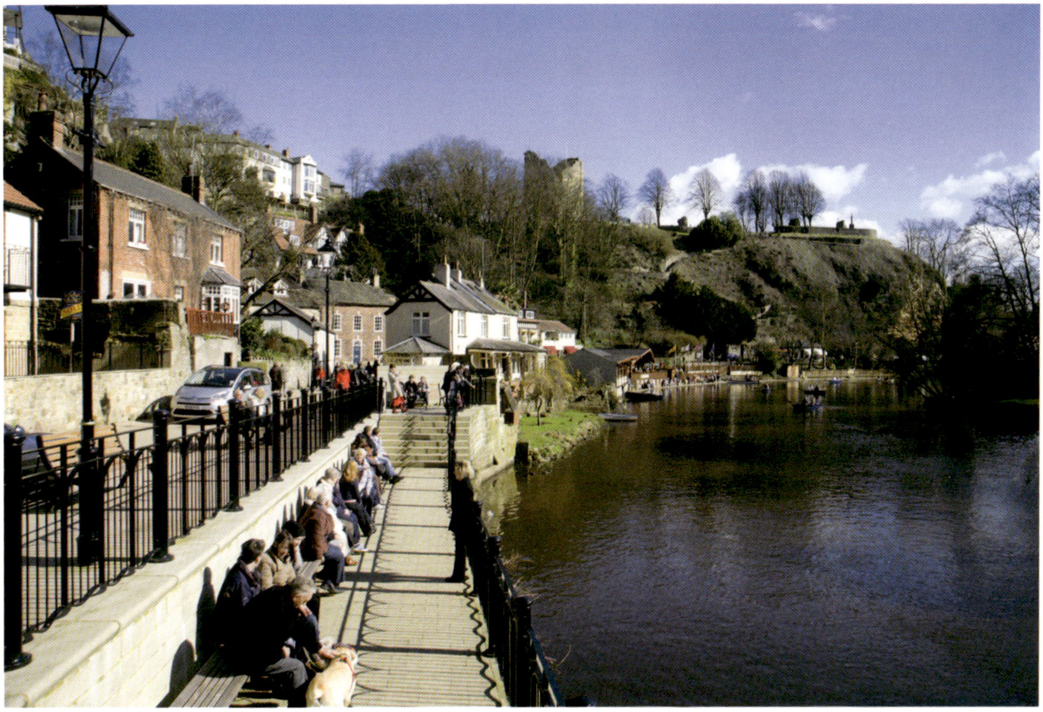

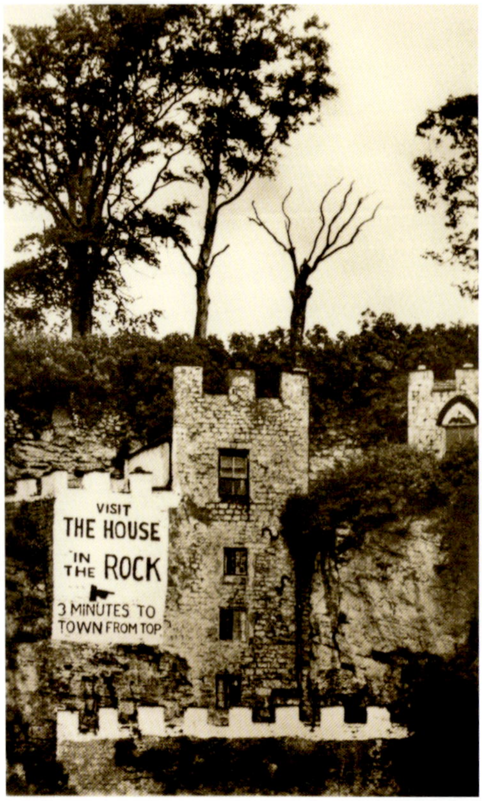

House in the Rock

Built into the rock opposite Low Bridge by 'Sir' Thomas Hill, a weaver, and his son between 1770 and 1791 it was originally called Fort Montague. Hill was something of an eccentric: flying the Union Flag from the Fort, firing gun salutes from a two pounder canon and issuing his own £5 banknotes with which he duped the Bank of Newcastle. Although a major attraction for many years, health and safety concerns forced Harrogate Borough Council to close it in 1994 and, despite a spirited attempt to keep it open for the public led by Nancy Buckle which attracted international media attention, it passed into private hands in 2000.

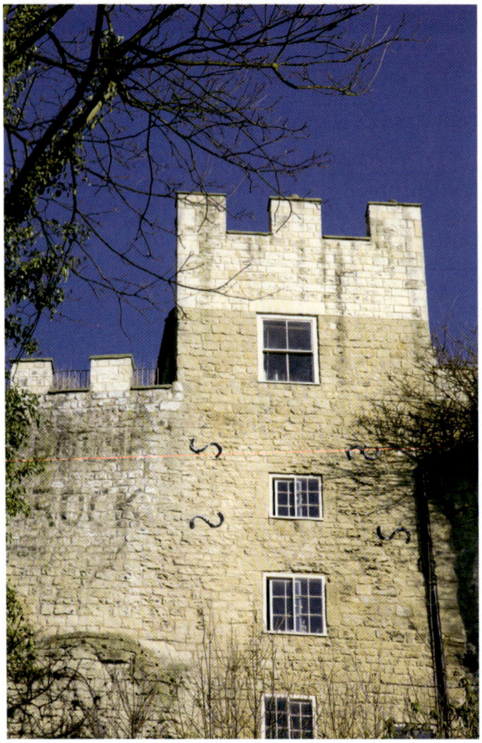

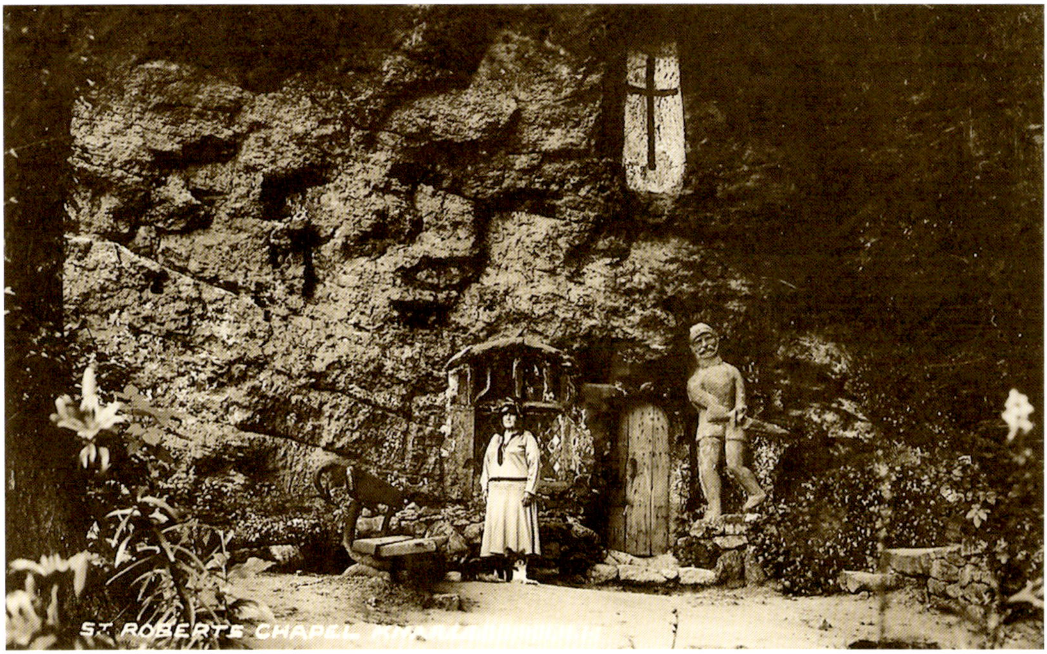

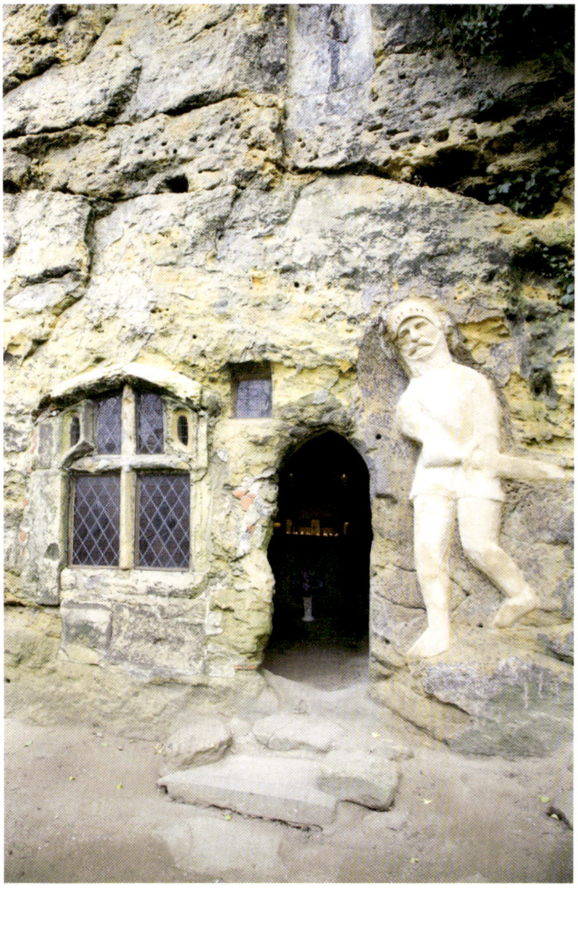

The Chapel of Our Lady of the Crag or St Robert's Chapel

10' 6" long, 9' wide and 7' 6" high this was 'elegantly hollowed out of the solid rock: its roof and altar beautifully adorned with Gothic ornaments' (according to an 1880s official guide to Knaresborough) by John the Mason in 1408. Allegedly it was in thanksgiving to the Blessed Virgin for his son's life after he survived a rock fall. Keeping the Knight Templar company (there was a Templar training camp at Little Ribston) is Annie Henshall, one of Nancy Buckle's aunts who died in 1993 aged 97. It is Britain's third oldest wayside shrine; the Knight is caught 'in the act of drawing his sword to defend the place from the violence of rude intruders'. Wordsworth visited in 1802, alluding to it in his *Effusion.*

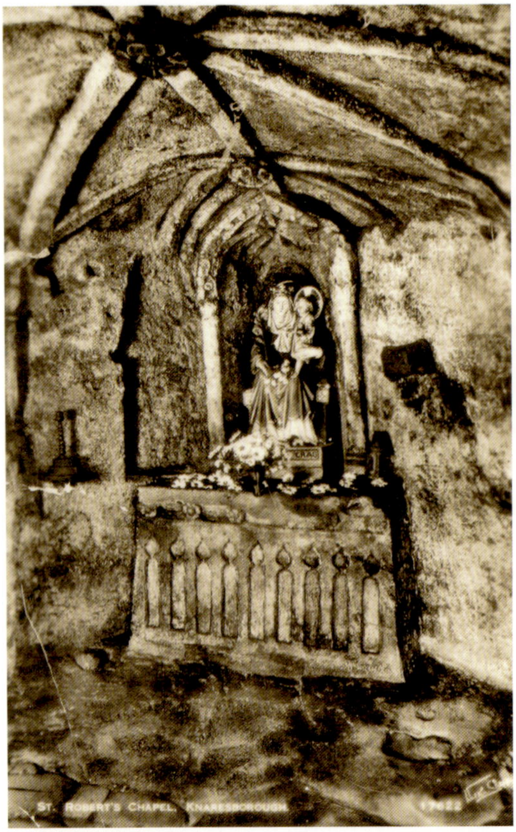

Interior of The Chapel of Our Lady of the Crag

Now officially recognised as a chapel by the Vatican the 1890 second edition of the guide referred to above goes on to describe the interior: 'Behind the altar is a large niche, where formerly stood an image; and on one side of it a place for the holy water basin. Here also are the figures of three heads designed...for an emblematical allusion to the order of monks (Sanctae Trinitatis) at the once neighbouring priory, by some of whom they were probably cut.' A later image of the Madonna and Child (depicted in the older photograph) dated from 1916 when the shrine was restored by John Martin. He gave it to Ampleforth Abbey on whose behalf it is now looked after by the parish of St Mary's, Knaresborough. The current statue shown in the newer photograph was carved by Ian Judd and dedicated in 2000.

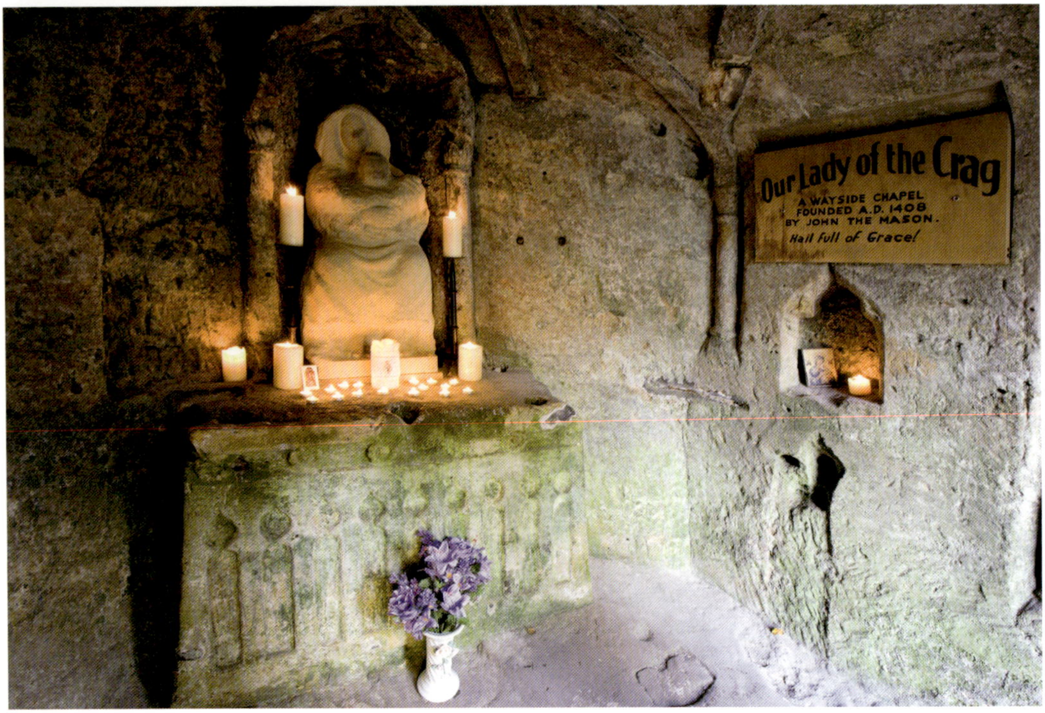

Mother Shipton

Born in 1488 (so predating Nostradamus by fifteen years) in a cave next to the River Nidd, the legendary Mother Shipton (née Ursula Southeil) is synonymous with Knaresborough and with the art of prophecy. Afflicted by what was probably scoliosis and variously branded a witch and the devil's daughter her predictions have included the demise of Cardinal Wolsey, the Gunpowder Plot, the Great Fire of London, her own death, and, as yet unsuccessfully, the end of the world (1881 and 1991)! Many of her prophecies seem to have been made up by an unscrupulous Brighton bookseller. The modern photograph shows Mother Shipton in one of the *trompe l'oeil* to be found around the town.

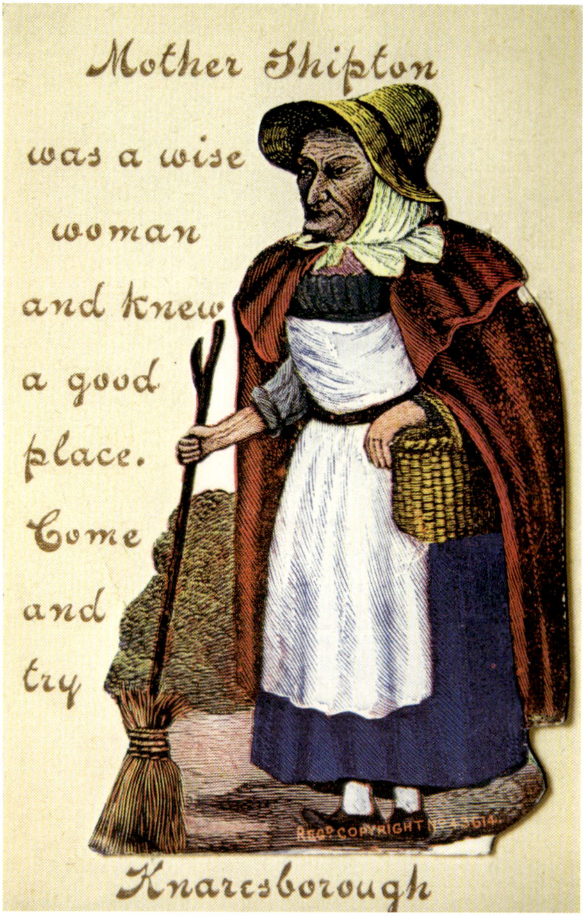

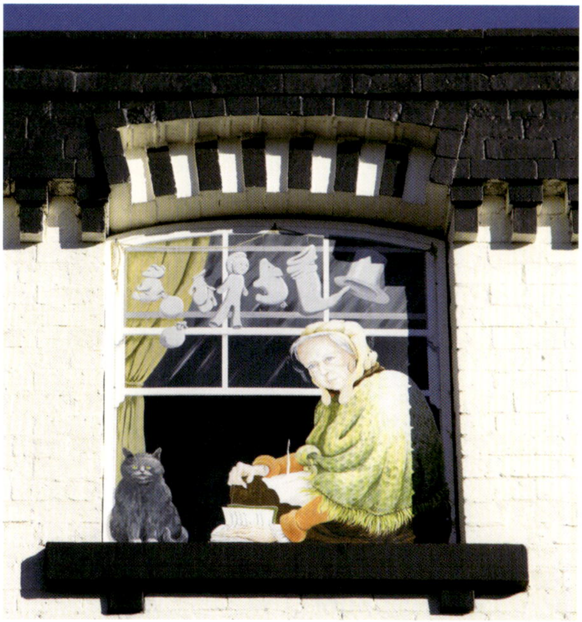

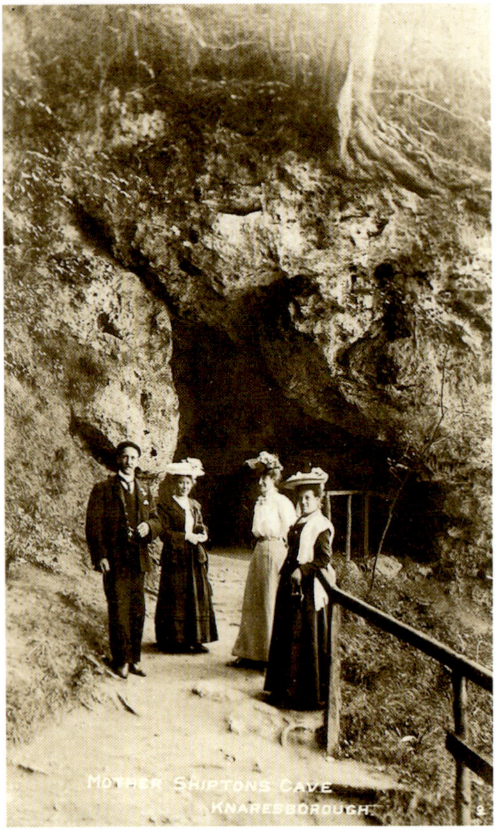

Mother Shipton's Cave
Despite claims by numerous other towns in the UK, this is where we like to think Mother Shipton was born – to Agatha during a violent thunderstorm. The Shiptons continue to fascinate to this day with the comparatively neglected Tobias Shipton celebrated by Middlesborough poet Bob Beagrie in his 2010 poem, *The Seer Sung Husband.*

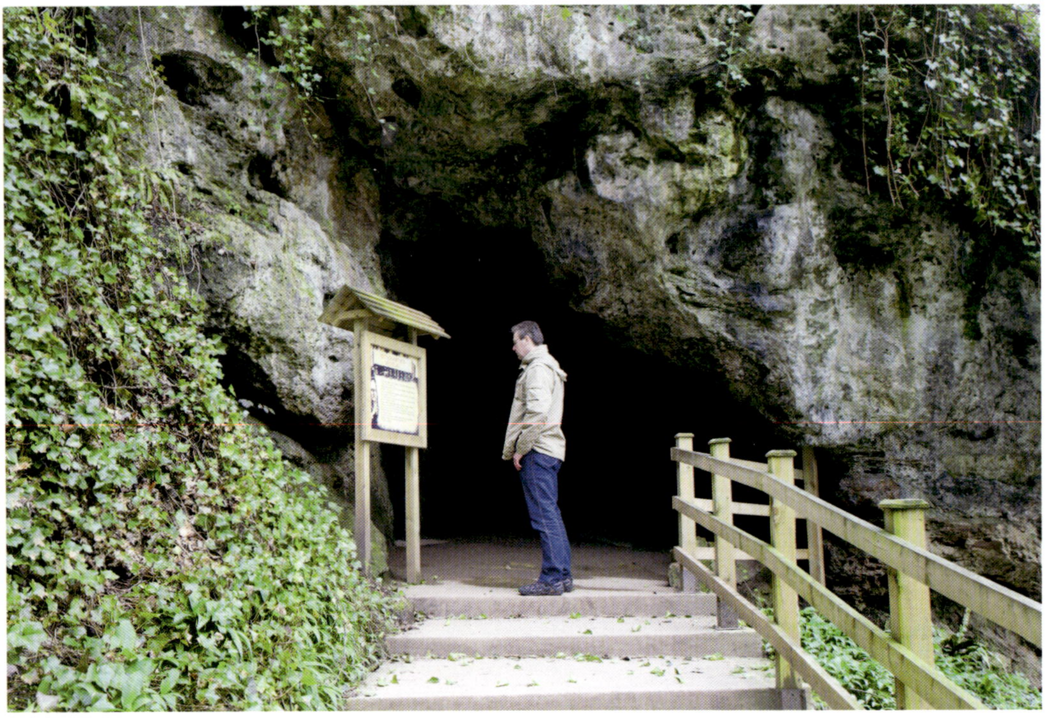

How to Petrify a Teddy Bear

A tourist attraction since 1630 the Petrifying Well has intrigued visitors with its seemingly magical ability to change everyday objects into stone by depositing layers of calcite. 700 gallons of water flow through every hour and it takes approximately six months to 'petrify' a teddy bear, for example. Today the well features a highly imaginative array of articles as the modern photograph shows. Those in the inset are in the museum. The overhang is nowadays regularly scraped to prevent collapse, as happened in 1704, 1816 and 1823.

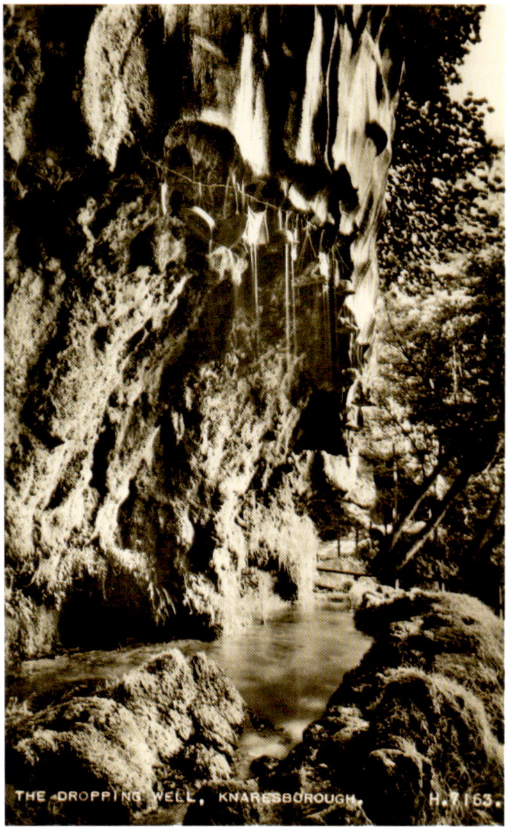

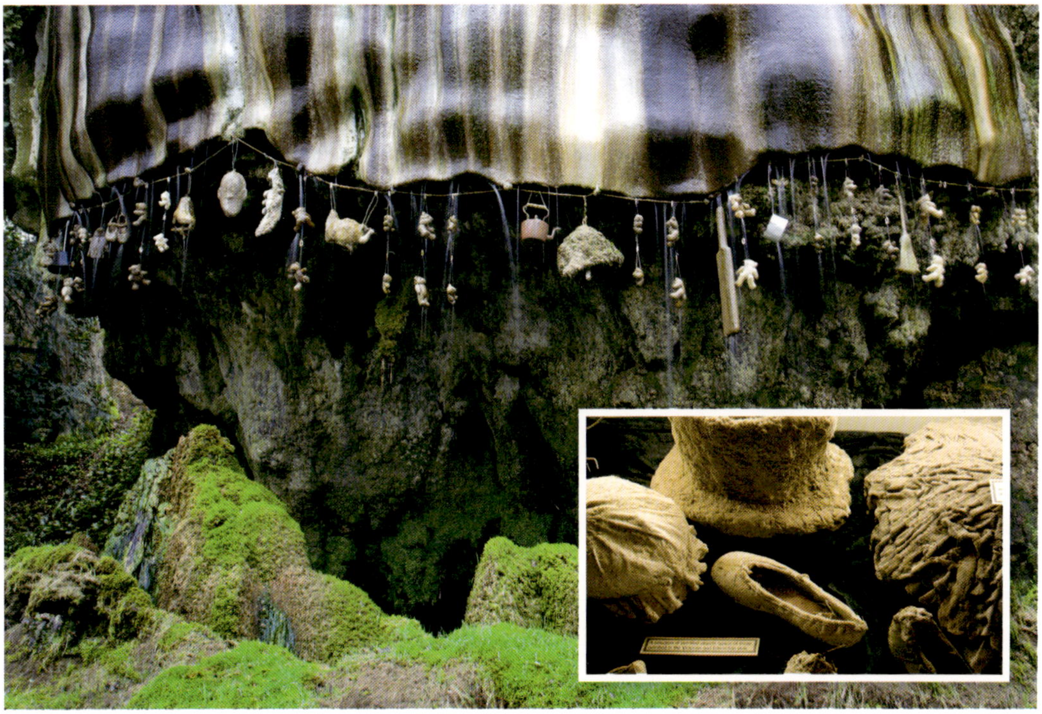

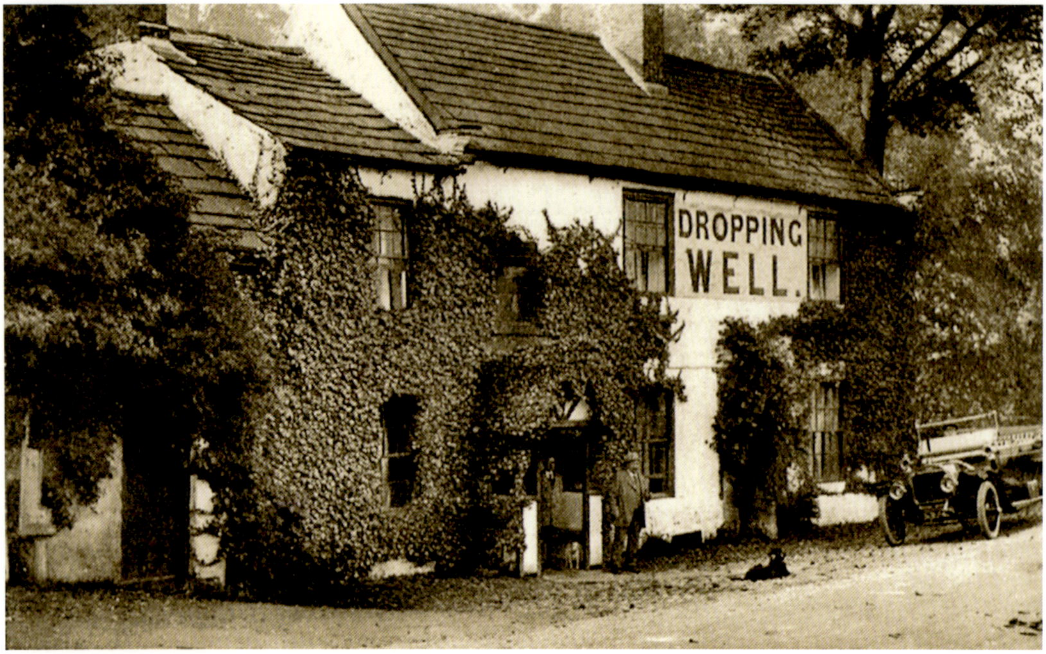

Dropping Well Inn

Also known as Mother Shipton's Inn, Mother Shipton features on the copper sign above the door in this 1914 photograph. The Dropping Well estate was run by a Mrs Comer and her five daughters in the early twentieth century until they were forced to leave when the Slingsby family lost the Slingsby baby case (concerning the legitimacy of their child and its right to the family's fortune) in 1916.

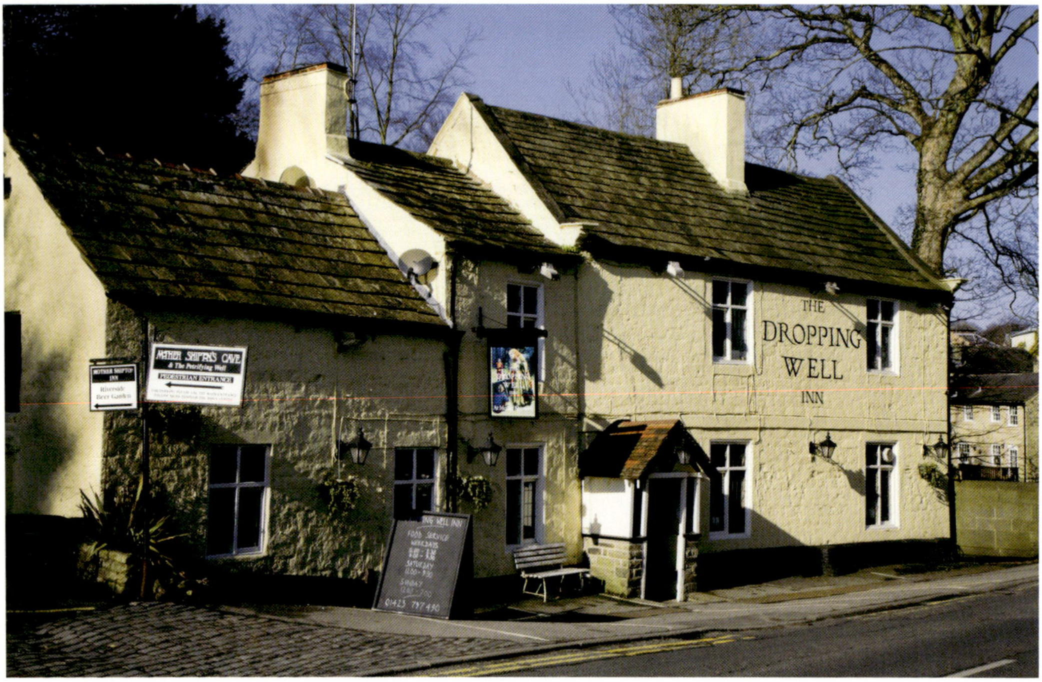

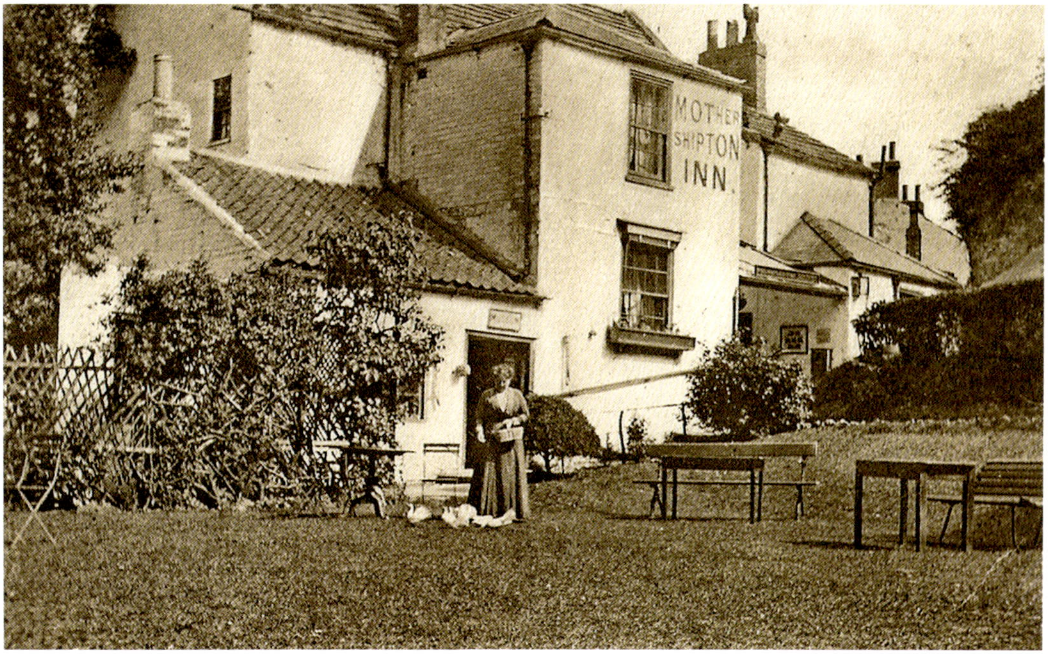

Feeding the Chickens in the Garden, Dropping Well Inn

The inn was part of the Slingsby estate. Sir Charles Slingsby was perhaps the most famous member of the family; he died tragically on a ferry on the River Ure at Newby Hall while out hunting in 1869 along with six other men and eight horses. His sister, Emma Louisa, dedicated a tomb to Sir Charles in the Slingsby Chapel in the parish church of St John the Baptist. The contemporary shot shows how little has changed in what is now the beer garden.

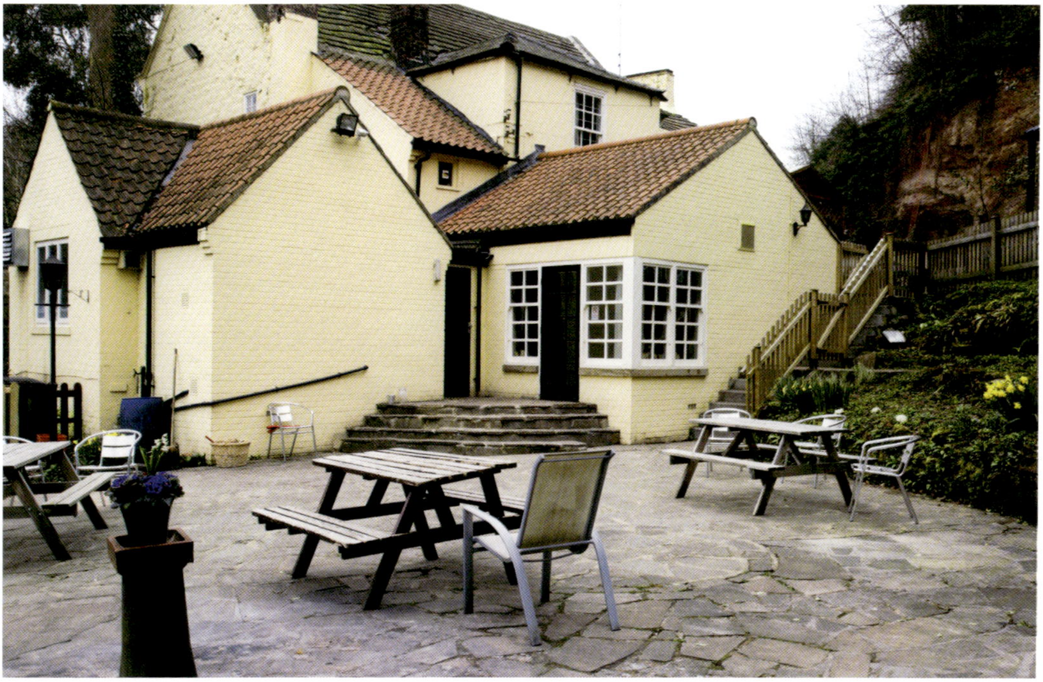

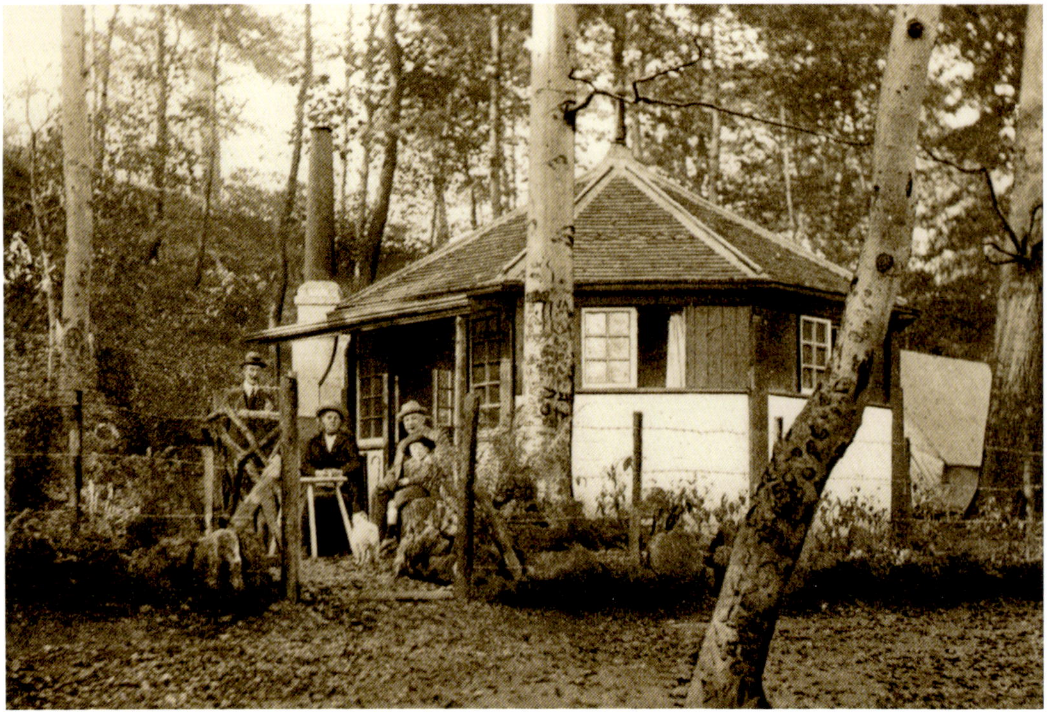

The Hut, Long Walk

This was used by Madame Doreen – palmist and clairvoyant – who gave special consultations, by appointment. Nothing exists today as the modern photograph so clearly shows.

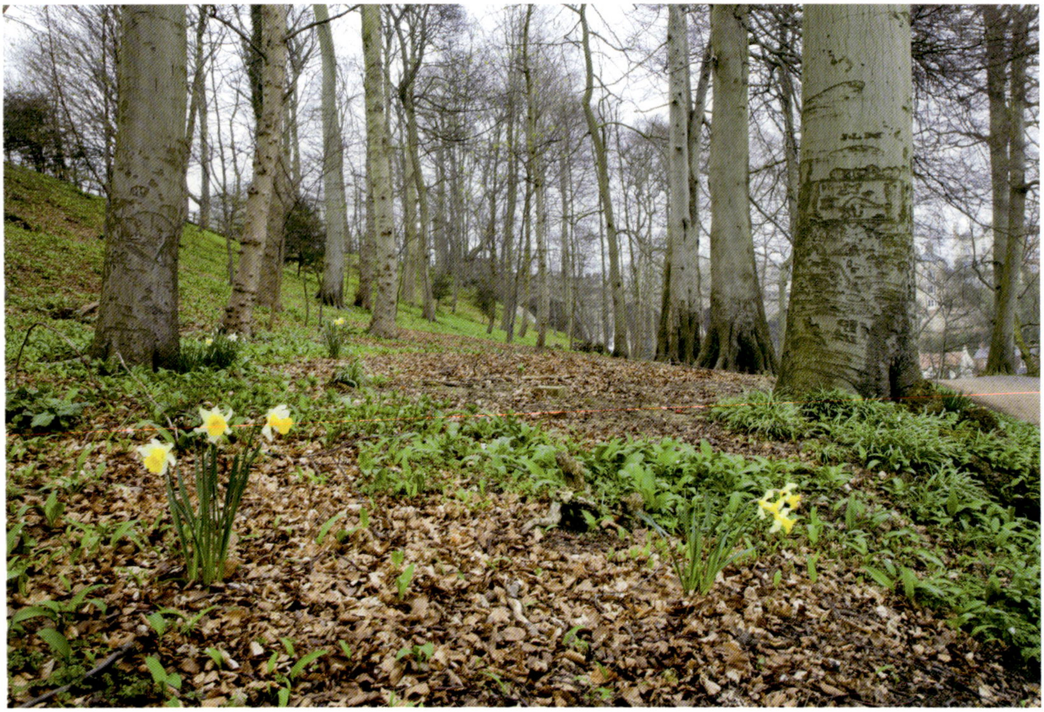

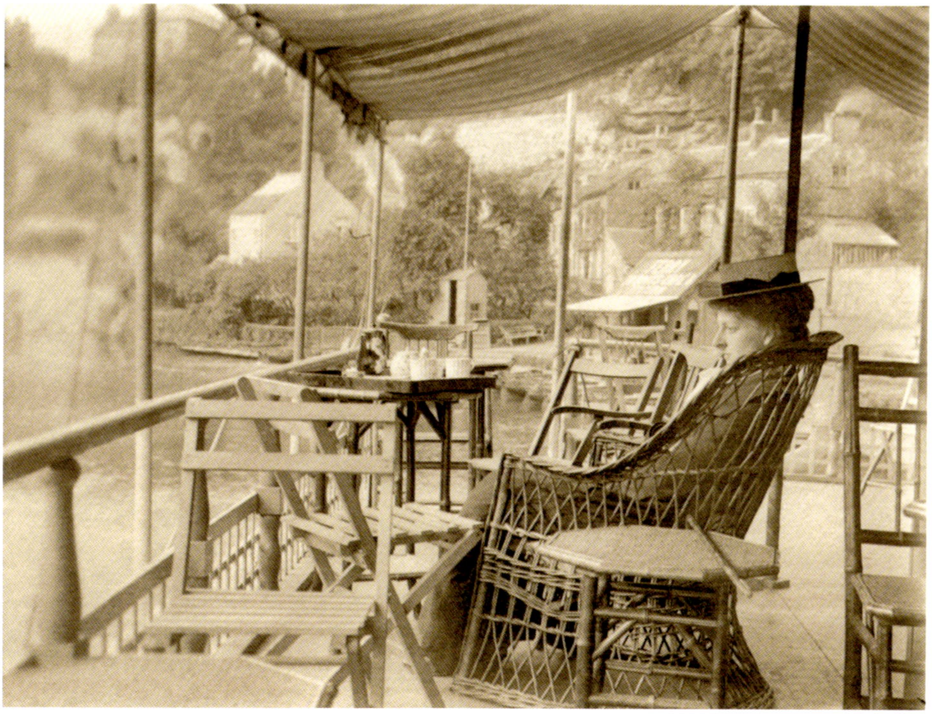

Pensive Lady on *Marigold*

The *Marigold* houseboat (along with the Moat Café) was owned by the O'Reilly sisters and spent most of its time as an Edwardian café restaurant moored between Sturdy's and Castle Mill. It played a key role in the annual Water Carnivals as the venue for a brass band; unfortunately it sank in 1920, hence its absence from the modern photograph taken in the Marigold Café on Waterside.

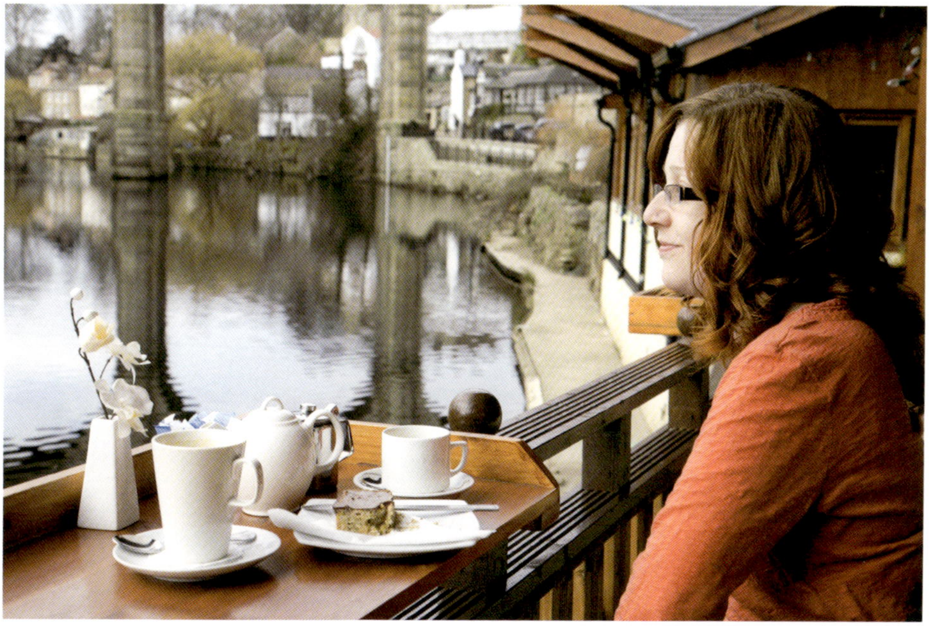

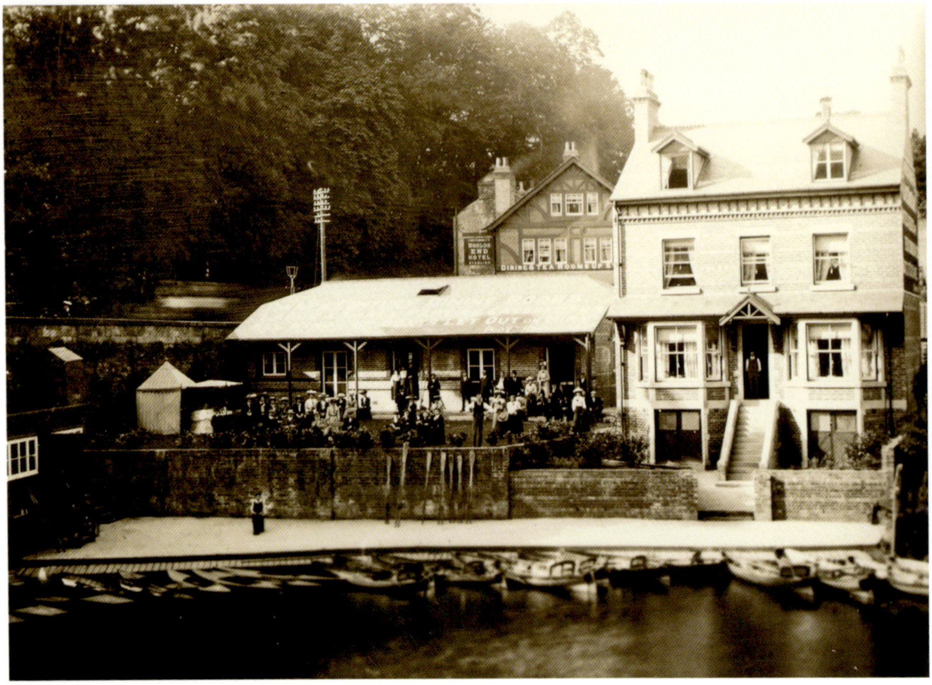

High Bridge Hotel

The hotel was opened in 1906 by Charles Blenkhorn and called the High Bridge Private Hotel; next door is Blenkhorn's Boat House Café, originally named the New Century Dining Rooms after the date of its opening in 1900. Blenkhorn's boats are in the foreground, the World's End in the background. A veritable hive of activity and a tourist trap in those days, as today.

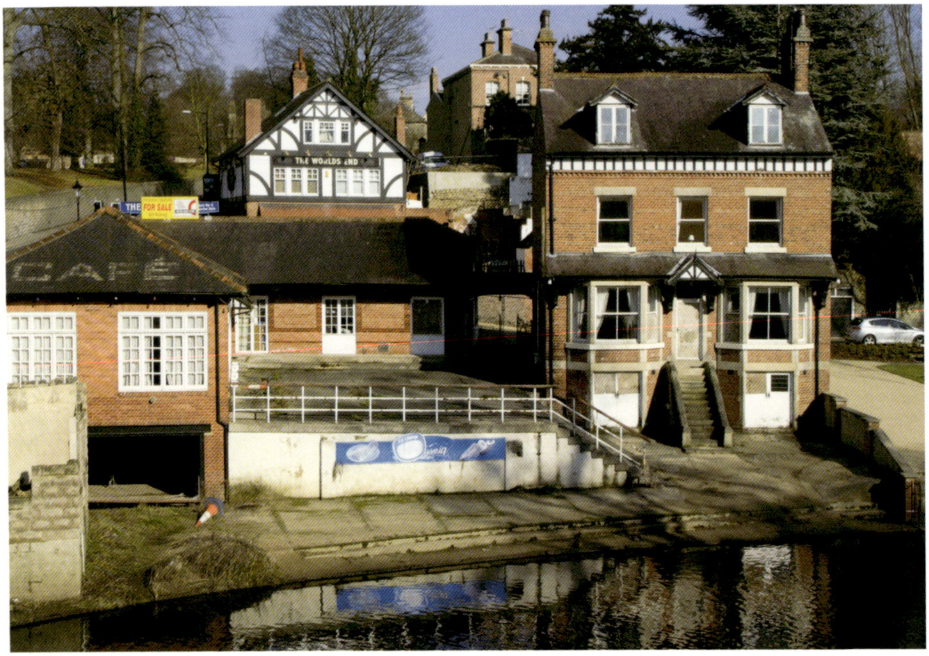

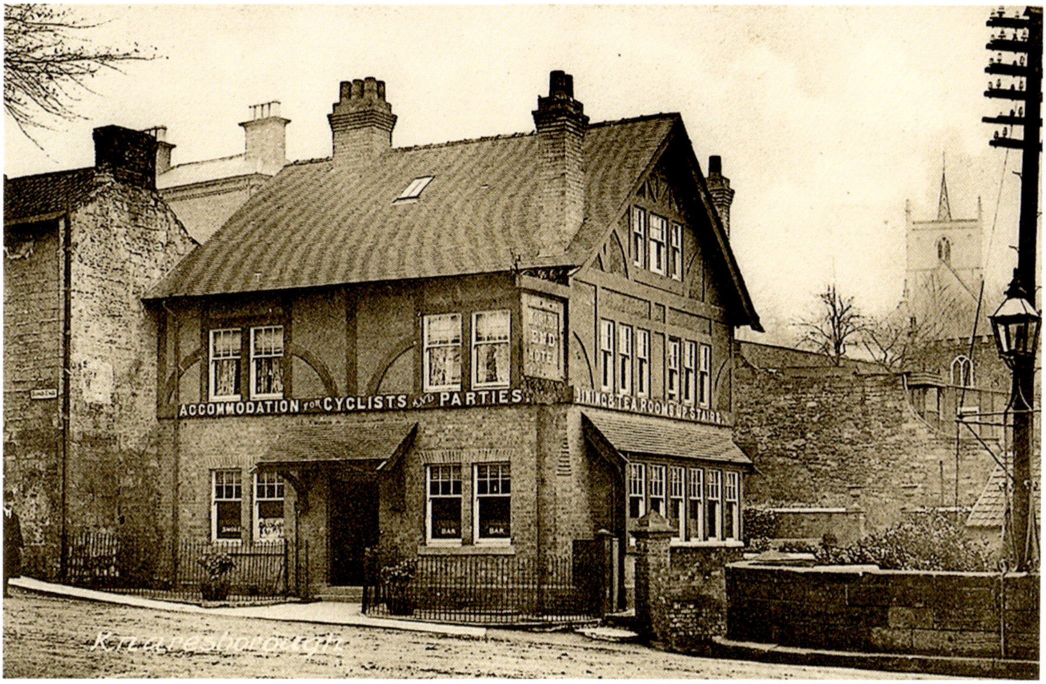

World's End

This pub on High Bridge dates from around 1898 when it replaced the original tavern. It was owned by Charles Blenkhorn who also had the boats, hotel and café mentioned above and was postmaster; his sister was postmistress. The new photograph shows the exterior to have been tastefully restored.

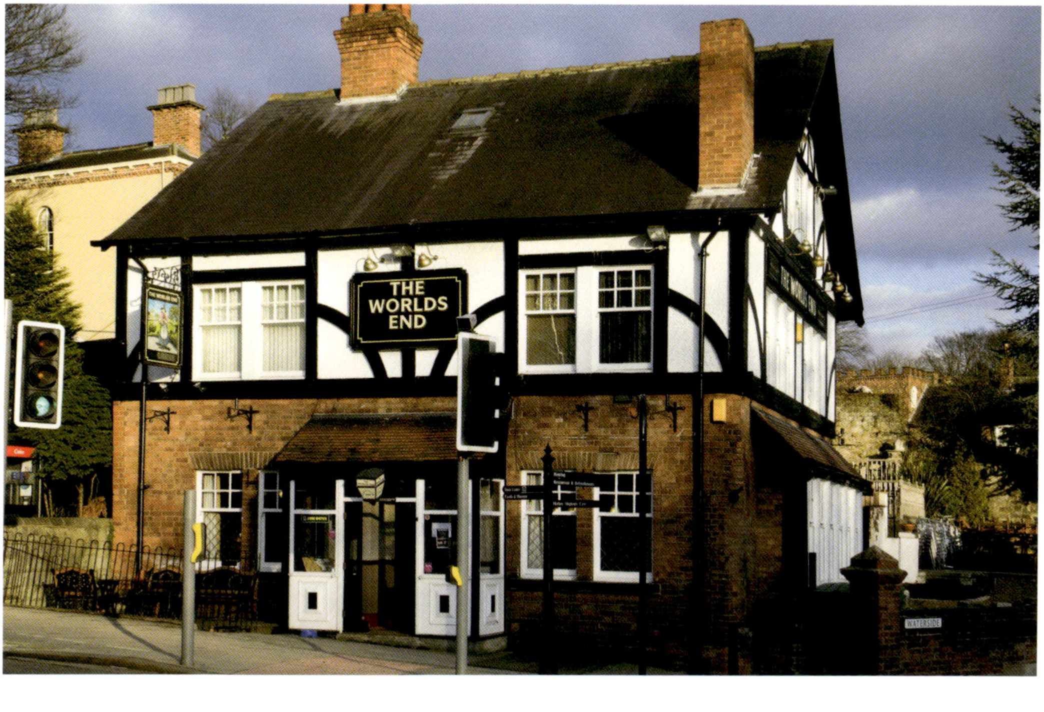

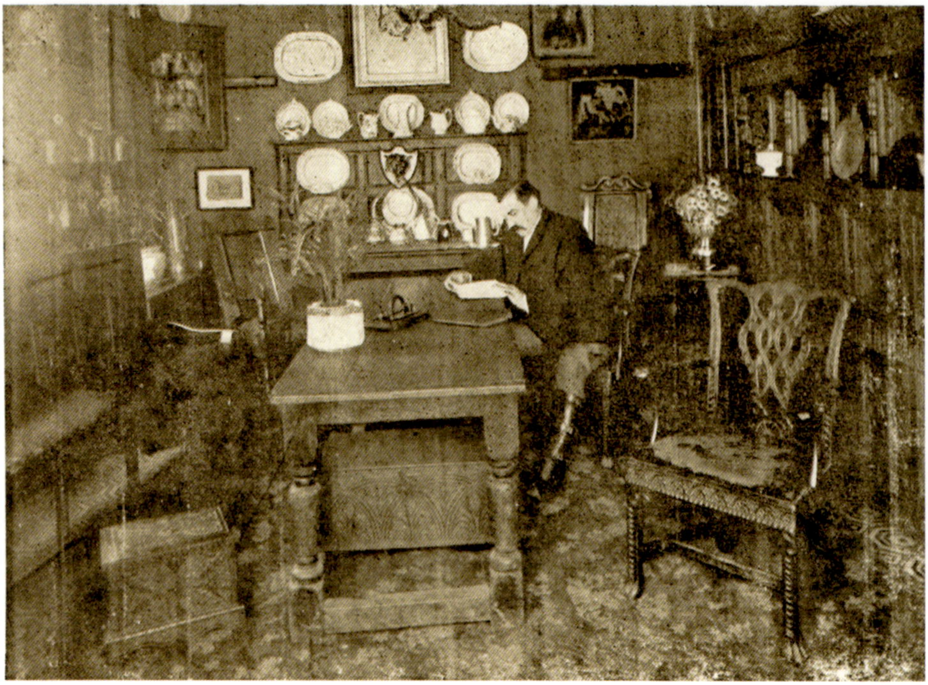

Old Oak Room, Crown Hotel

A wonderful photograph from the early 1900s showing the wood-paneled room inside this pub with a customer enjoying a quiet read; the only thing missing is a pint of ale – not so on the new photograph where today's drinkers can enjoy a blizzard of media entertainment with large screen television and tableside TVs. *Baines Directory 1822* lists 39 other pubs and hotels in Knaresborough. Around this time the Crown boasted an impressive external clock, was owned by Tetley's and the landlord was a W. Broadley.

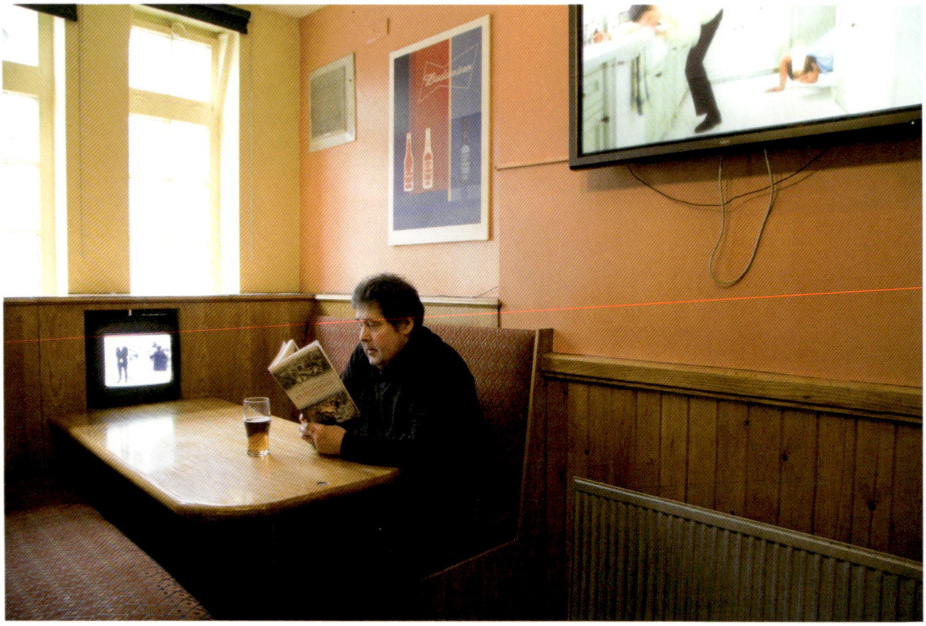

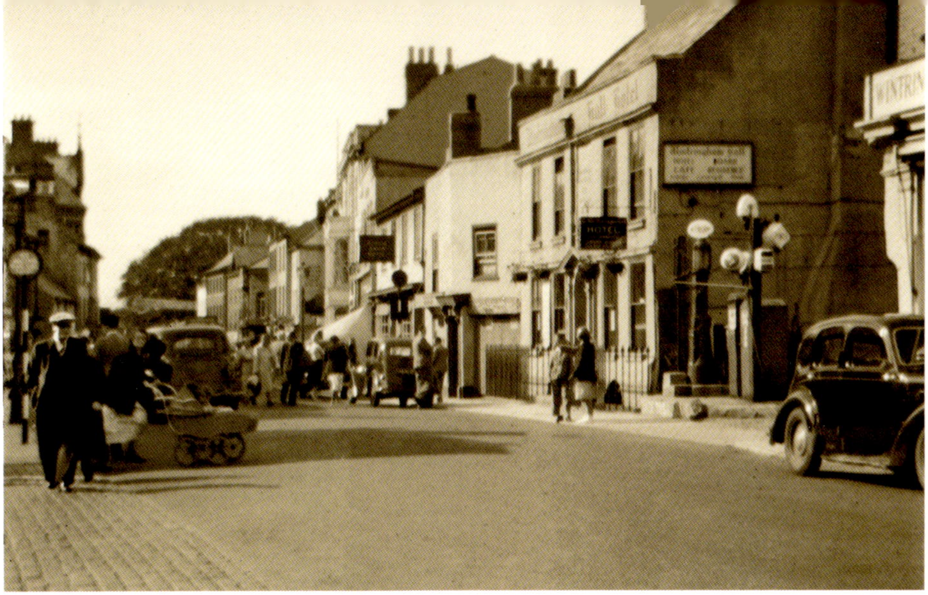

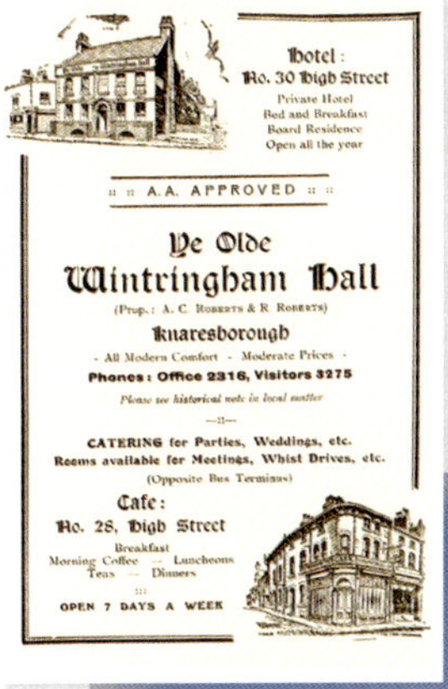

Wintringham Hall, 30 High Street

Tragically demolished in 1957. What was originally a Tudor building was rebuilt in the 1800s and became a popular local haunt for many years. The buildings were originally the home of Alice and Joan Wintringham; Joan then lived there with Sir William Plumpton, Master Forester and High Sherriff of Yorkshire. They married in 1451 although William tried to keep this, his second marriage, a secret for many years. Cobbles apart, not much survives from the original scene.

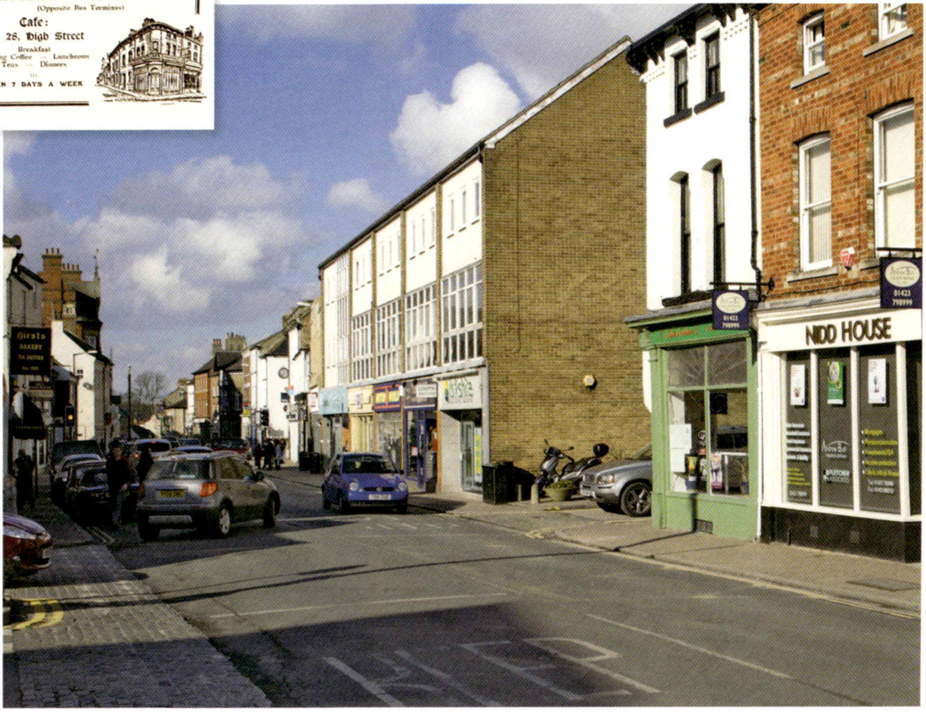

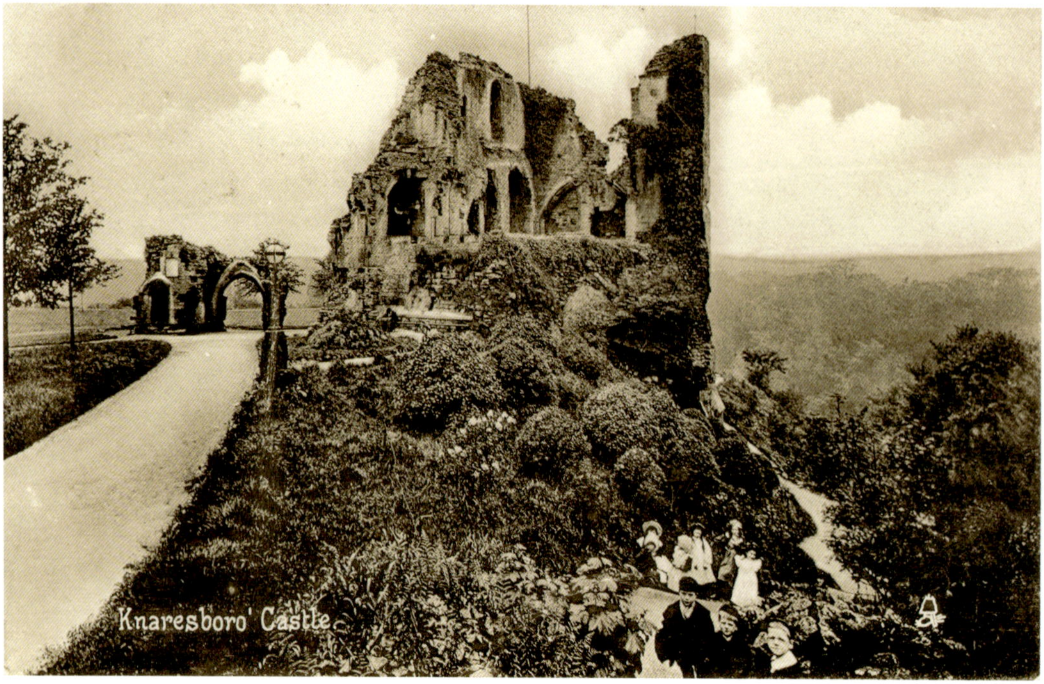

Knaresborough Castle, a Turbulent Priest and a Civil War Slighting

This 1905 photograph shows the impressive remains of the King's tower and porch, originally Norman and costing £11.00, it was rebuilt in 1312 by Edward II; in those days it had twelve towers and a fine keep. In 1170 it was refuge for Hugh de Morville and his accomplices in the slaughter of Thomas Becket. Captured in 1644 by Cromwell in the Civil War it was 'slighted' in 1648. In April 2010 the 800th anniversary celebrations of the first Maundy giving by King John were held there, the very first giving having taken place in Knaresborough in 1210.

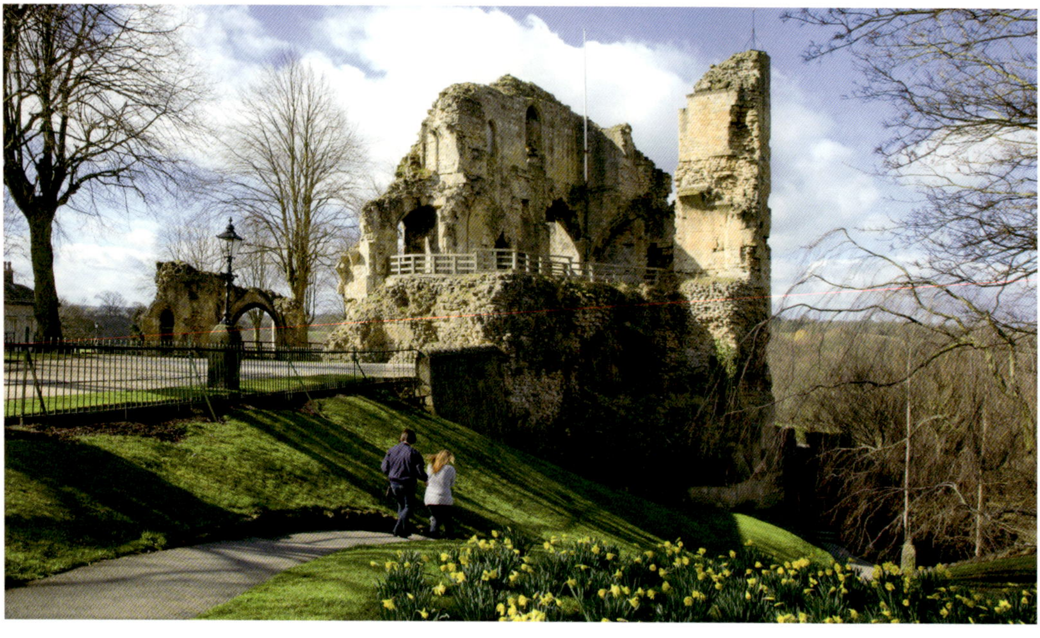

The War Memorial

Erected in 1921 the original top (pictured here) was blown off in a storm some ten years later – and again in 1956 (when the existing top was introduced). The memorial remembers 156 casualties from the First World War and 55 from the Second World War: *'Greater love hath no man than this, that a man lay down his life for his friends.'* [John 15:13]

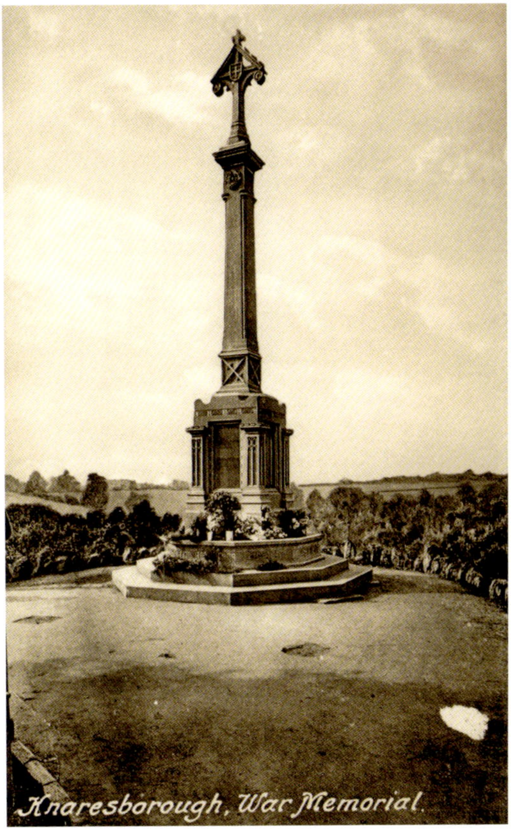

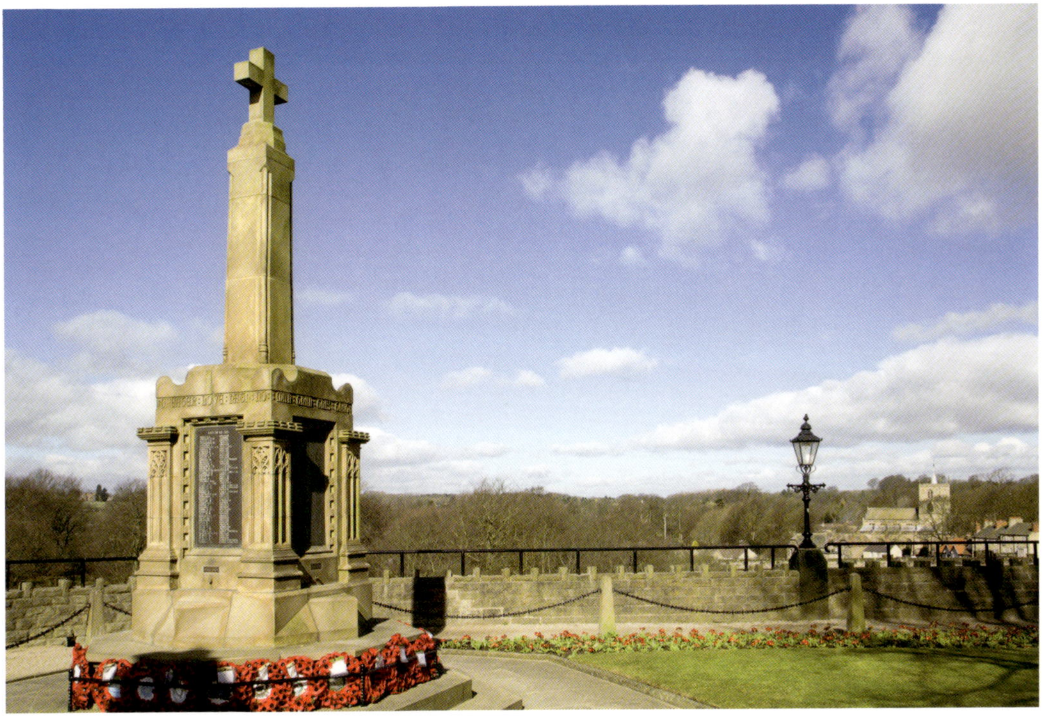

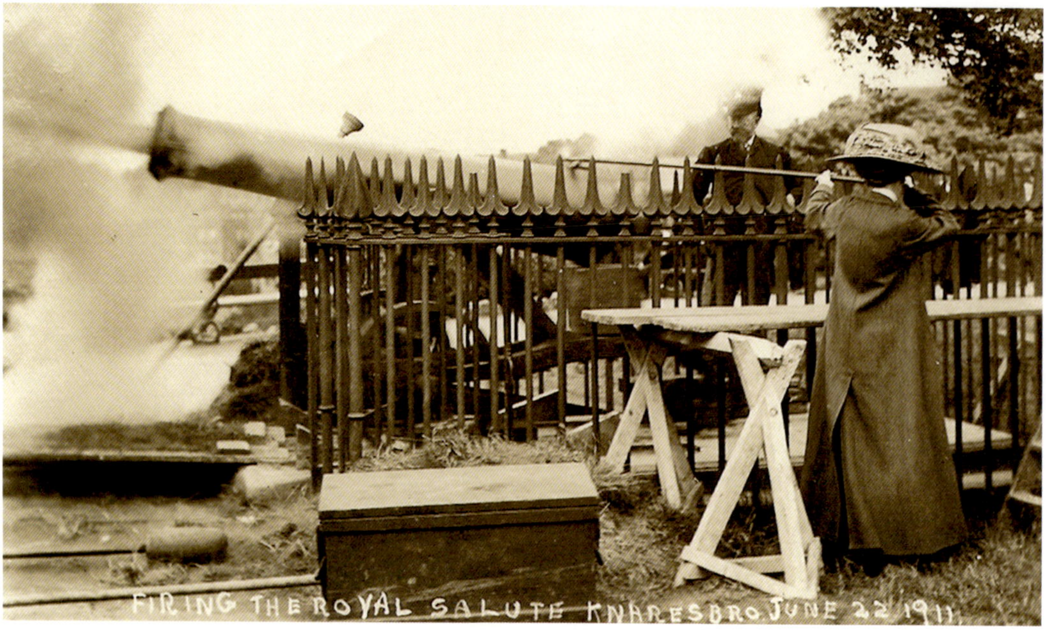

Firing the Royal Salute

This 24-pounder muzzle loader canon was captured at Sebastopol during the Crimean War and presented to Knaresborough in 1857; ironically, demand for war effort metal claimed it during the Second World War. A few yards to the left of the War Memorial this photograph shows a salute being fired to mark the Coronation of George V in June 1911. The contemporary scene is somewhat more peaceful, though considerably less dramatic.

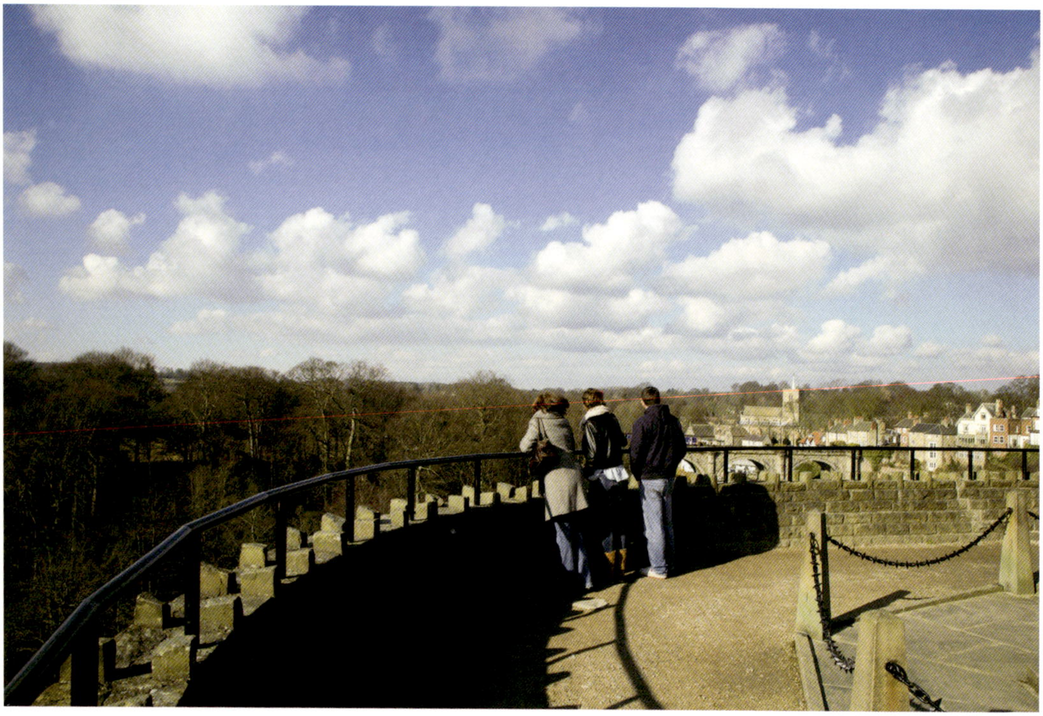

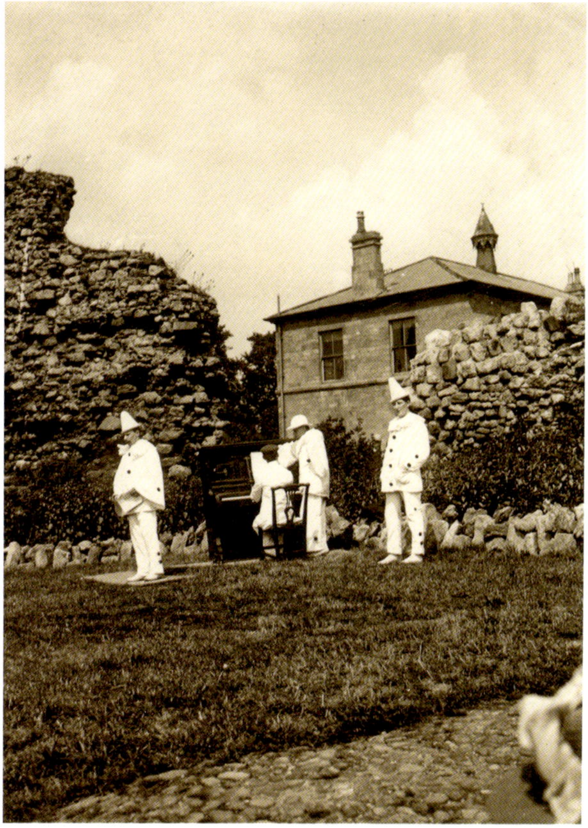

Pianist, Pierrots and a Yarnsmith
Pierrots and a pianist performing on the lawn in front of the Castle School for boys – a frequent sight in the thirties. The annual Mediaeval Day could be described as today's modern equivalent, as this picture of the 2009 event shows, transporting us back to life in Knaresborough during the Middle Ages. The story teller's poster reads: "teller of tales, merry jests for old, young, rich and poor... listen for the drum".

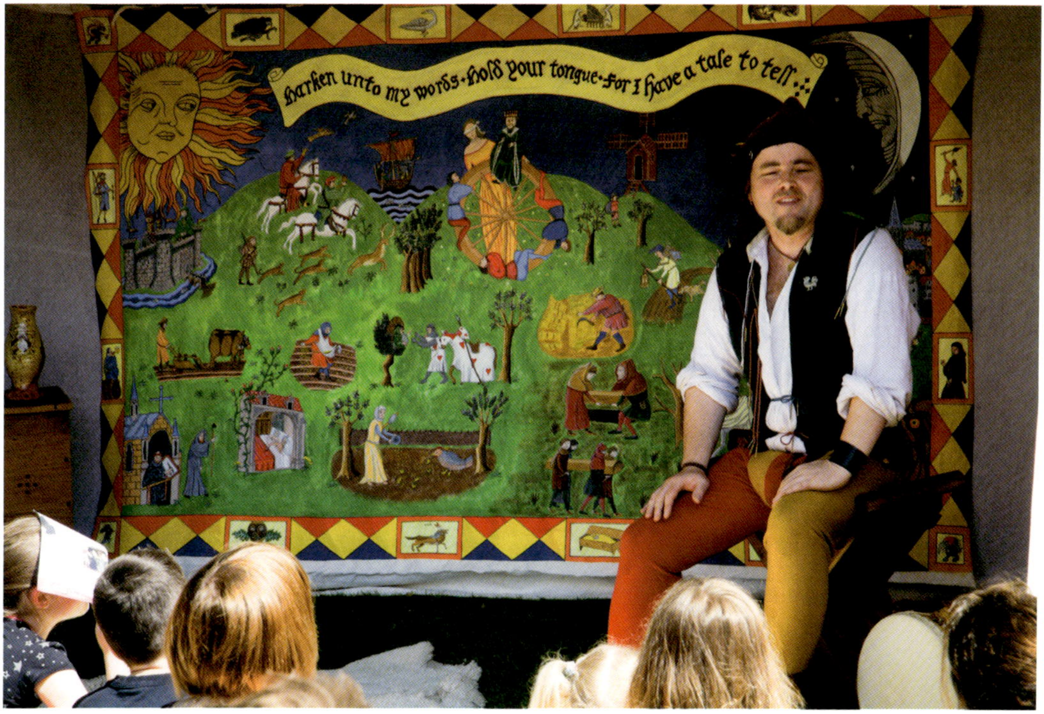

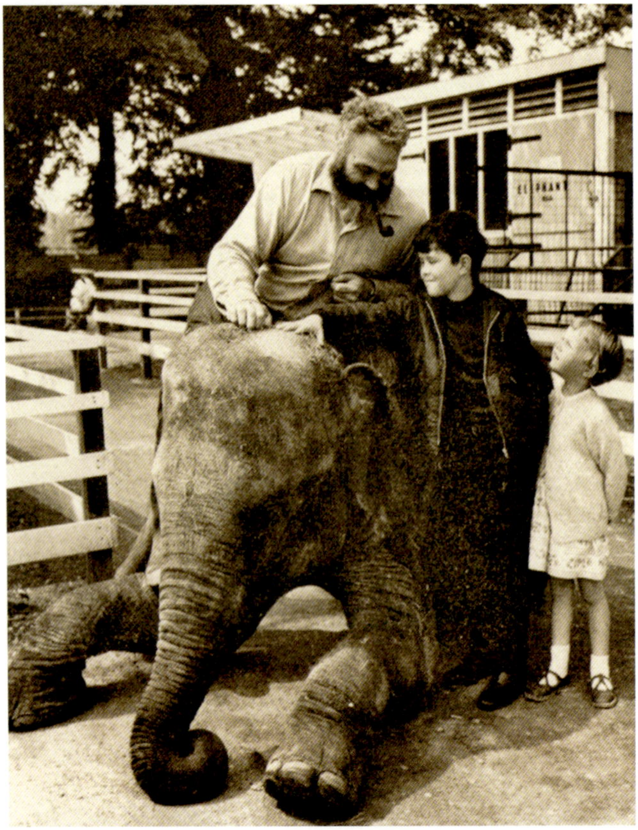

Knaresborough Zoo; Giraffe Looks out of Window

A popular attraction for many years this 1969 shot shows the zoo's owner Edward Milborrow with Irma the elephant. Irma was something of a film star and shared her home with breeding bears, lions, tigers, llamas, wallabies, penguins and monkeys. In its heyday the zoo attracted 150,000 visitors each year, 10000 of these in school parties. The giraffe looking out of the window above the Paragon Takeaway in the High Street is one of a series of striking and attractive trompe l'oeil to be seen around the town commissioned as part of Renaisssance Knaresborough Town Windows project in 2008. There are thirteen paintings on eight buildings each depicting an aspect of Knaresborough's history.

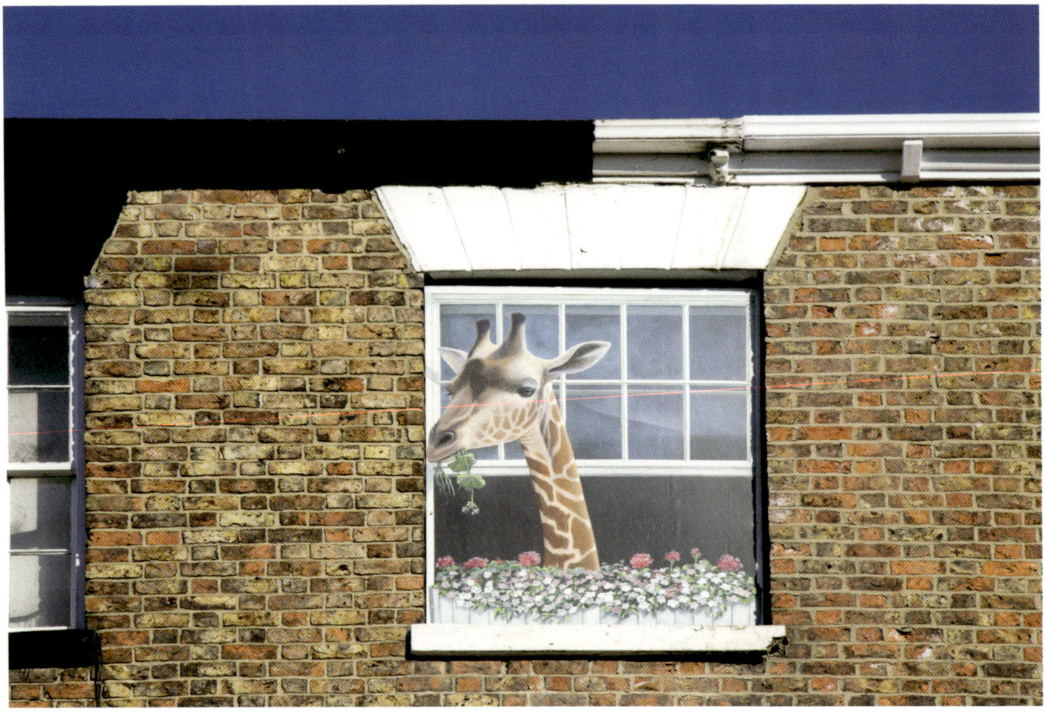

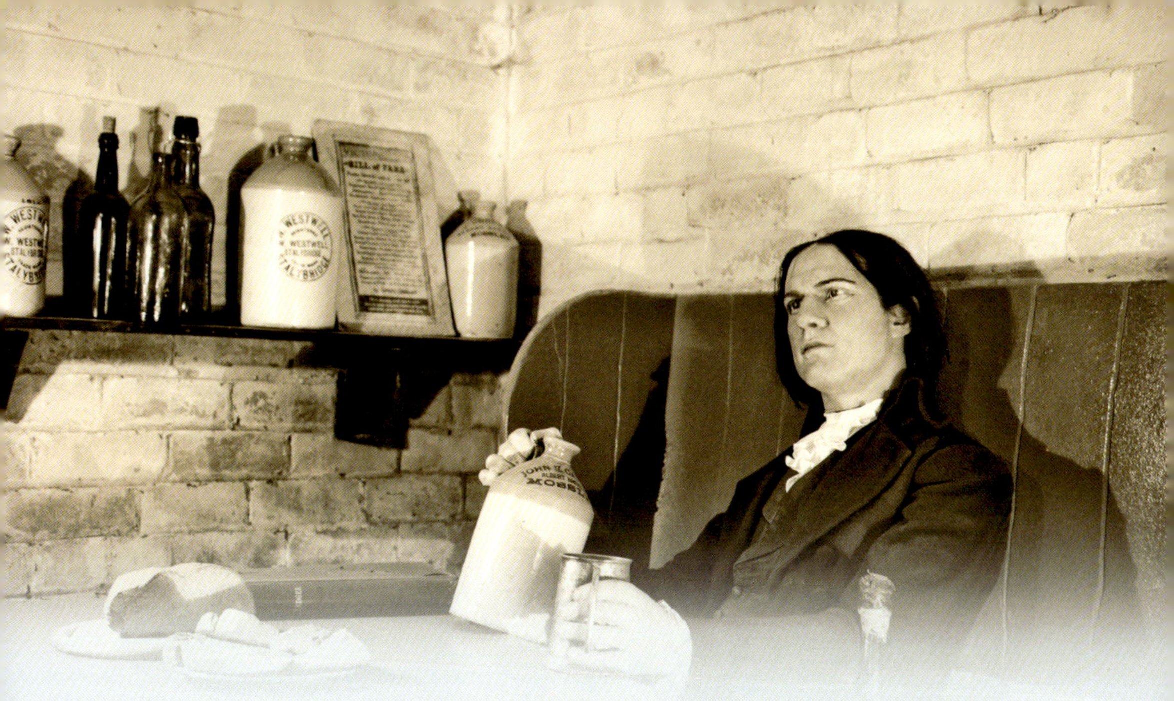

CHAPTER 2

Knaresborough People

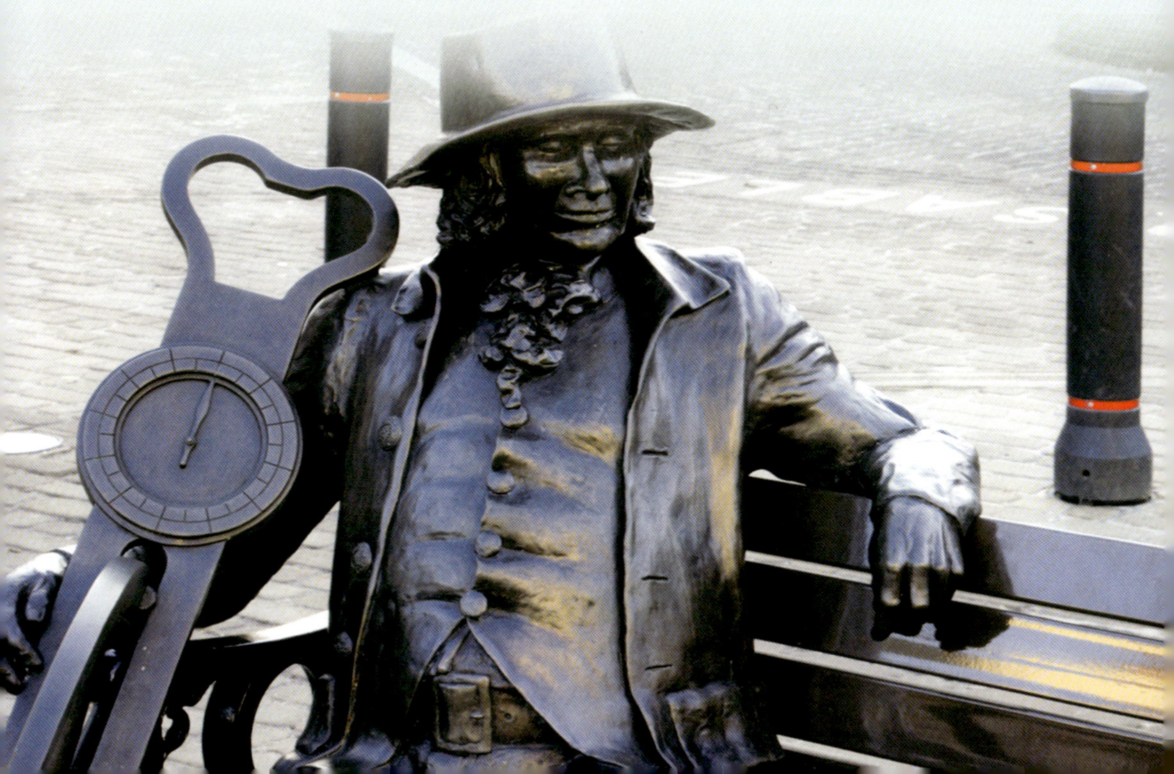

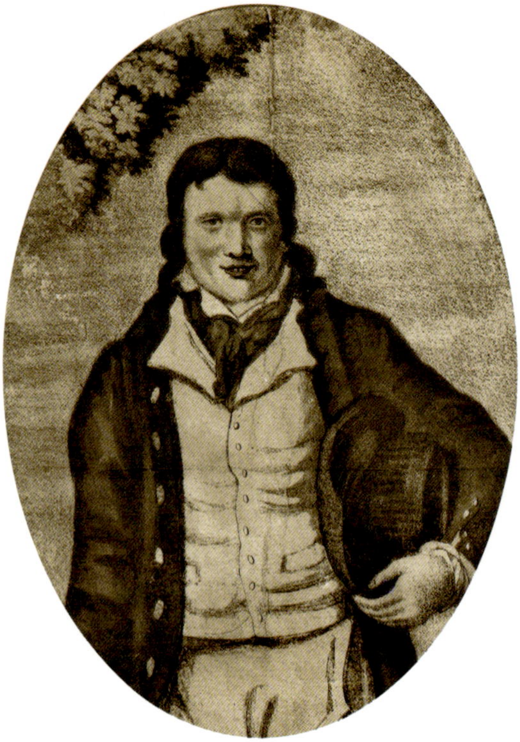

Duchess of Buccleugh, Thomas Hill and Nancy Buckle

'Sir' Thomas Hill was charged by His Majesty's Command as follows in January 1791: 'you shall faithfully serve, watch and maintain our commands against any lawless audacious depredators, robbers and night strollers who dare villainously assemble themselves...'
The inset painting by Sir Joshua Reynolds shows the Duchess, daughter of the Duke and Duchess of Montague who helped finance the House in the Rock. The little girl is Lady Mary, later Countess of Courtown. Thomas Hill is the great-great-great-great grandfather of Nancy Buckle; the photograph below shows Nancy in her role as Town Crier (the first and only woman to hold the post). As a teenager Nancy auditioned for and was accepted into the Bluebell Showgirls; however the aunt with whom she lived refused to sign her papers to allow her to travel to Las Vegas with them.

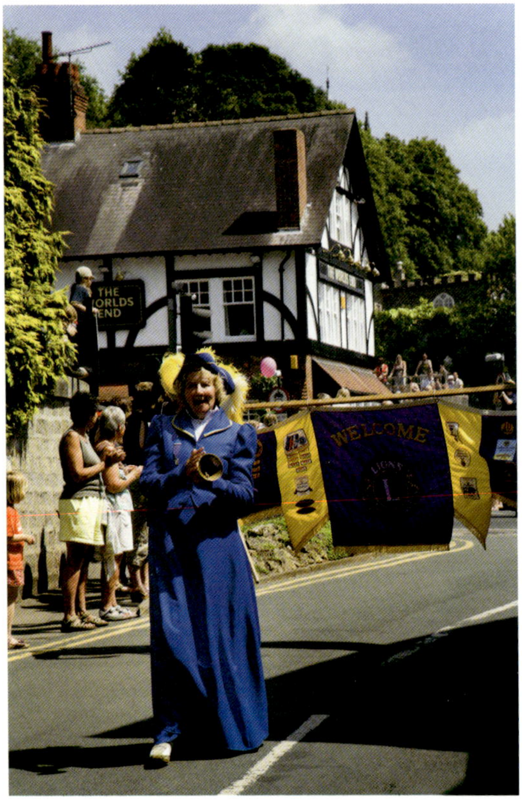

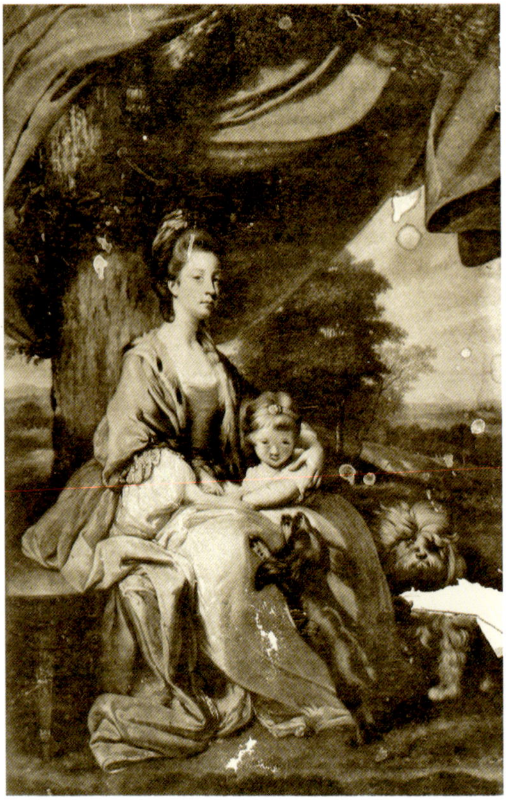

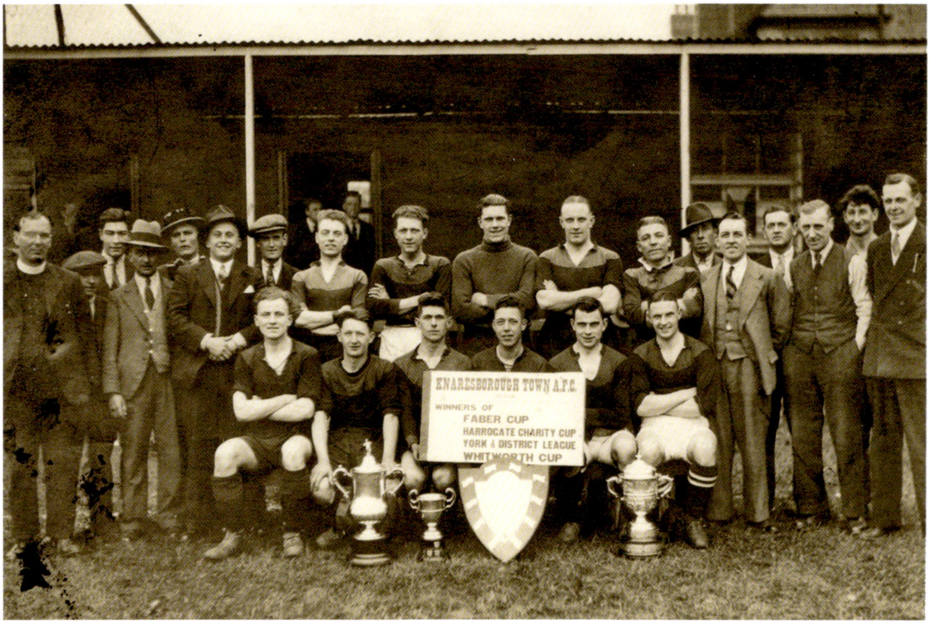

Knaresborough Town AFC – Champions!

Founded about 1900 the first chairman was Frank Sturdy (of boating fame) and the HQ was the Marquis of Granby. This photograph from the 1934-35 season shows the team proudly displaying their haul of silverware. More recently they were West Yorkshire League Premier Division Champions 2008/2009; the modern shot shows a goalmouth incident in the league game against Otley Town February 13 2010; Knaresborough, eighth in the table at the time won 2-0.

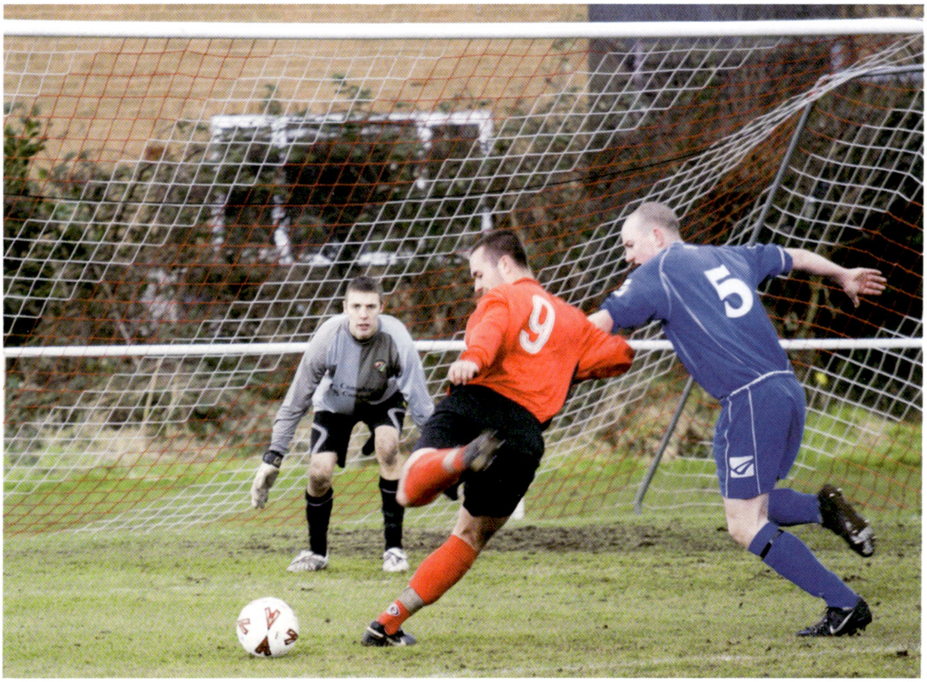

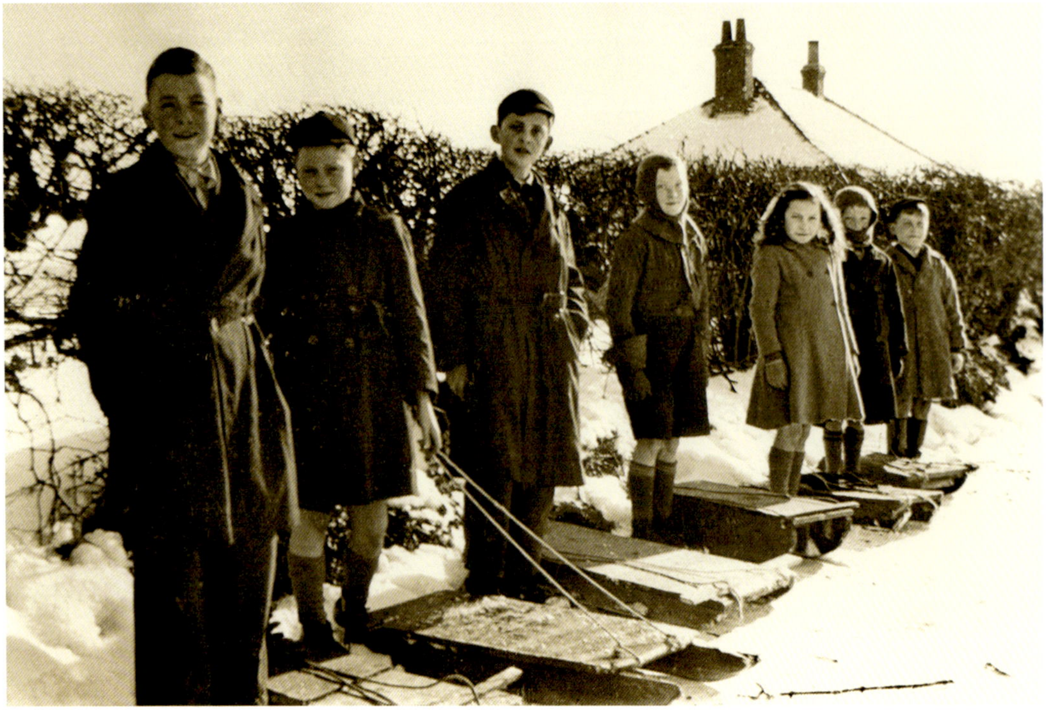

Sledgers in Carmires Avenue

This group of children, all well wrapped up with caps, macs and balaclavas, and equipped with wooden home-made sledges in the 1947 freeze all lived around Carmires Avenue. Gerald Hardwick, who provided the photograph is third from the left; the new photograph shows Gerald today roughly where the older photograph was shot.

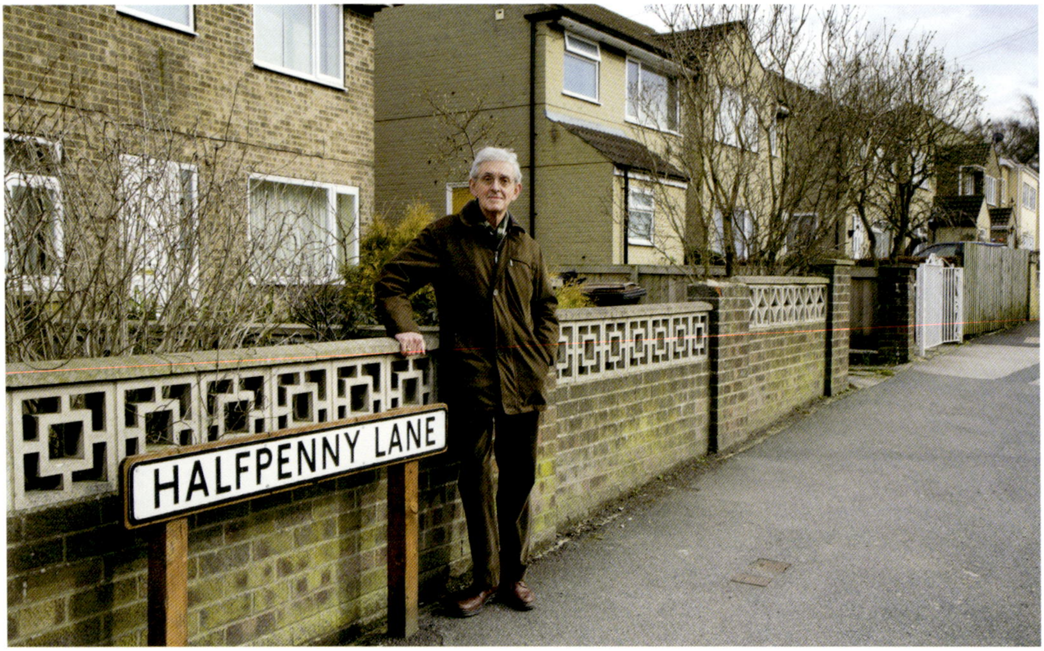

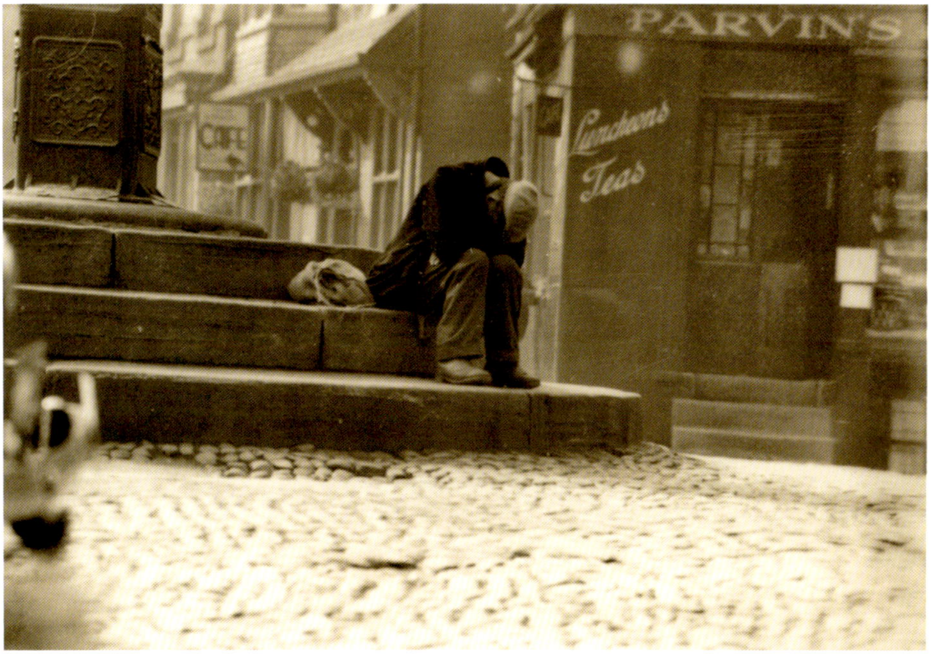

'Down and Out' and Blind Jack

This emotive photograph was taken just before the Second World War and entitled 'Down and Out' – a stark reminder of the poverty which existed at the time. Local legend Blind Jack (really John Metcalf 1717-1810) now occupies a bench nearby, impressively cast in bronze by local artist Barbara Asquith in February 2009. Metcalf was a Jack of All Trades – despite his disability – and at various times was musician, drinker, road-builder, hunter, cock-fight gambler, horse-dealer and smuggler. He constructed 180 miles of road earning £65k.

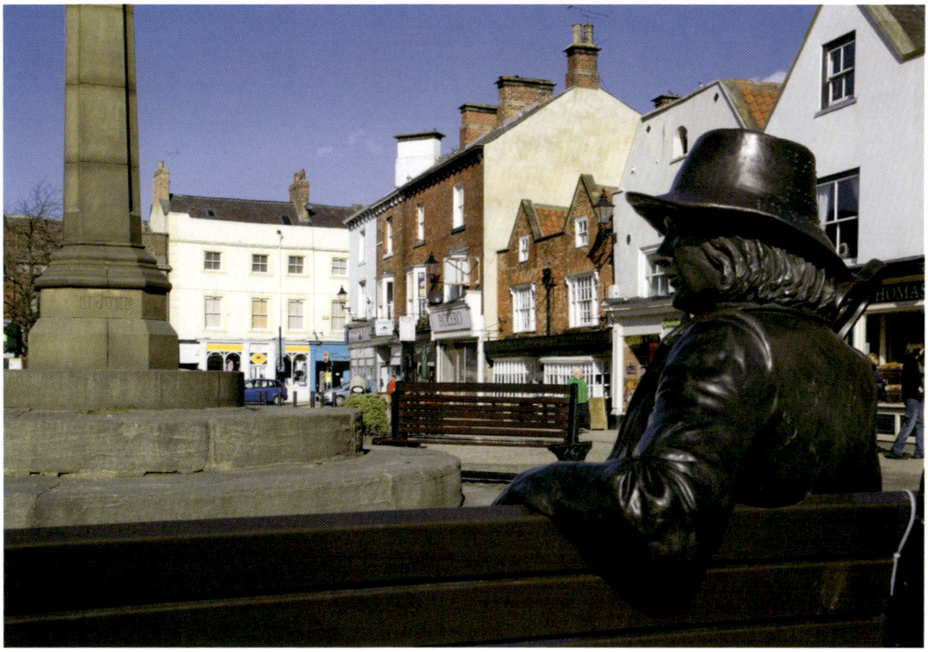

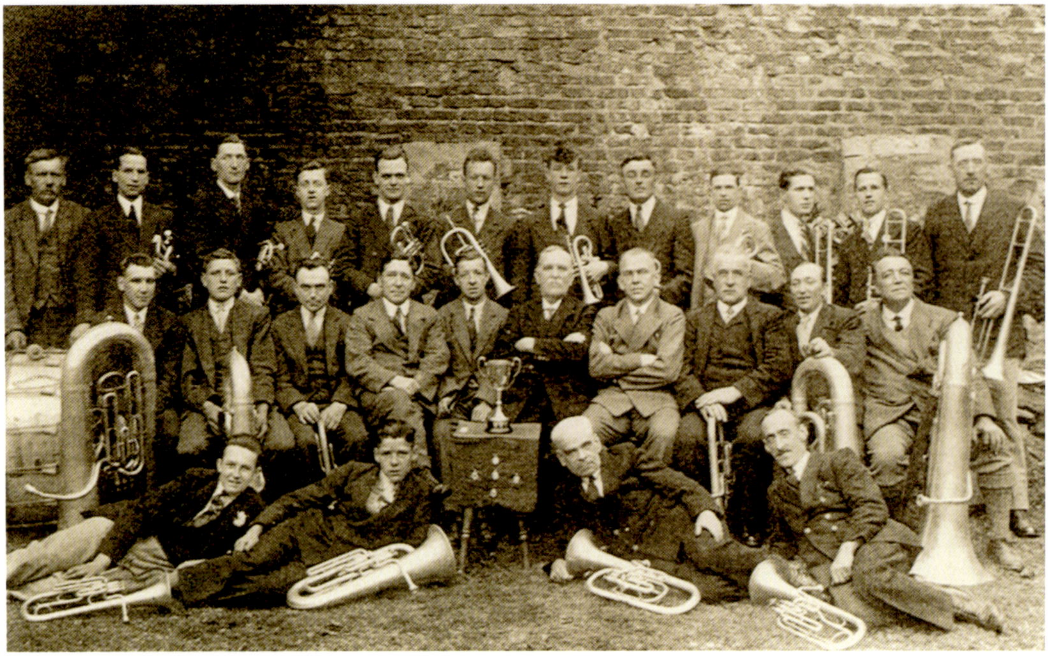

Knaresborough Silver Band

A 1930 photograph of the prize-winning band proudly showing off a new set of instruments. Established in 1879 as the Volunteer Band the Silver Band has provided a constant accompaniment to significant Knaresborough events for 130 years. The 2009 Edwardian Christmas market is the occasion for the modern shot; note the absence of women in the older one, typical for the time.

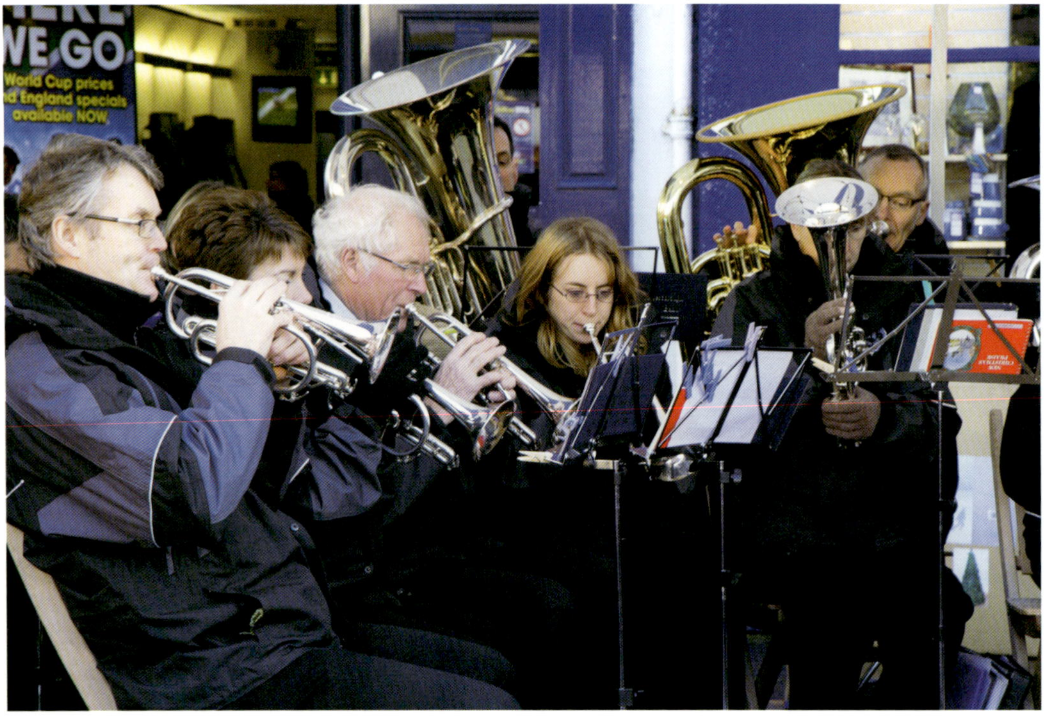

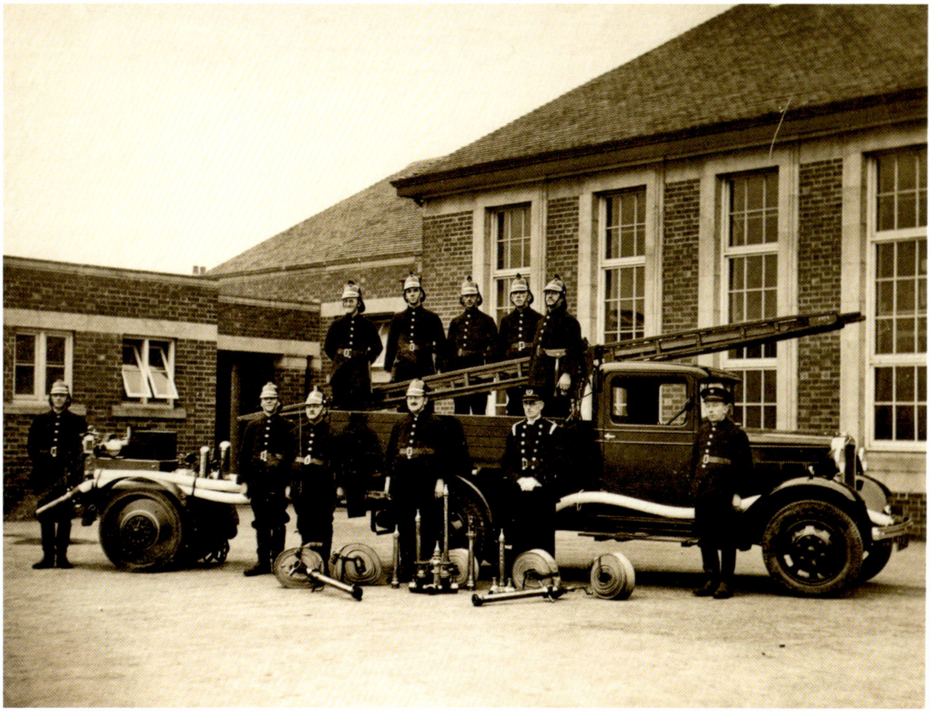

Knaresborough Firefighters

Organised firefighting in Knaresborough goes back to at least 1774; this photograph is from the late 1890s when the firemen were all unpaid volunteers; annual wages of £2.00 started in 1920. The fire engine was stationed behind the Borough Bailiff (along with the emergency bell) and can still be seen in the Courthouse Museum. The modern picture shows today's firefighters in action at the 2010 duck race.

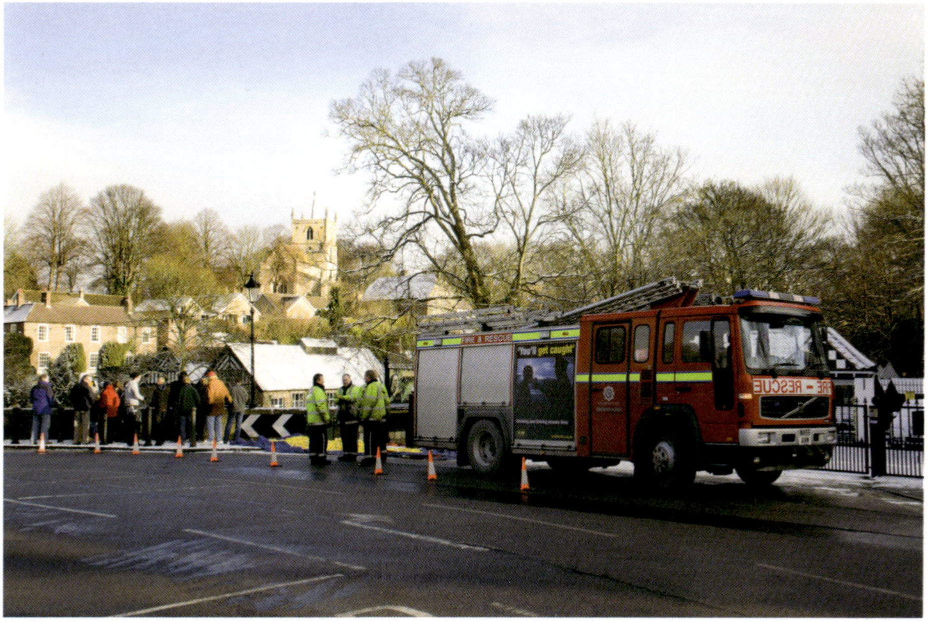

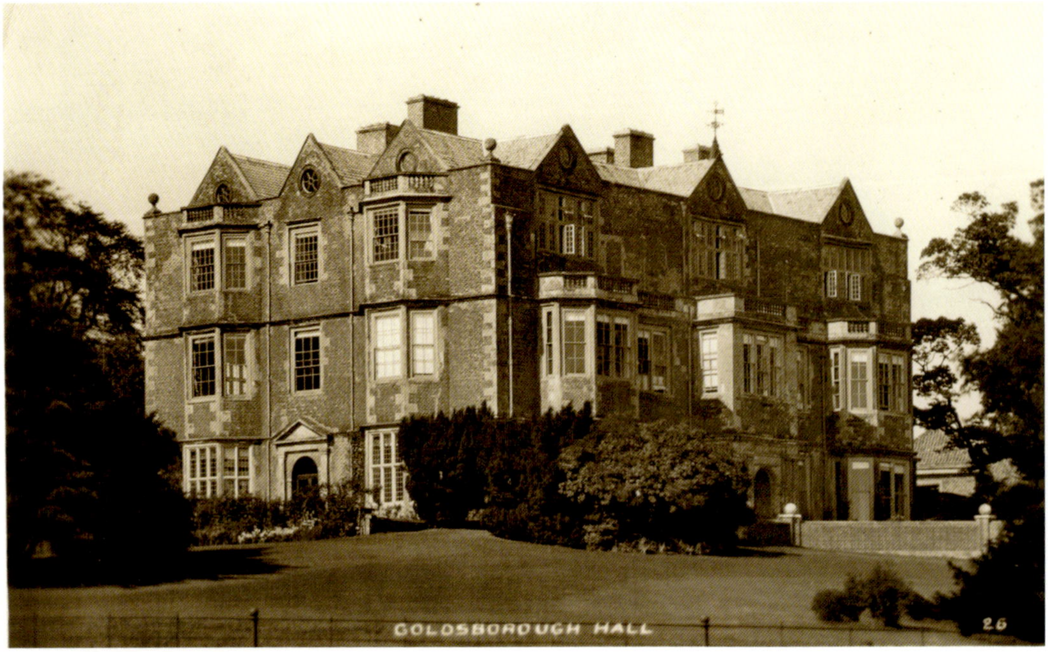

Goldsborough Hall and Princess Mary

Built in the 1620s this has been the home of the Lascelles family and of Princess Mary the Princess Royal in the 1920s and '30s. The modern photograph shows the Hall today during a charity event in March 2010 – the first time the 11 acres of gardens have been opened to the public since 1930 and a dress rehearsal for its opening in July 2010 as part of the National Garden Scheme.

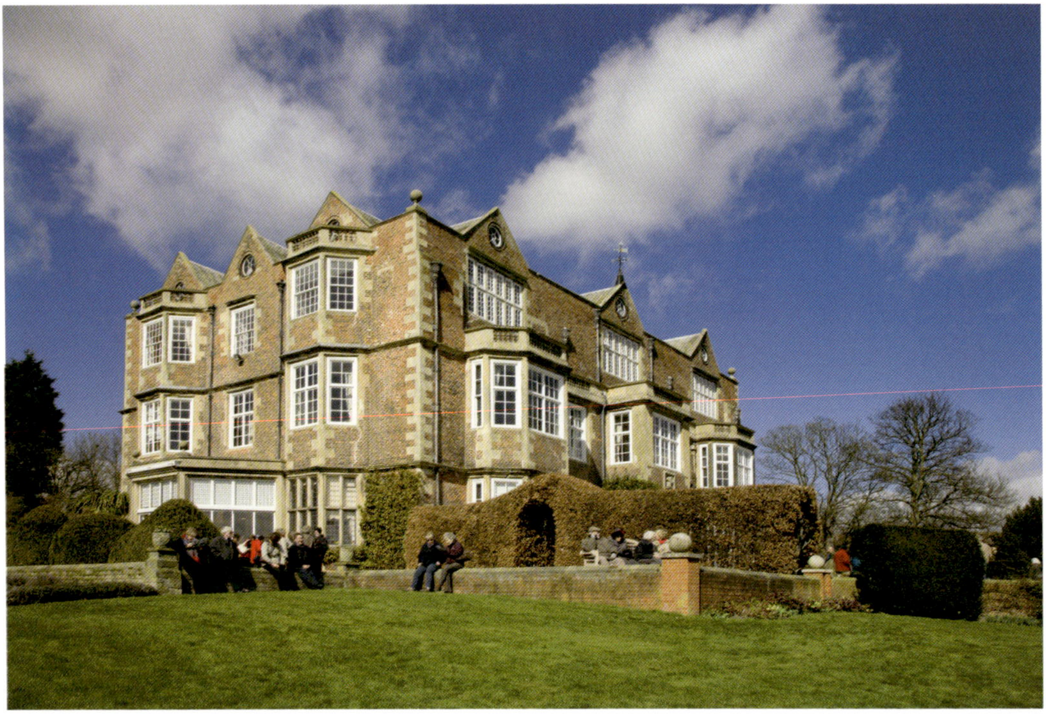

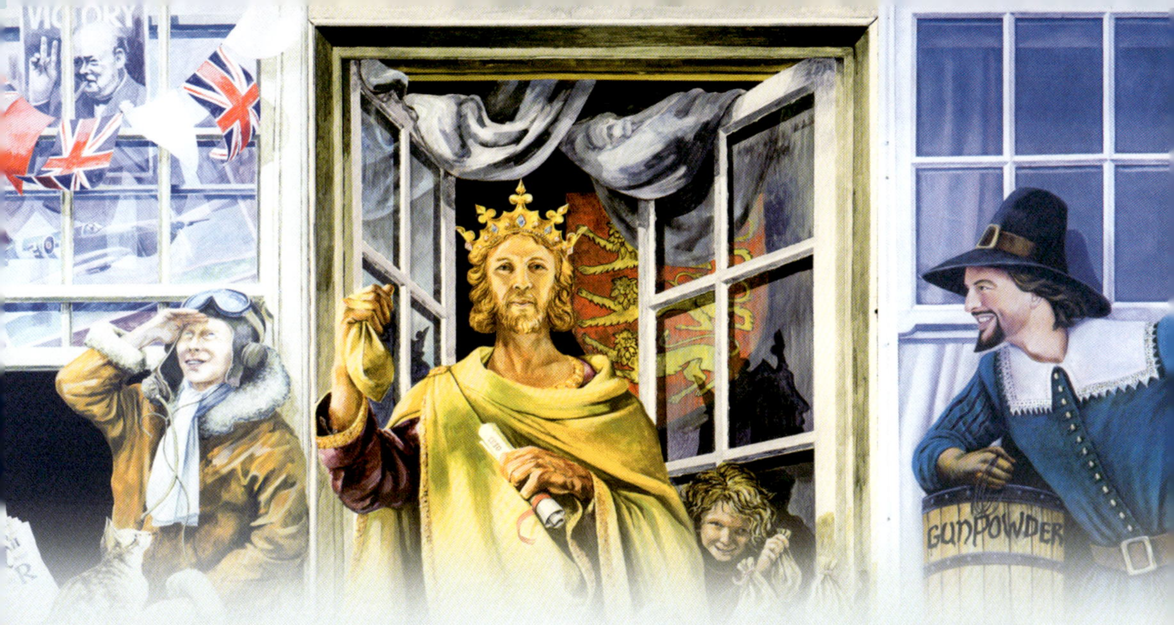

CHAPTER 3

Special Events

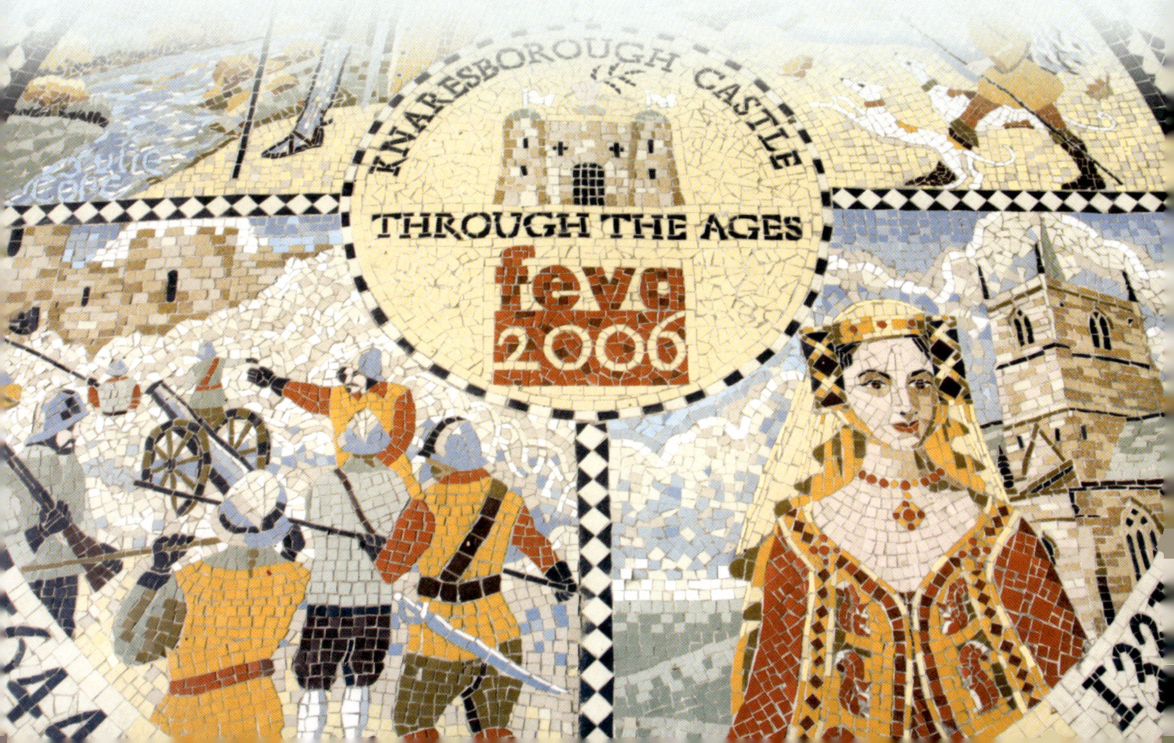

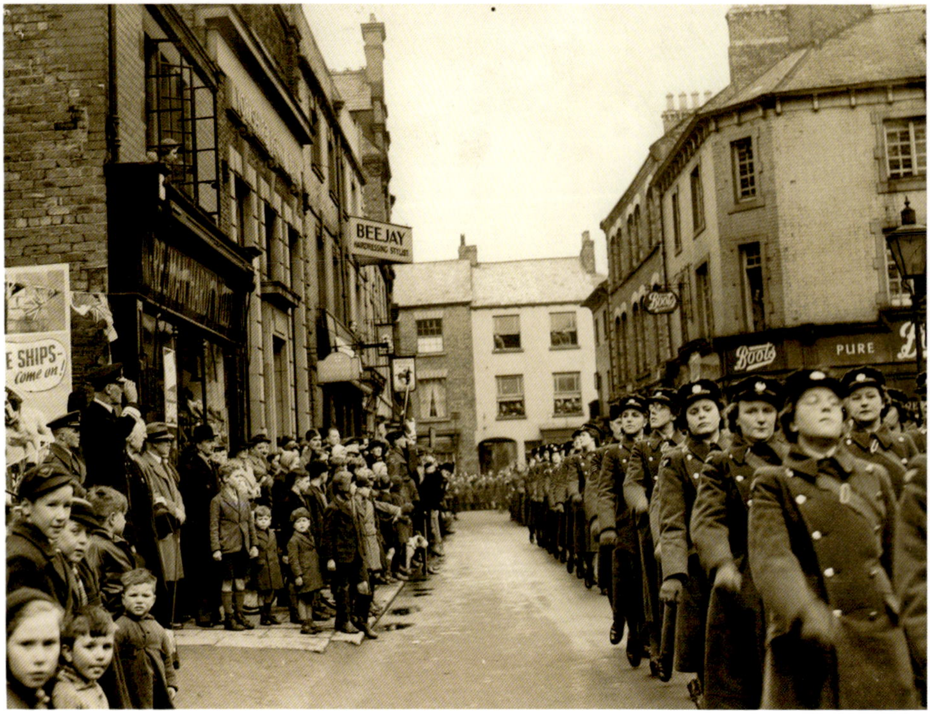

Warship Week 1942

WAAFs processing into the Market Place from the High Street during Warship Week March 1942; the officer taking the salute was Rear Admiral L. Forbes-Sempill. Boots is still there in the building on the right as can be seen in the remarkably unchanged scene showing the 2009 Remembrance Day parade sixty-seven years later.

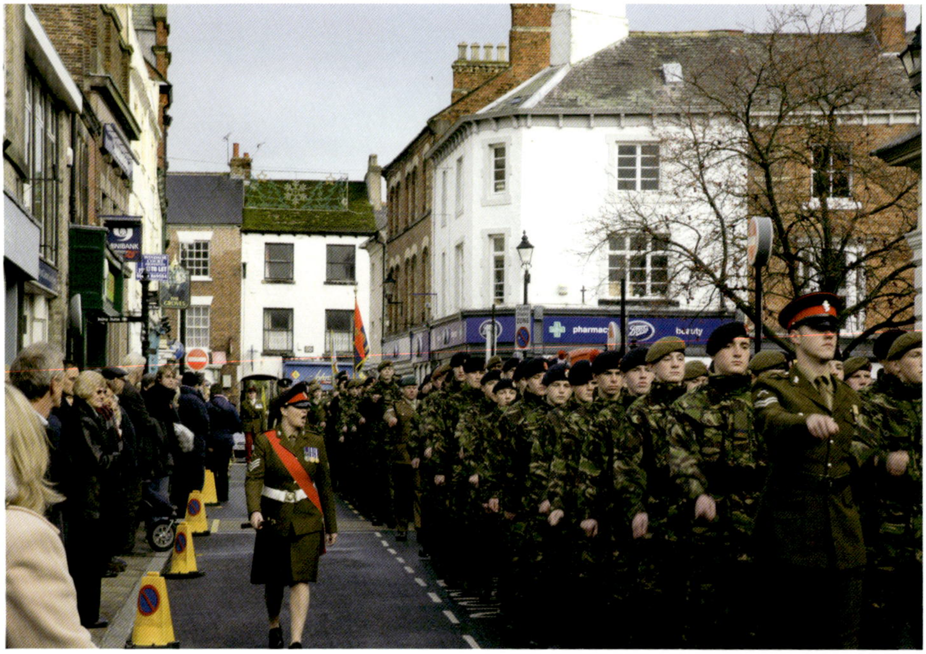

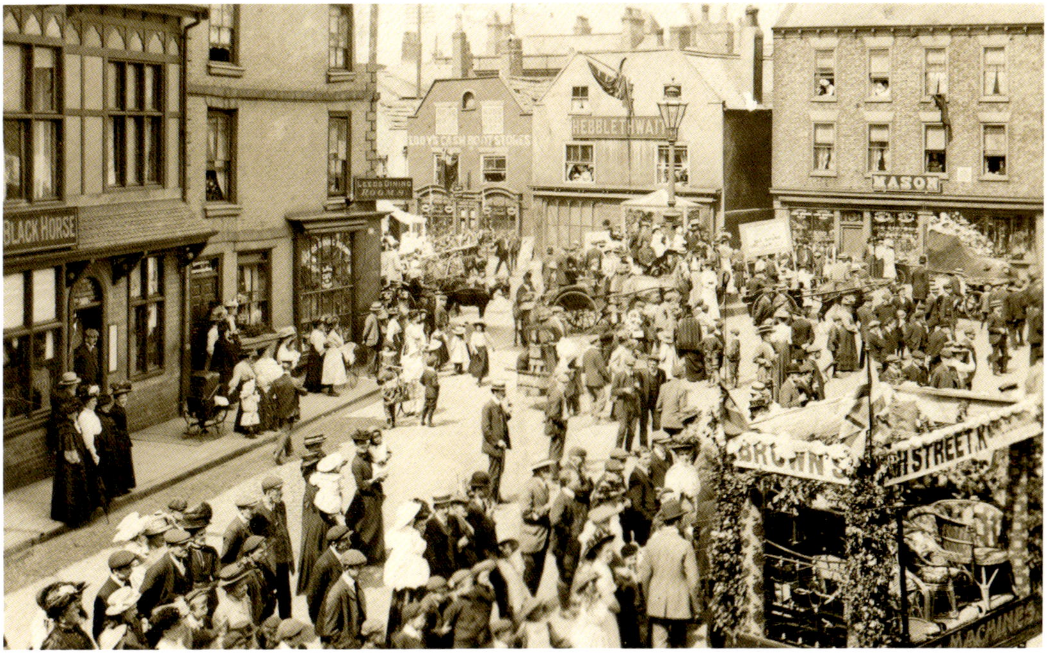

Tradesmen's Procession

One of the annual Tradesmen's Processions which took place every June before the First World War. Here we see the float from Brown's, the High Street furnishers, in the Market Place. In the background we can see a number of shops: Mason's was an ironmongers (now Clinton's) and hardware shop, Hebblethwaites a draper's (now Thomas the Bakers), Eddy's Cash Boot Stop to the right is now the Oxfam shop; the Black Horse pub is now the Halifax Building Society; the Leeds Dining Rooms on the corner and popular with cyclists is now Hi-Spirits, a specialist off-licence famous for artisan beers and fine wines from around the world. A bed from a recent bed race provides an apt modern equivalent.

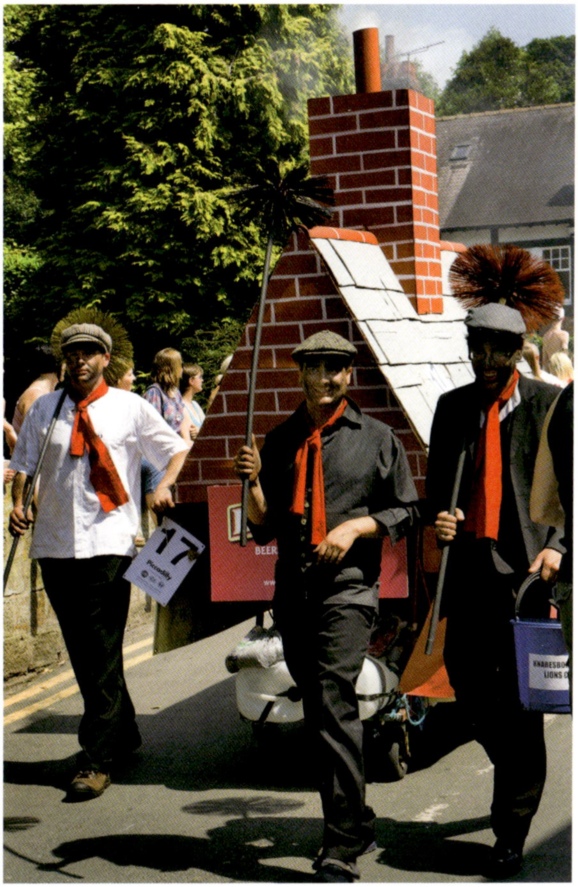

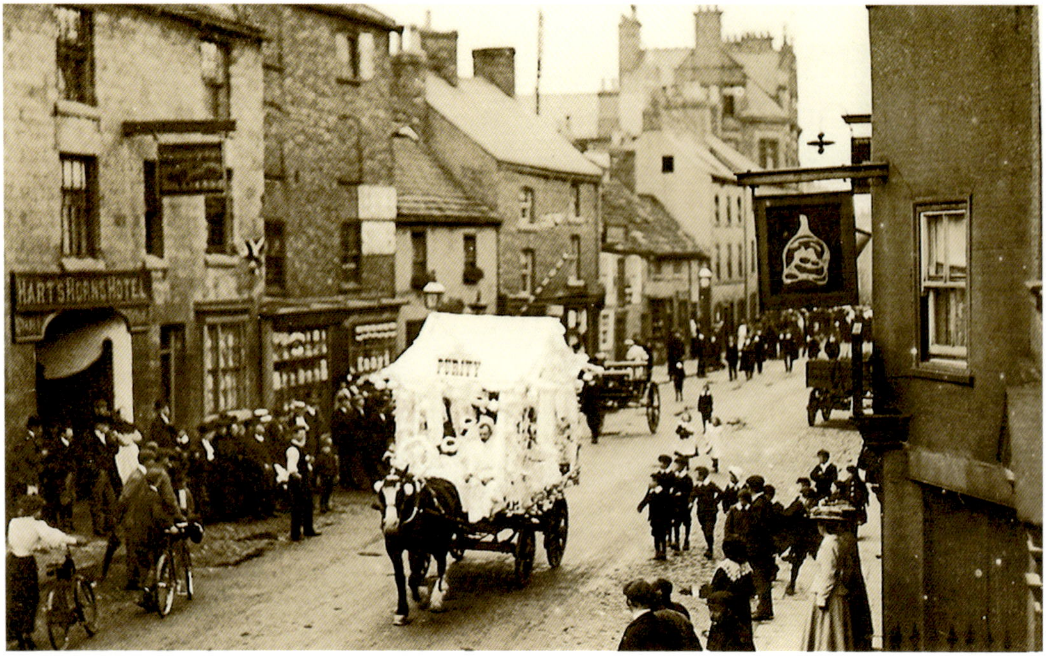

Purity

Another float from another Tradesmen's Procession, this time in the High Street just passing the Hart's Horns Hotel entrance (now the Hart). Note the barber's pole on the left at what is now the Knaresborough Bookshop which has been in the town in various locations on the High Street for over forty years. The pub on the right was the Shoulder of Mutton – now demolished.

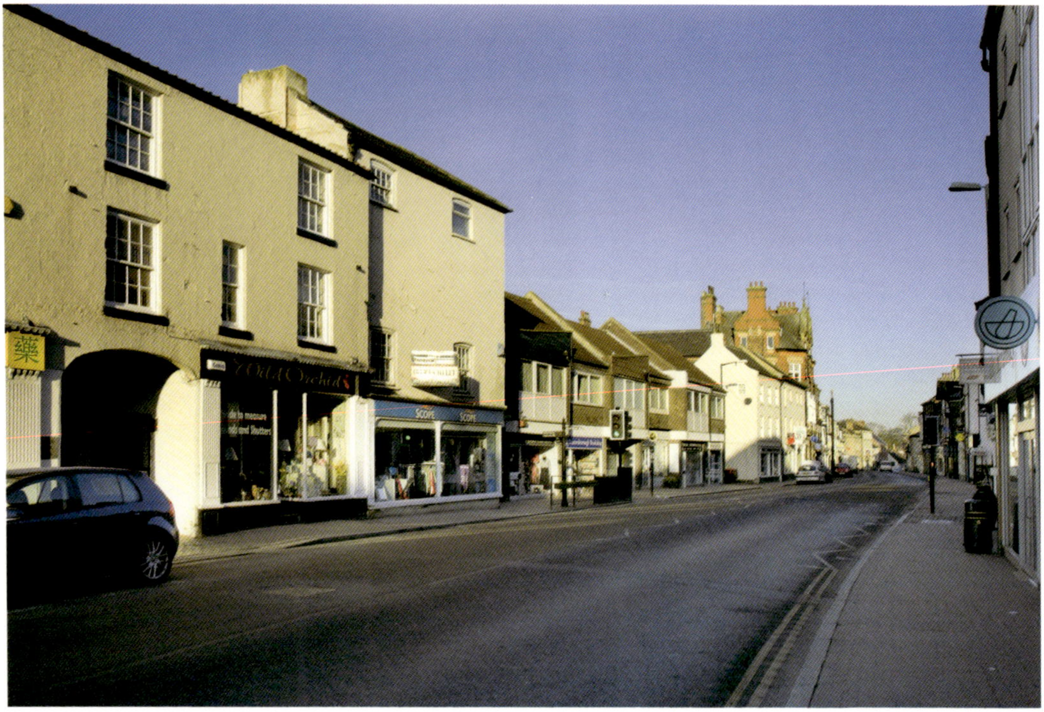

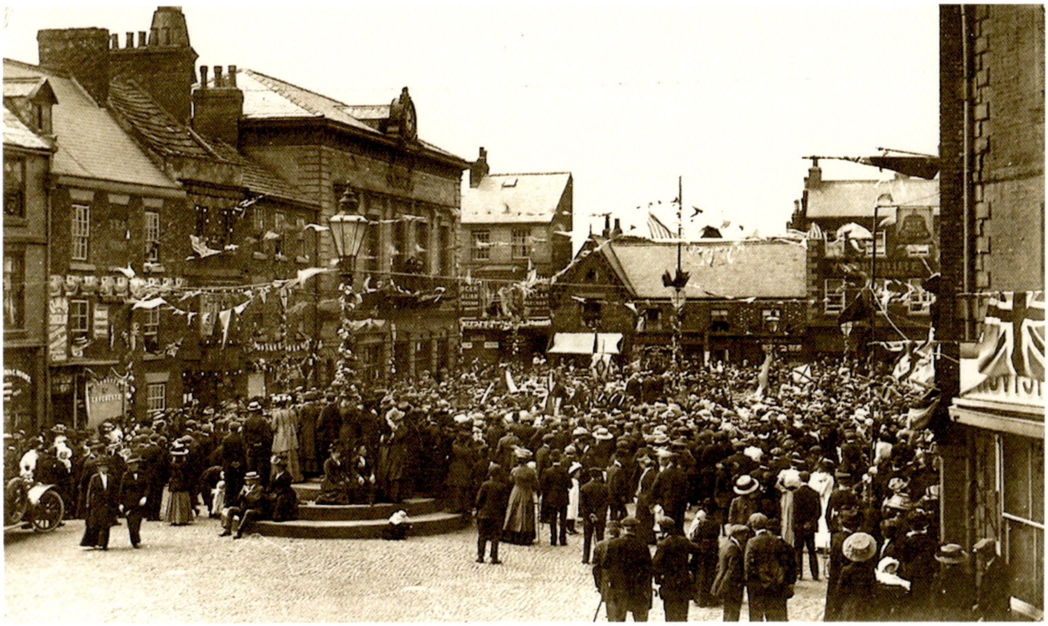

The Coronation of George V

June 1911 saw celebrations to mark George V's coronation centred on the market cross, or rather the 1824 gas lamp erected there by John Malam. This in turn was replaced in 1954 to mark the coronation of Queen Elizabeth II by L. H. Clark's fourteenth century style cross. Market Place remains the focus for Knaresborough events: this picture shows Morris dances performing at the 2009 Edwardian market.

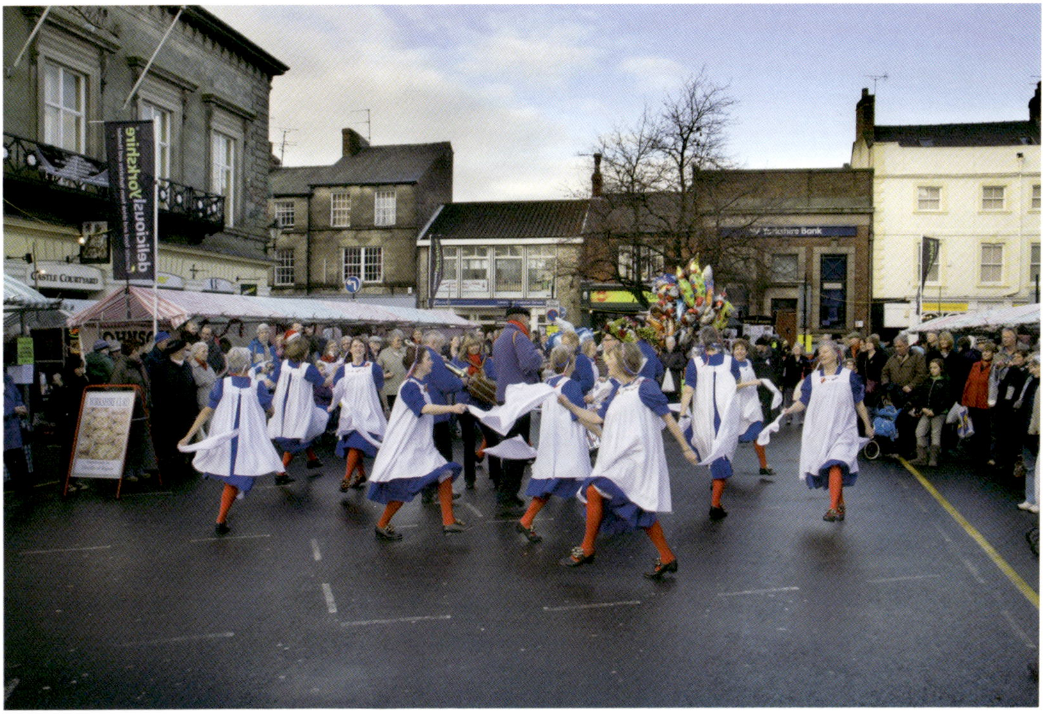

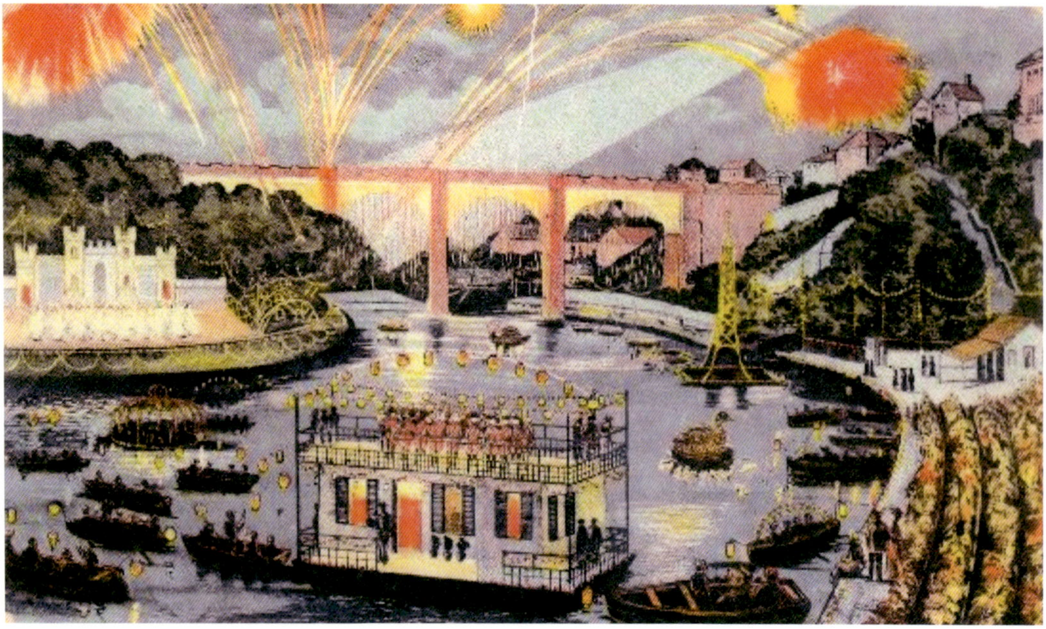

'England's Unique Water Pageant'

Knaresborough Water Carnival: a magnificent spectacle which really came to life after nightfall when Brock's provided a fantastic firework display. The viaduct was transformed into Niagara Falls (cost in 1903: £58.00). Don Pedro crossing the river by tightrope, a fairy castle, the Eiffel Tower, the houseboat (The Marigold) with forty dancers and a brass band, and a spotlight picking out notable local characters such as Mother Shipton, completed the scene. A century later and Knaresborough's close association with the Nidd is undiminished as this photograph of the 2010 New Year's Day charity duck race at High Bridge shows.

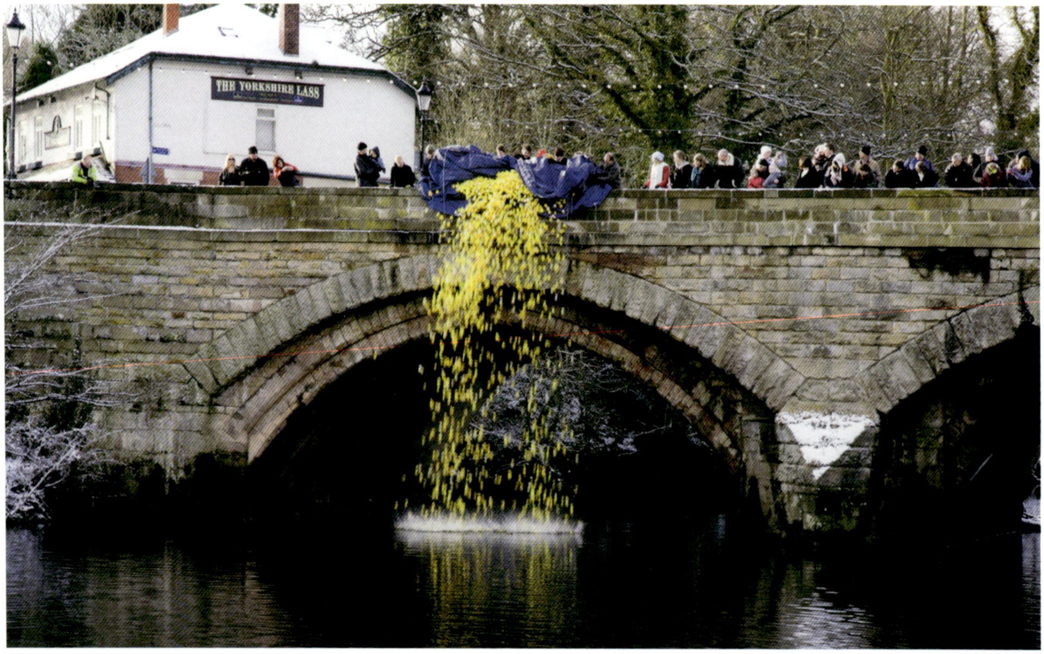

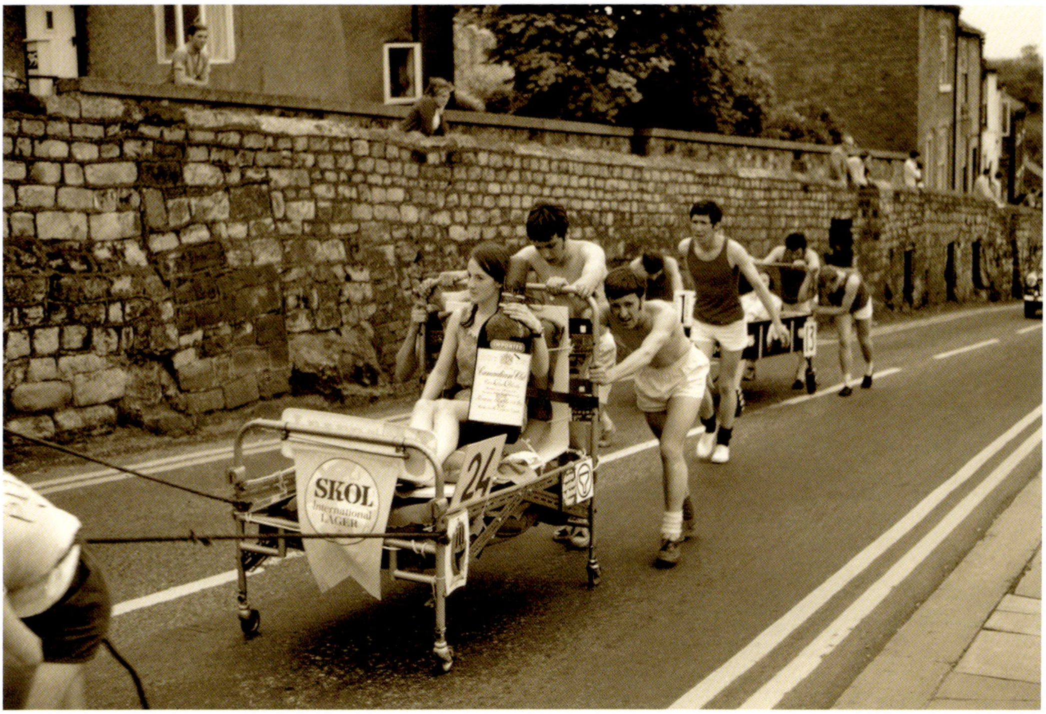

The Great Knaresborough Bed Race
The world famous bed race was started by the Knaresborough Lions in 1966 and was originally restricted to the Services and the fire brigade. In 1968 it was thrown open to the wider community; a record ninety teams are competing in the 2010 event to bring in about £80,000 for charity. The newer photograph shows the dramatic river stage of a recent race.

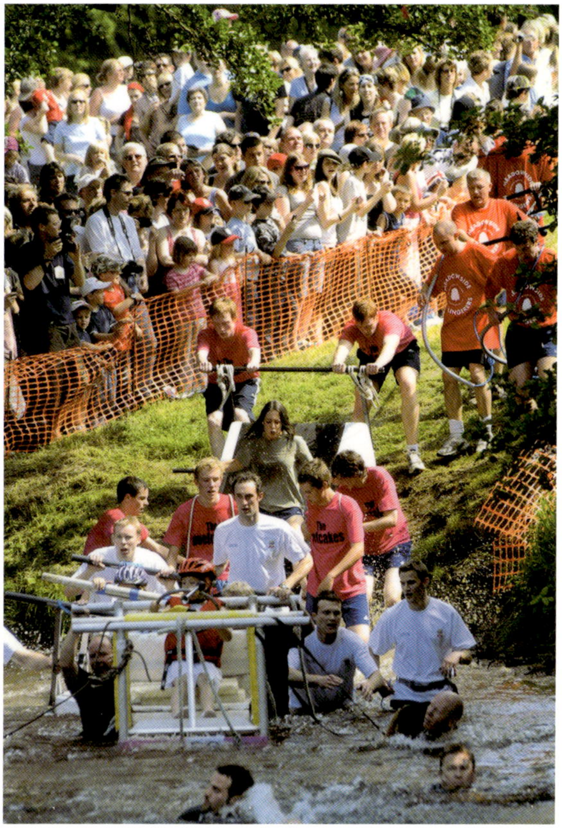

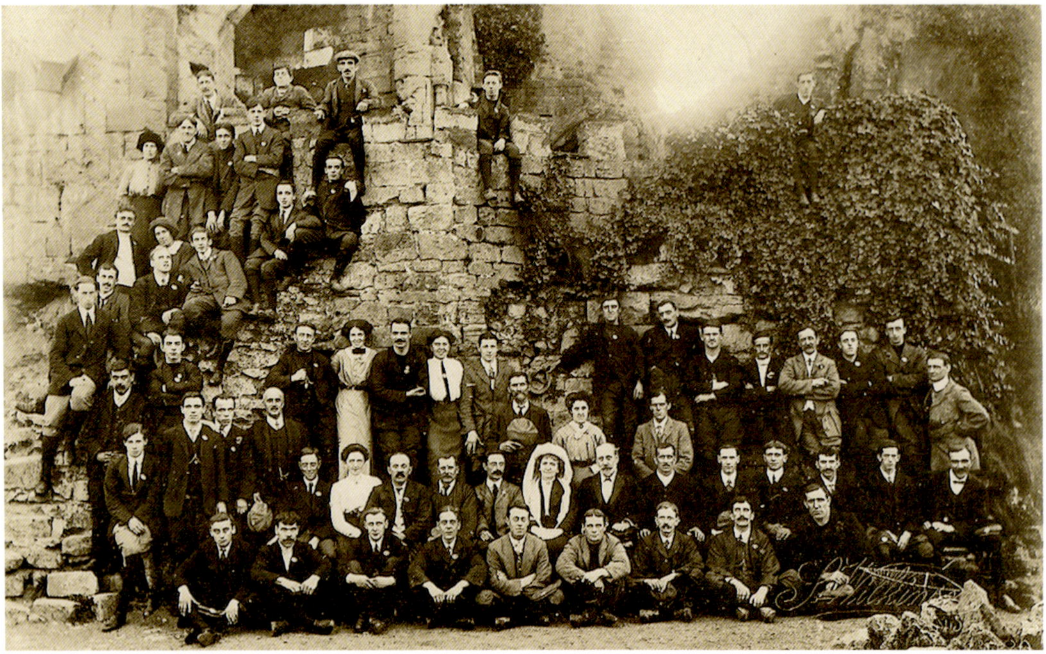

The Very First Maundy Giving in Knaresborough in 1210

The old photograph shows an unknown event at the castle which was important enough to warrant Sunday best and badges and involved both men and women. Anyone know what it was and when? In April 2010 the 800th anniversary celebrations of the first Maundy were held at the castle, the very first giving having taken place in Knaresborough in 1210. The modern photograph shows King John, Queen Isabelle and retainers handing out the Maundy gifts to thirteen Knaresborough people.

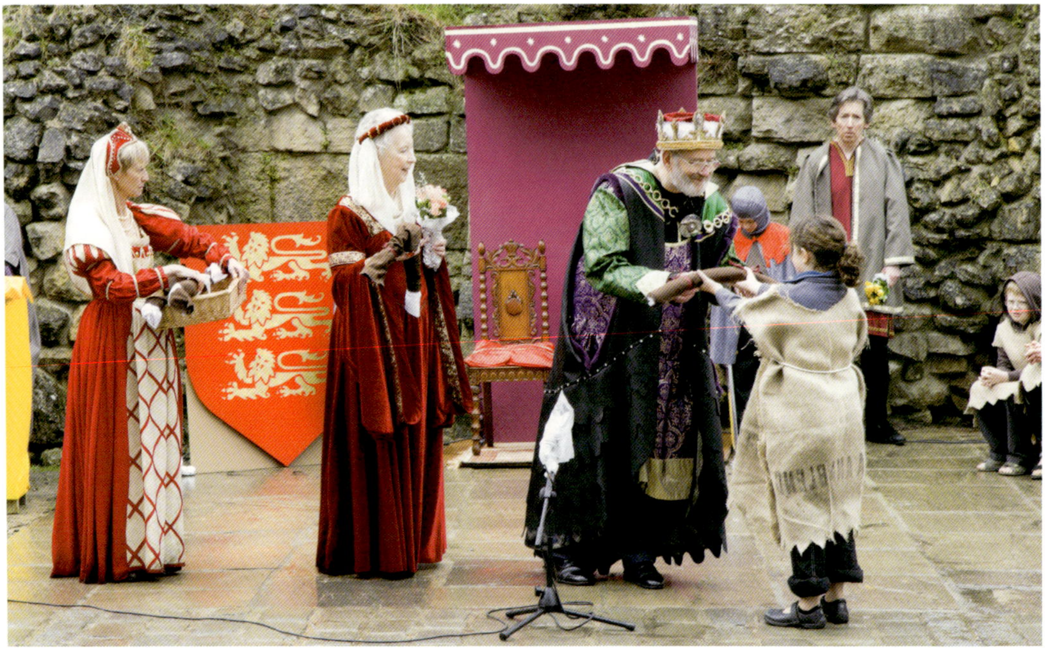

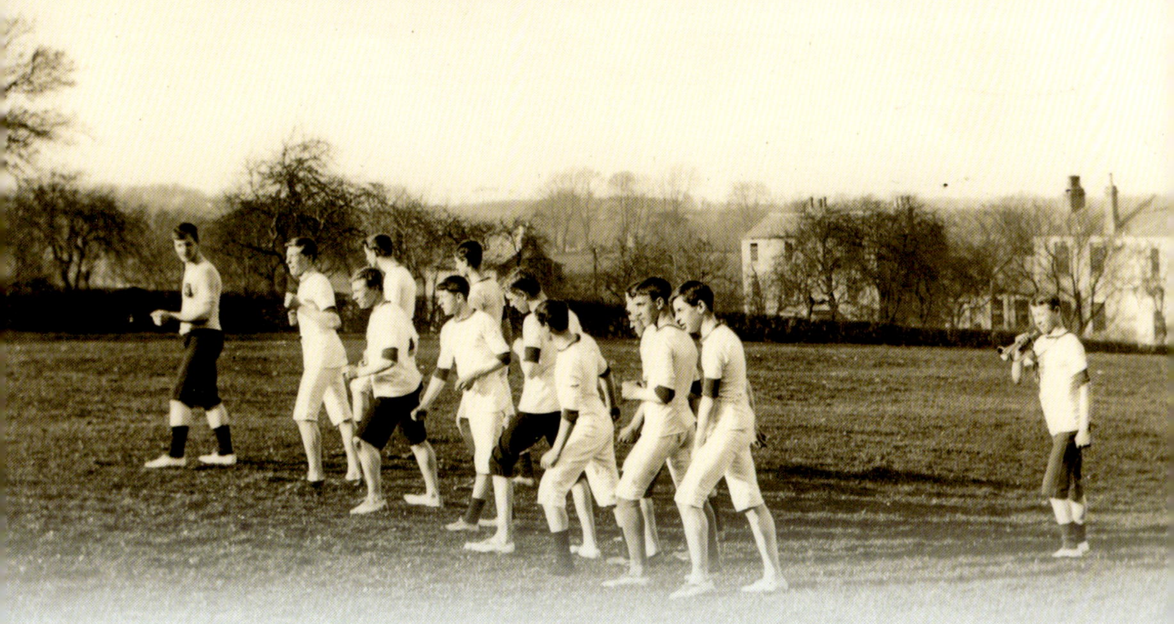

CHAPTER 4

School

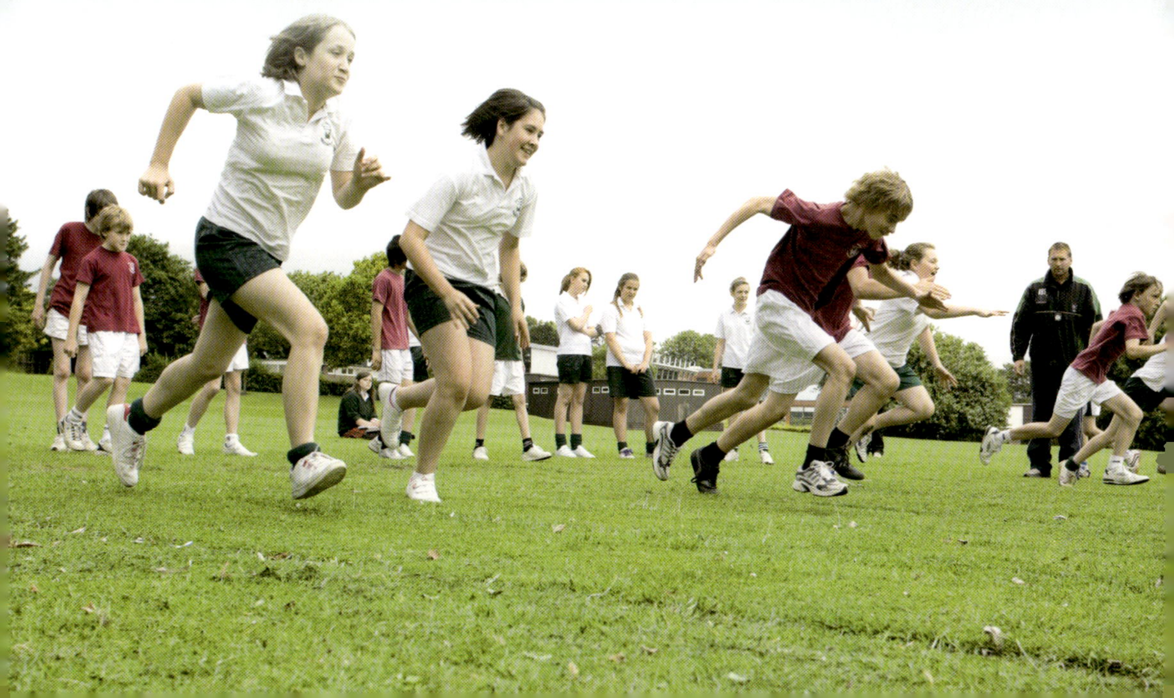

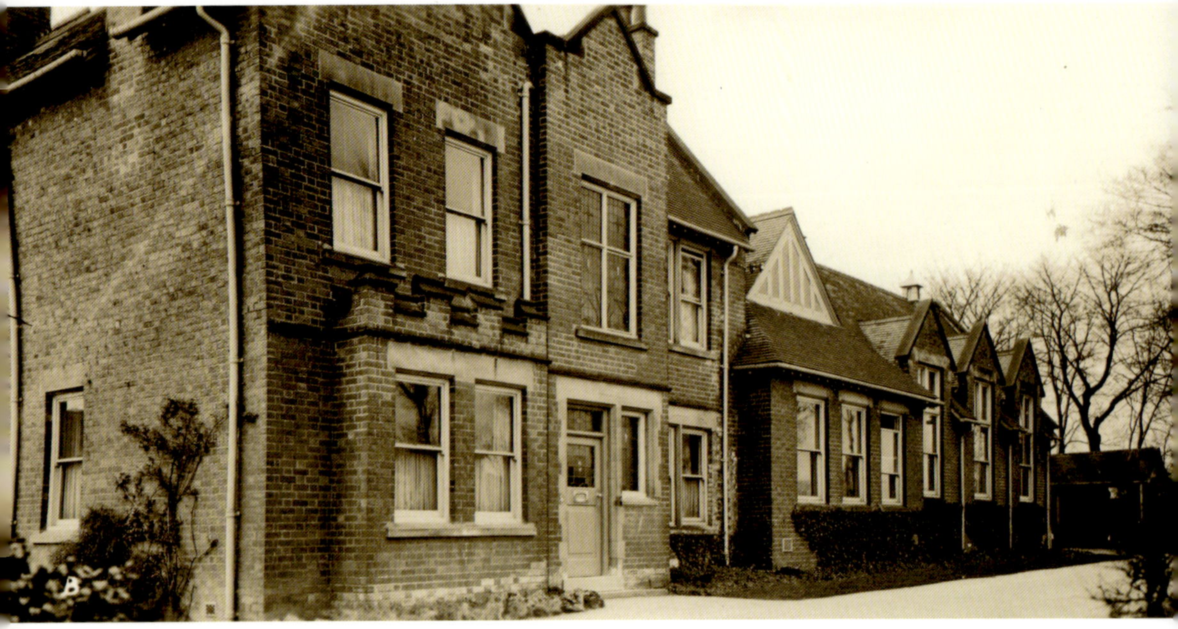

King James's School: *Quid Retribuam Domino?*

A 1952 picture of what was then King James's Grammar School; the Head was Mr D. J. Stevens. The school had been founded in 1616 by permission of the King on the instigation of the Revd Dr Robert Chaloner; he was 'to take paines with all indifferently, as well poore as rich.' Anyone 'unapte to learne' after a year was expelled. Zero tolerance too on absenteeism: 'he shall be utterly expelled' – unless caused by illness. The newer photograph shows the impressive new extension.

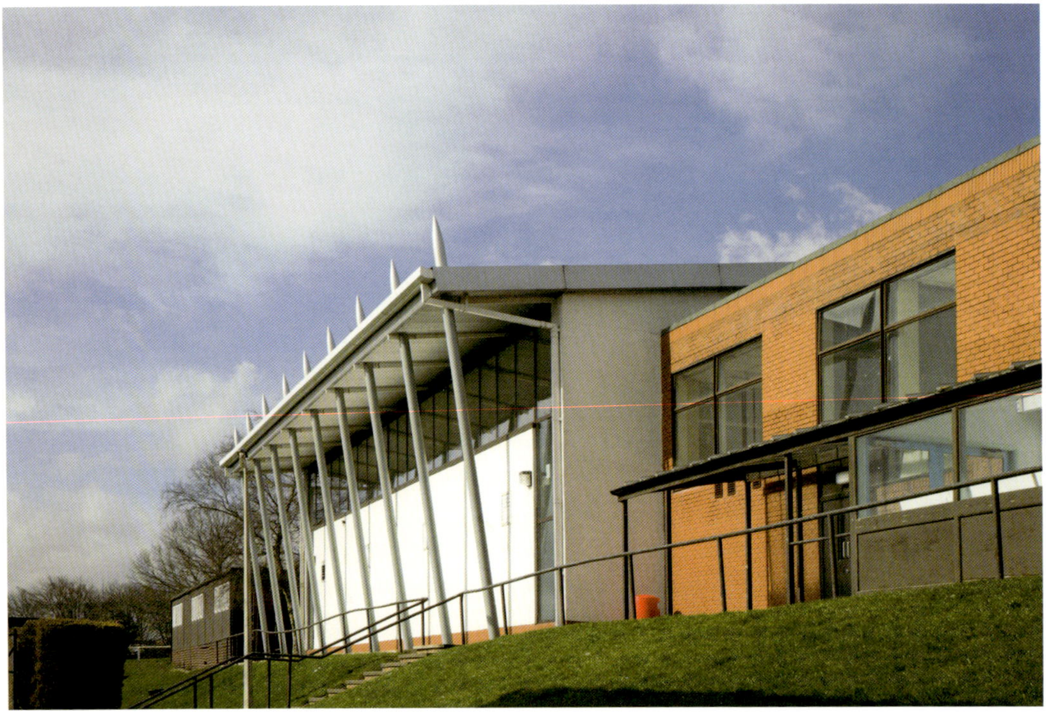

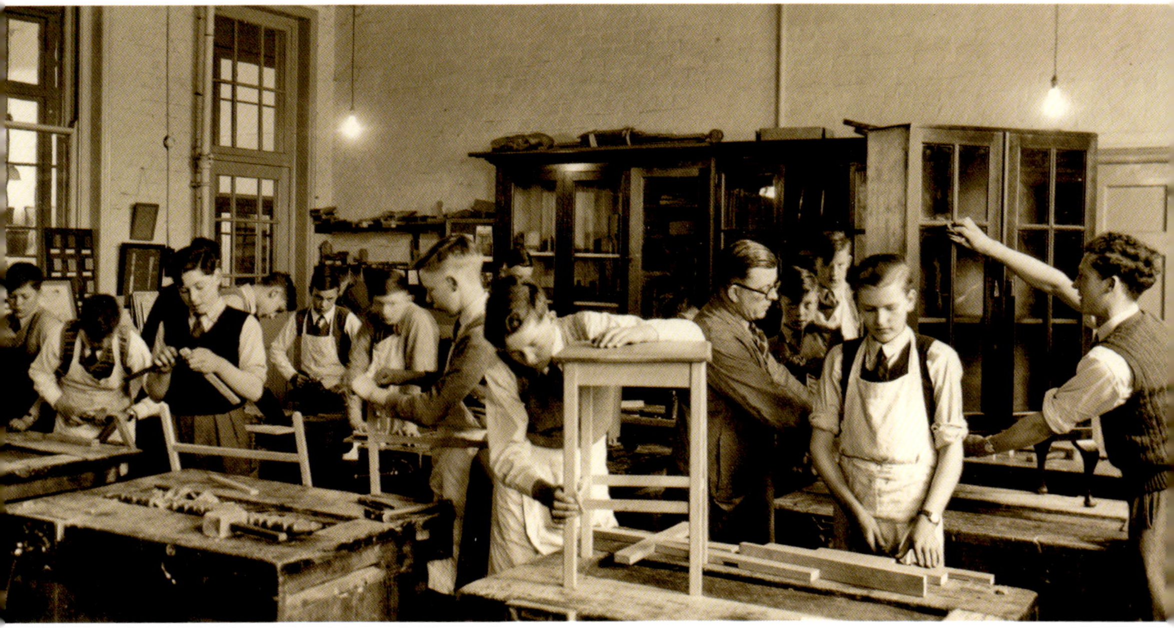

Design and Technology 1952 Style

A woodwork class in 1952. The modern picture taken in the Design and Technology department demonstrates how school equipment nowadays must be state of the art and compatible with that used in industry, so that students are familiar with machinery they would go on to work on either at university or in employment.

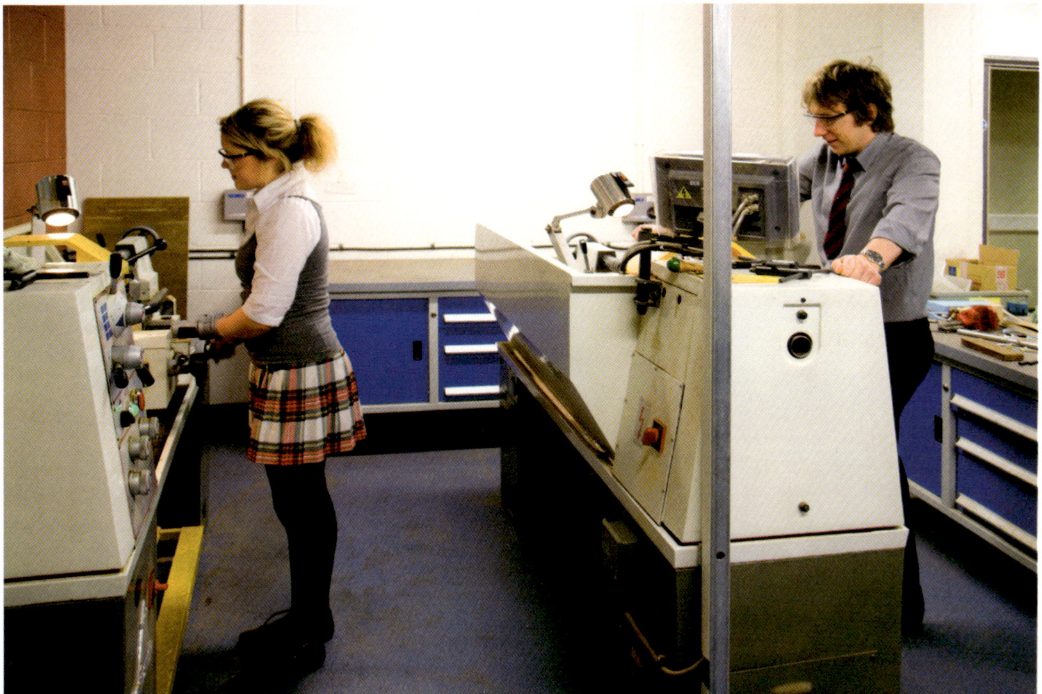

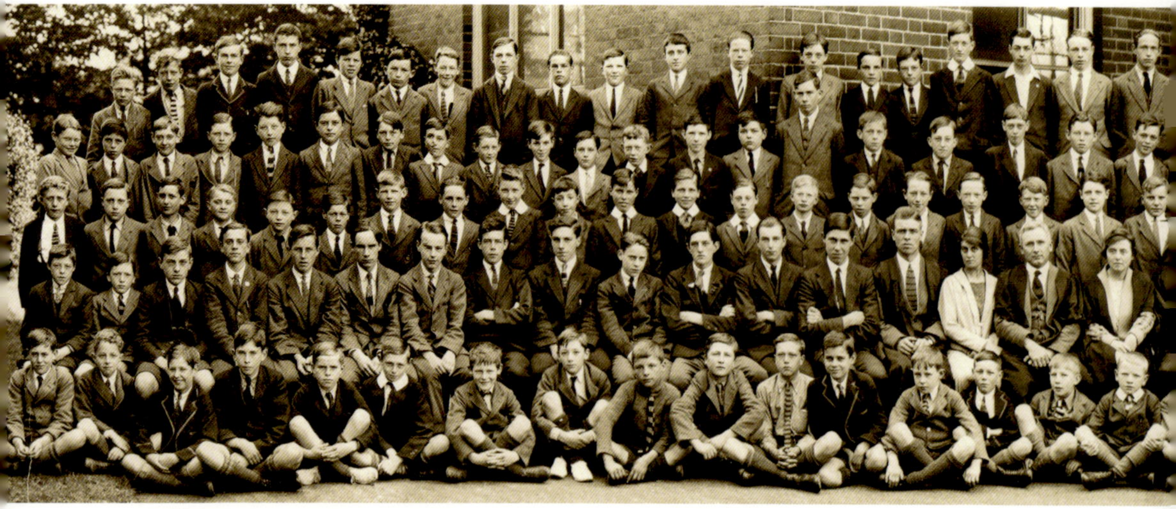

King James's School photograph 1925 – the Men and Boys

The original school rules (Ordinances and Lawes) dictated that discipline be enforced by 'a rod, moderately': 'The Maister...shall severely punish swearing, lying, picking, stealing, fighting and quarrelling, wanton speech and unclean behaviour.' Today's photograph shows a somewhat more relaxed headmaster, Carl Sugden, with a group of students.

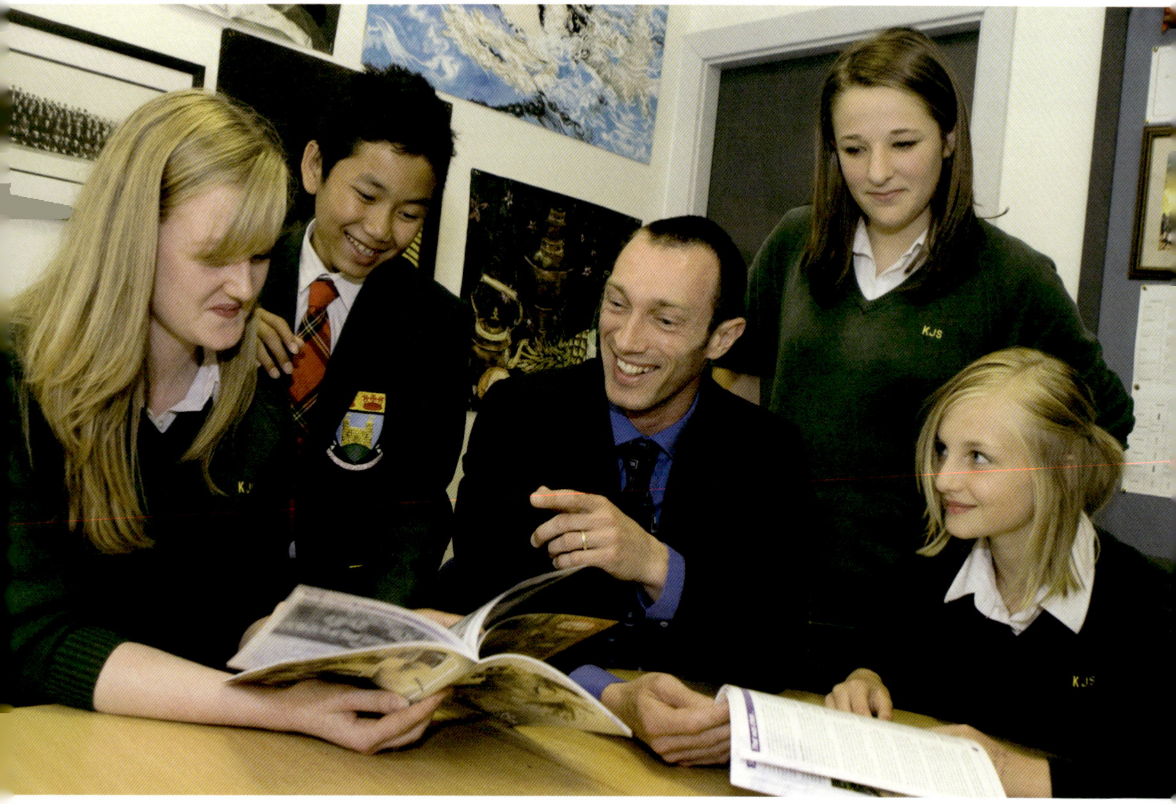

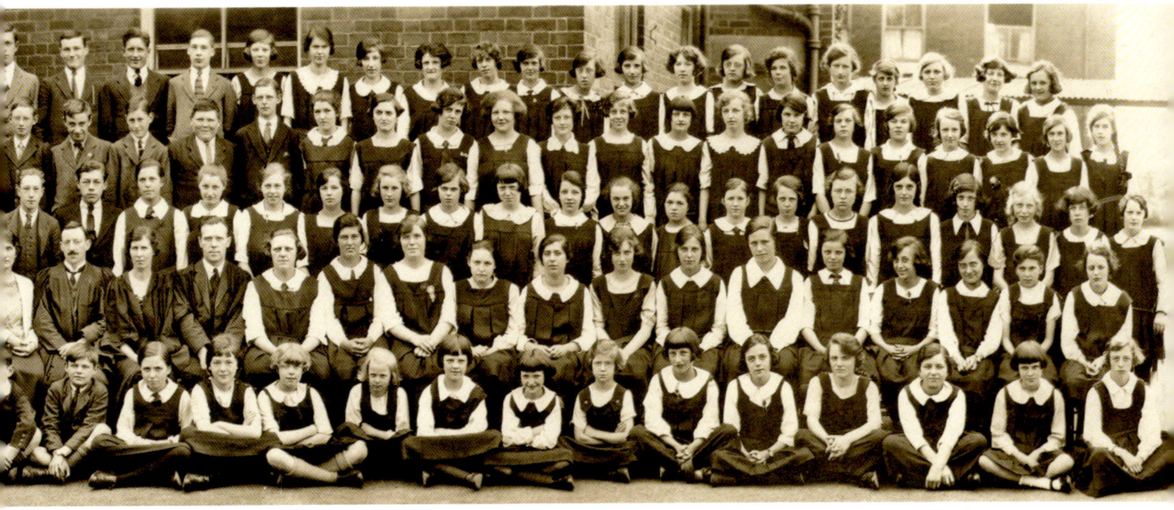

King James's School photograph 1925 – the Women and Girls

In the early days school started at 6.00 am in the summer, 7.00 am in the winter with an assembly in which the boys recited, on their knees, not just any old Psalm but the longest of them all: Psalm 119 (176 verses); the Creed, the Lord's Prayer and the Catechism. After Year 1 they had to converse in Latin *at all times including playtime.* Parents were responsible for the provision of bows and arrows (for practice, in case of war) as well as books and all writing materials, and candles in winter.

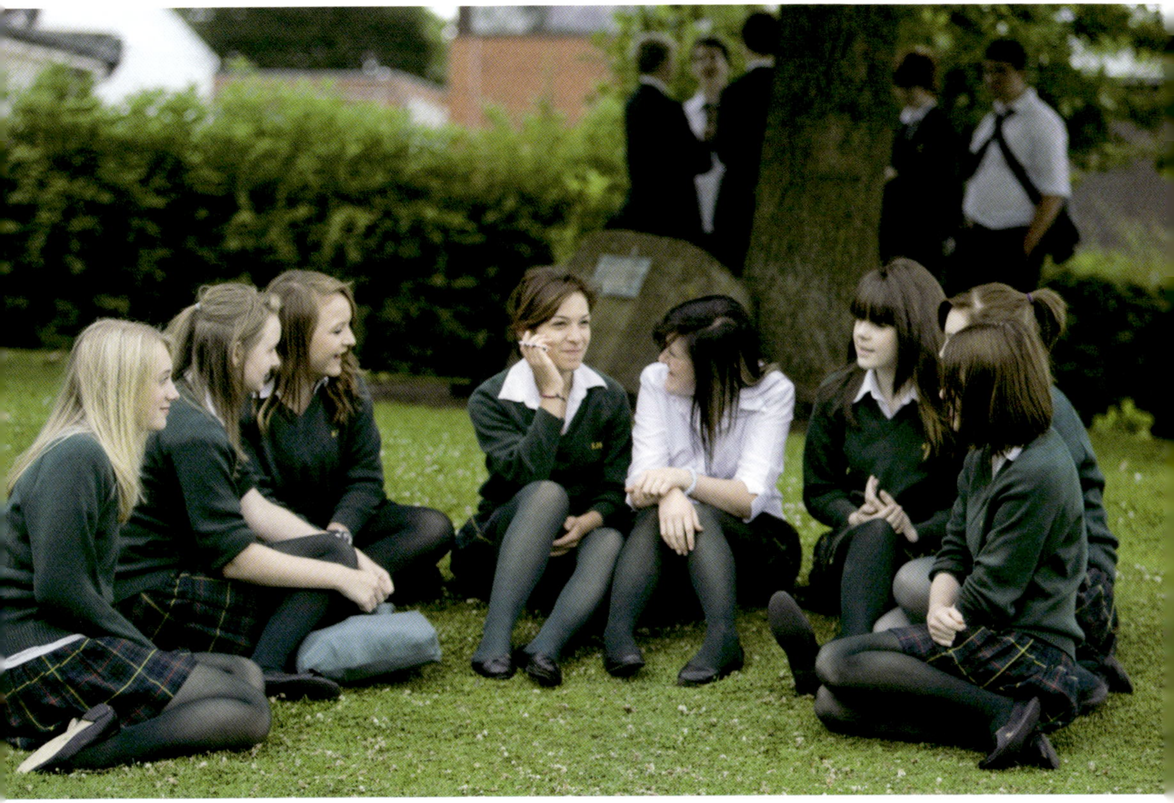

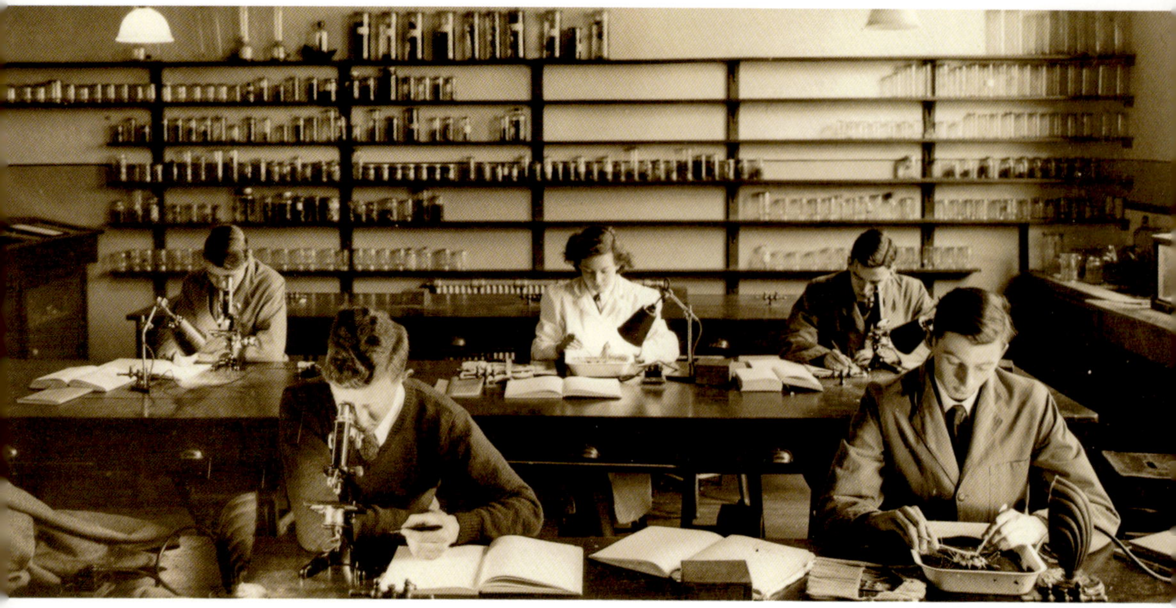

Biology Laboratory

Students working in the biology lab in 1952; over fifty-eight years later things have moved on a bit, not least safety in the laboratory, as the protective glasses show. A new science block was opened in 1963. *Baines 1822 Directory* tells us that there were ten other schools in Knaresborough at the time including Thomas Cartwright's (classical and commercial) and the aptly named Sarah Fairlass school for ladies, on the High Street.

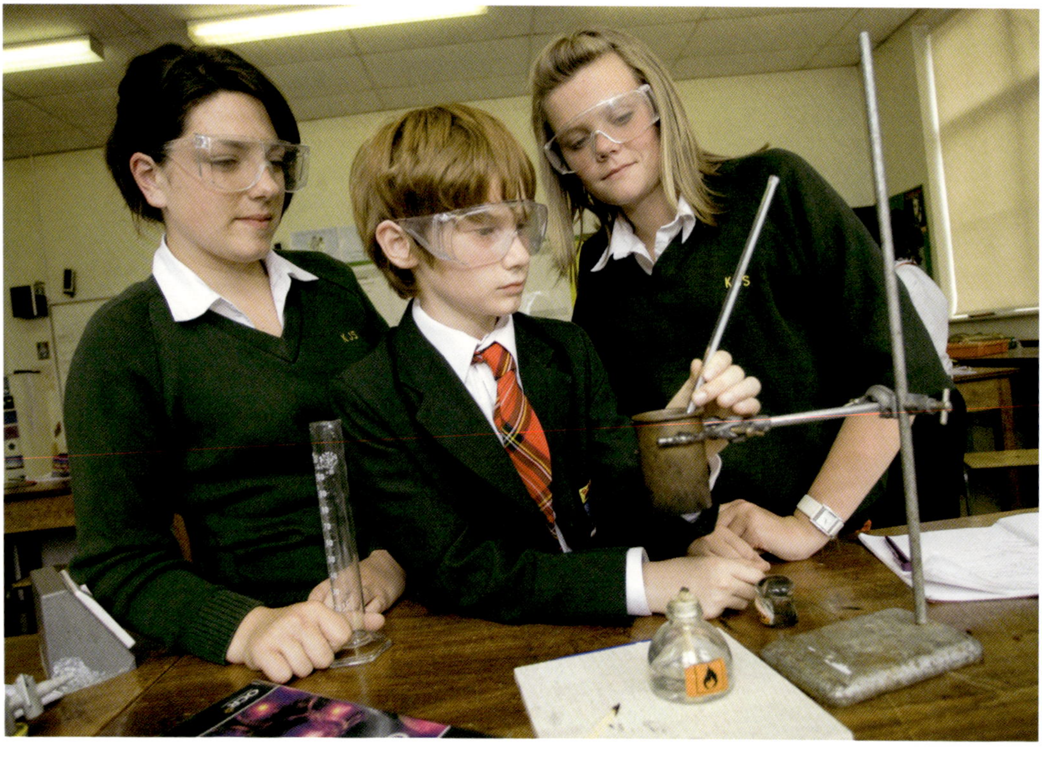

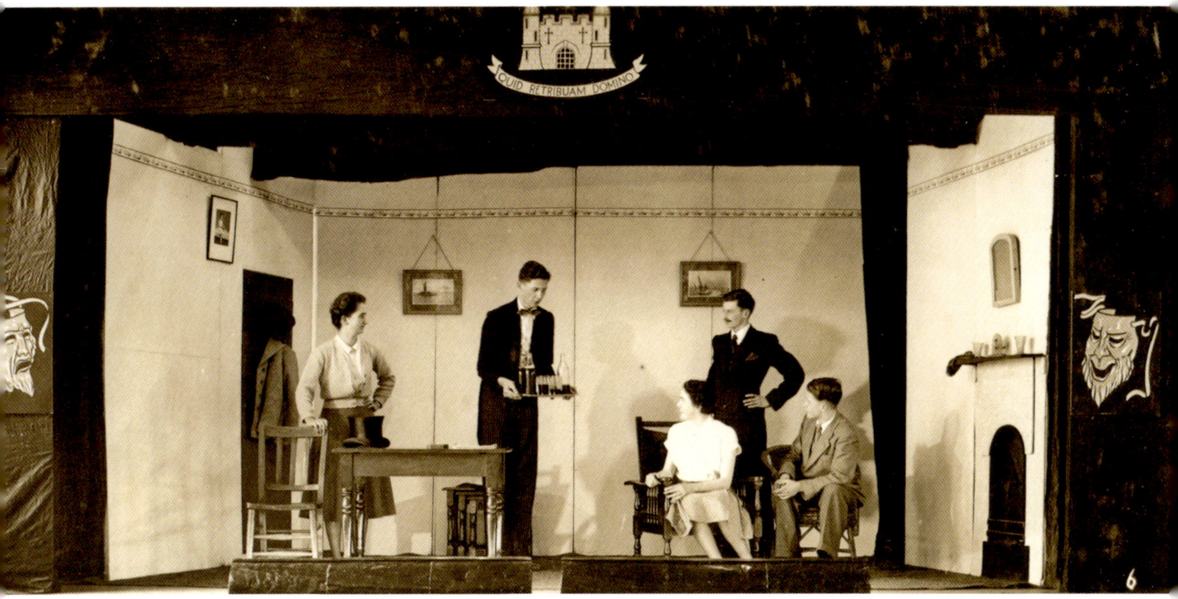

Domestic Drama

A 1952 drama production and a 2009 production written, performed and produced by drama students as part of their A level course work. Both photographs are very much of their time, showing as they do domestic scenes. In 2005 a drama tower was built complete with stalls, circle and balcony classroom.

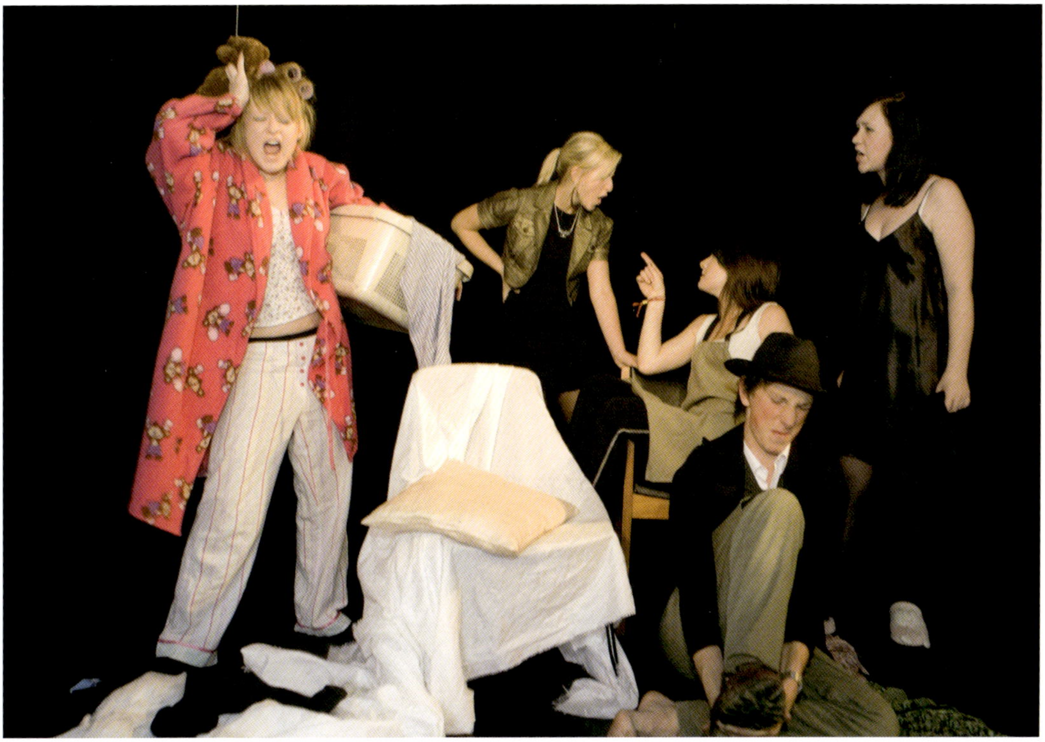

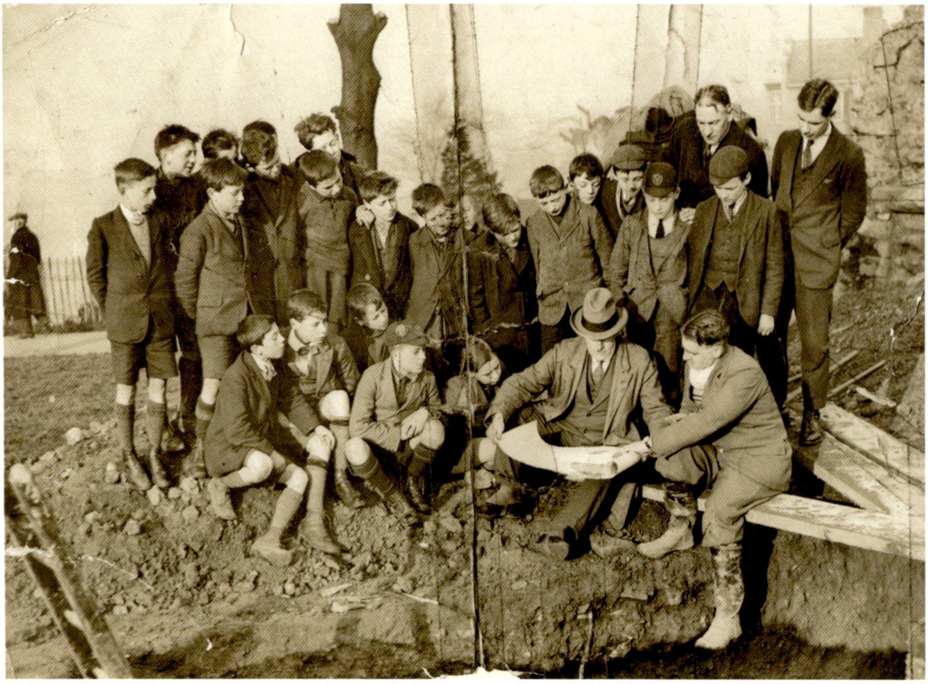

Castle School Excavation at the Castle

Boys from the Castle School (originally the Boy's National School founded in 1814 by public subscription) showing avid interest in the excavation of the second sally port in 1961. Today's students show just as much enthusiasm but with more independence.

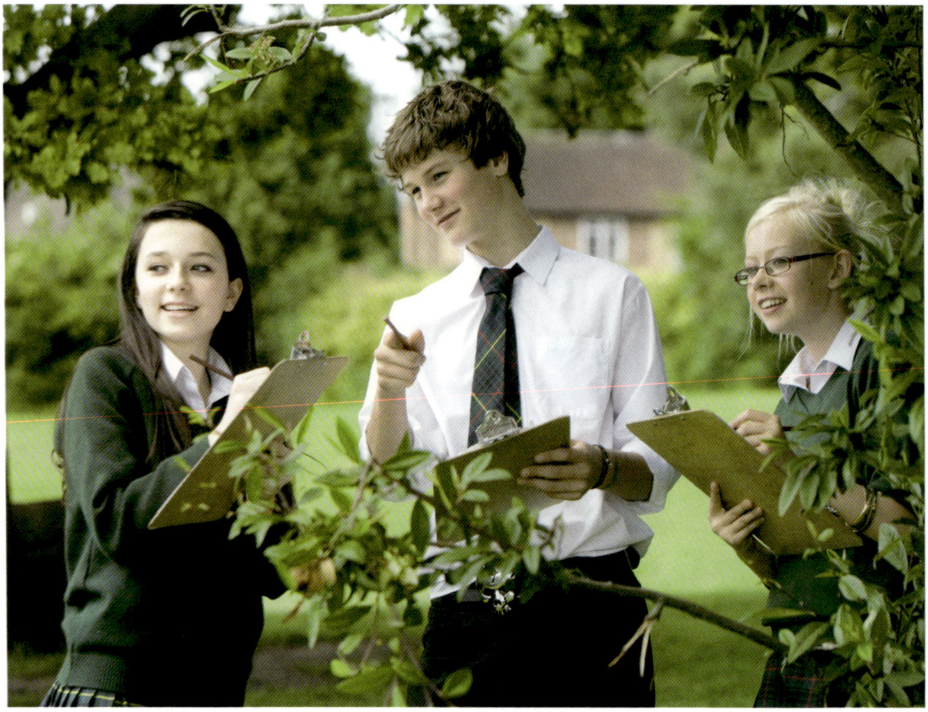

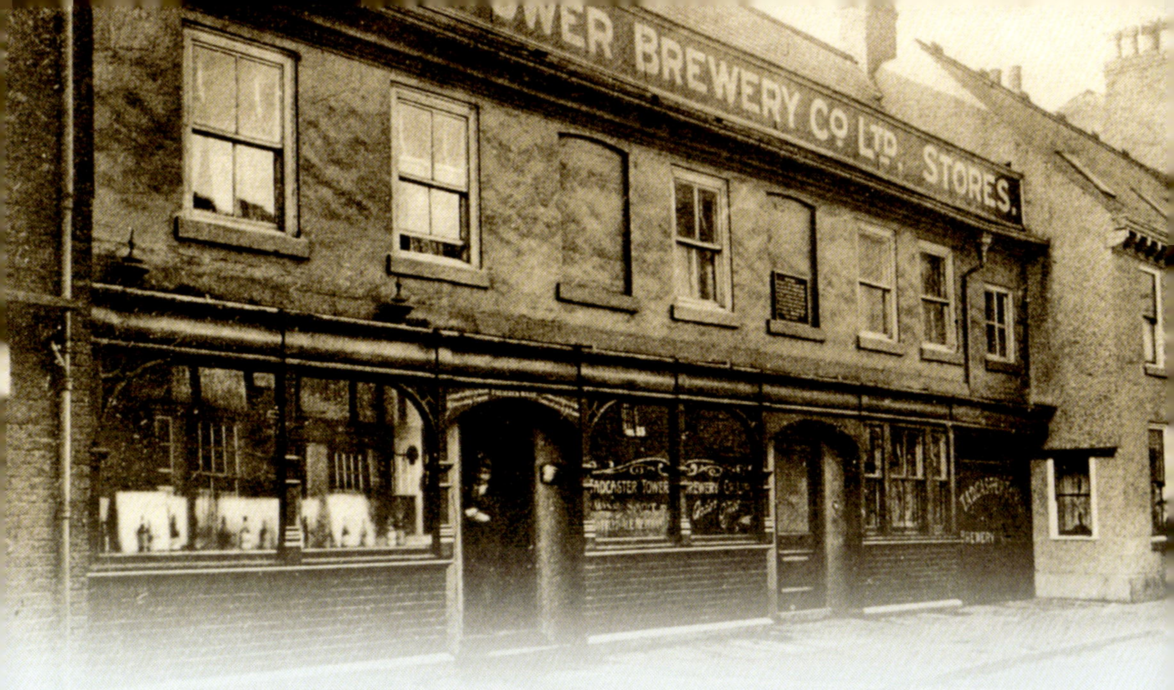

CHAPTER 5

Knaresborough's Trade and Industry

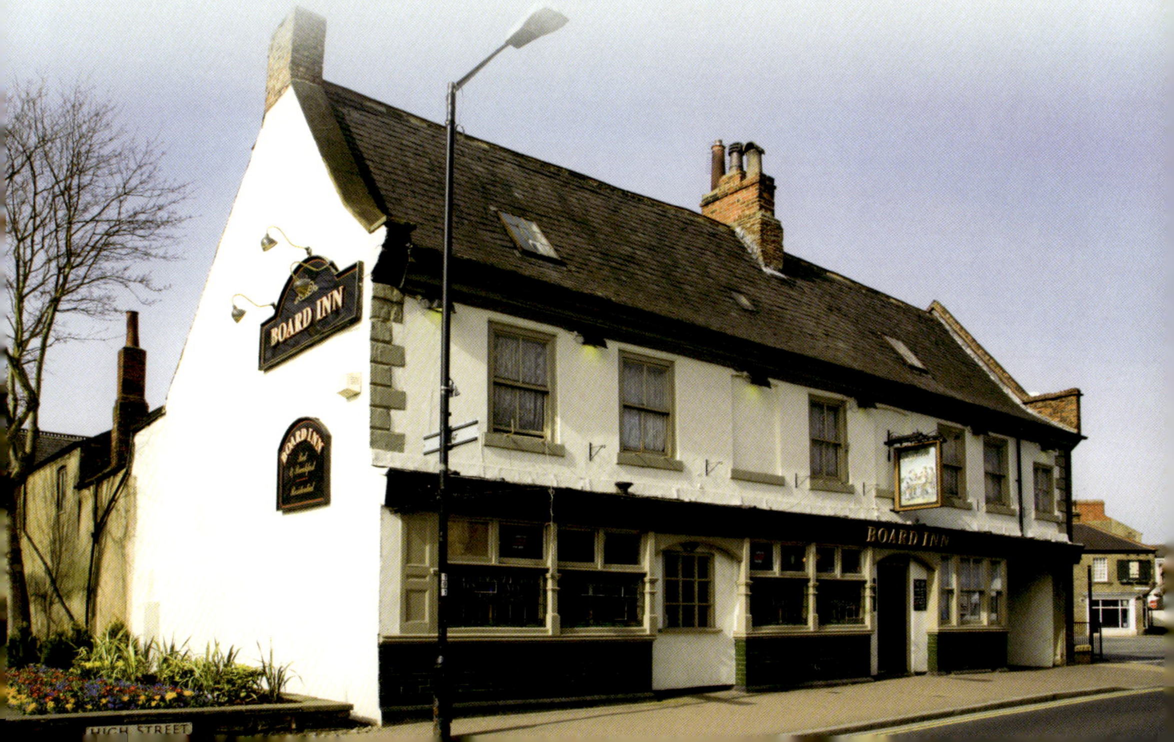

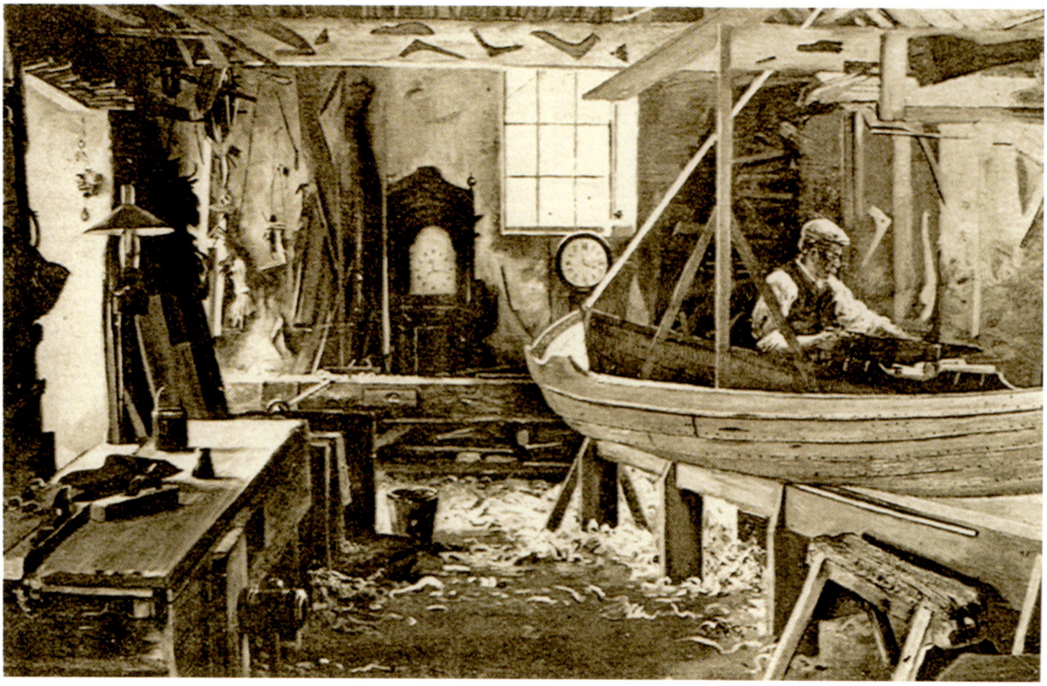

Sturdy's Boats

Sturdy's built the boats they hired out; this 1914 photograph shows Frank Sturdy (son of the founder Richard) at work; Frank did his apprenticeship in York. At this time Frank had taken on George Smith, an apprentice aged twelve. The contemporary photograph shows today's boats in storage for the winter.

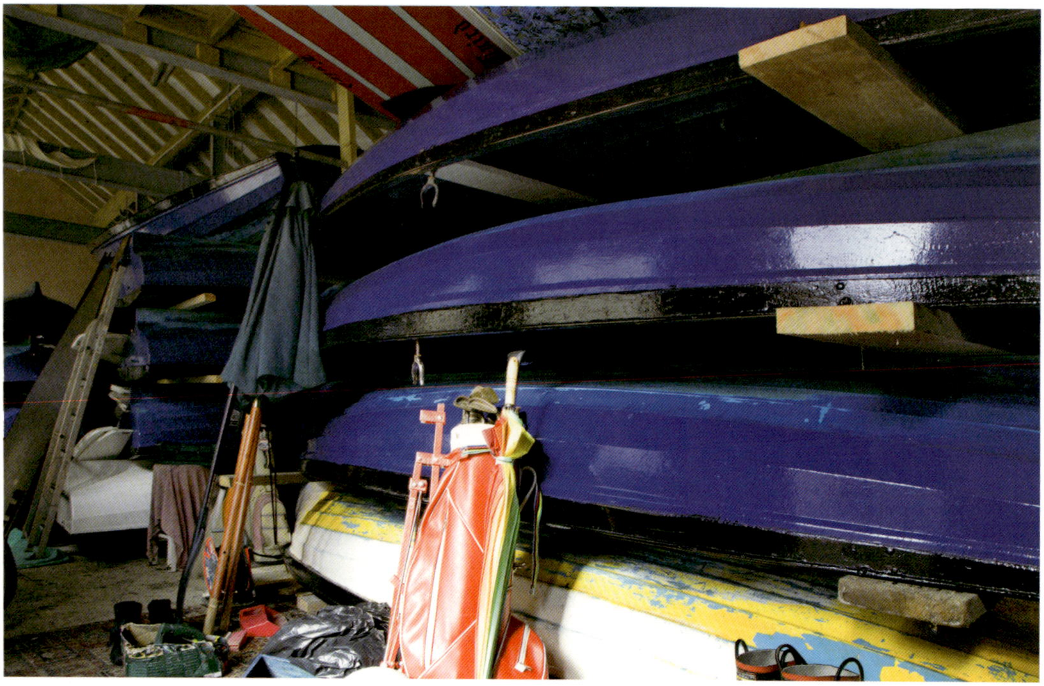

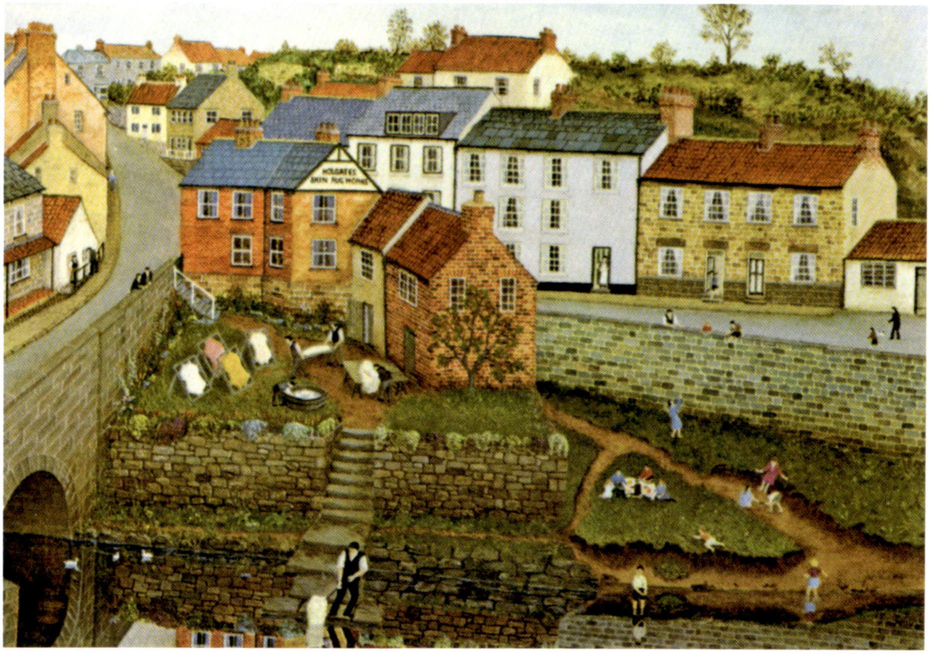

Rug Works

Knaresborough's main industry was linen but this shows the Knaresborough rug works (Holgates) as painted by Joseph Baker Fountain (1907-1992) with fleeces being washed and drying in the garden; *Pigot & Co. Royal, National and Commercial, 1841* tells us that the companies based at Low Bridge in the mid nineteenth century were J. Clapham, William Clapham and Co. (both of whom specialised in sheep skin), and William Hartley with Jacob Edmondson in Market Place. Clapham's is next to the gas works in a building which was formerly a soap factory run by Joe Clough.

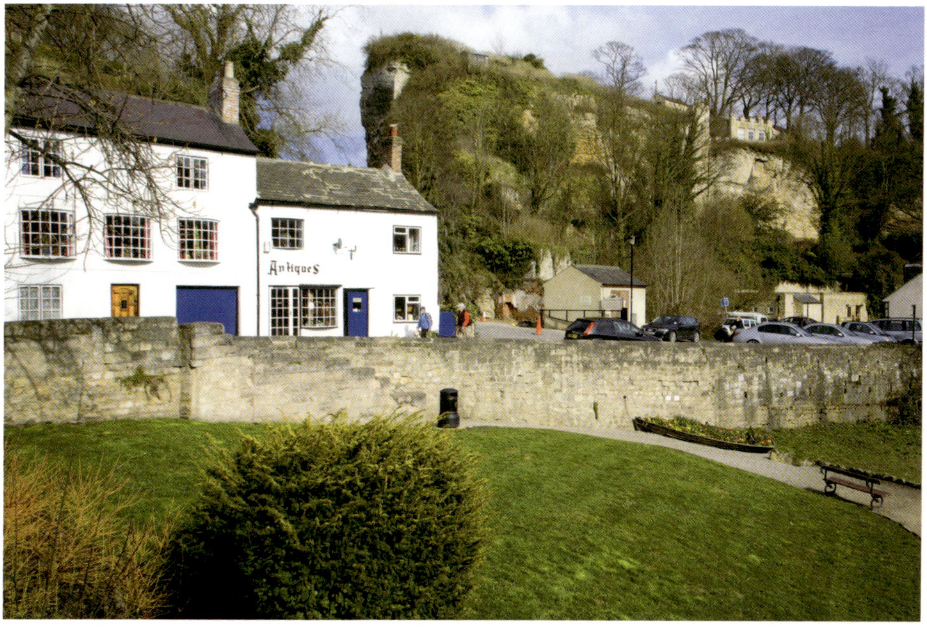

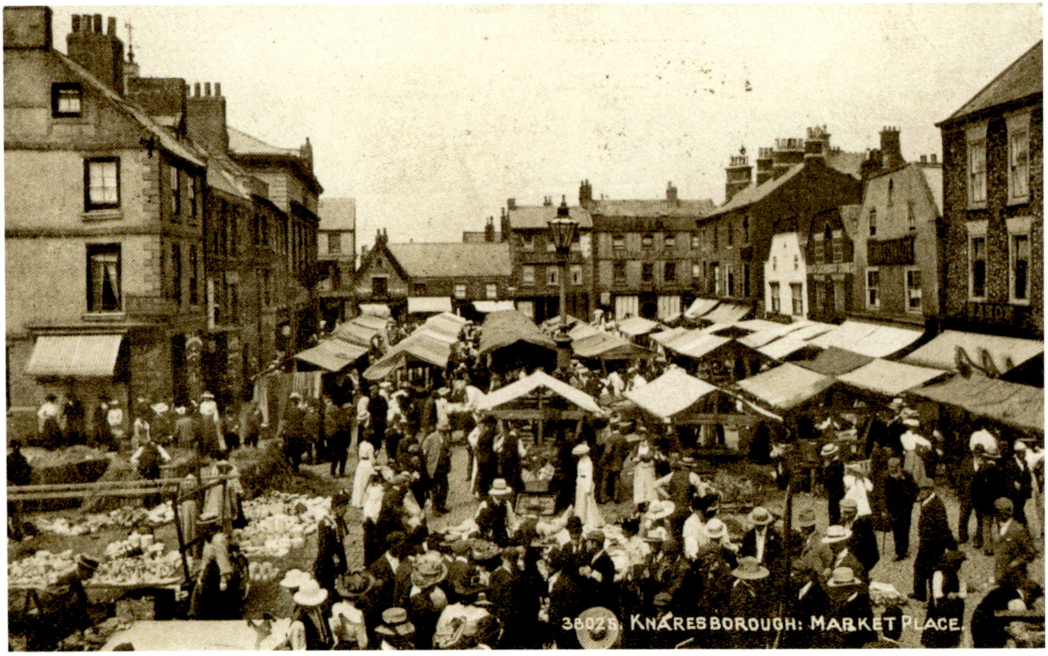

Wednesday Market

Not that much has changed since this was shot in 1916 – the market still takes place each Wednesday and has been complemented since 2009 on every fourth Sunday by a Farmer's Market. The Wednesday market was established in 1310 by royal Charter of Edward II and has continued more or less ever since.

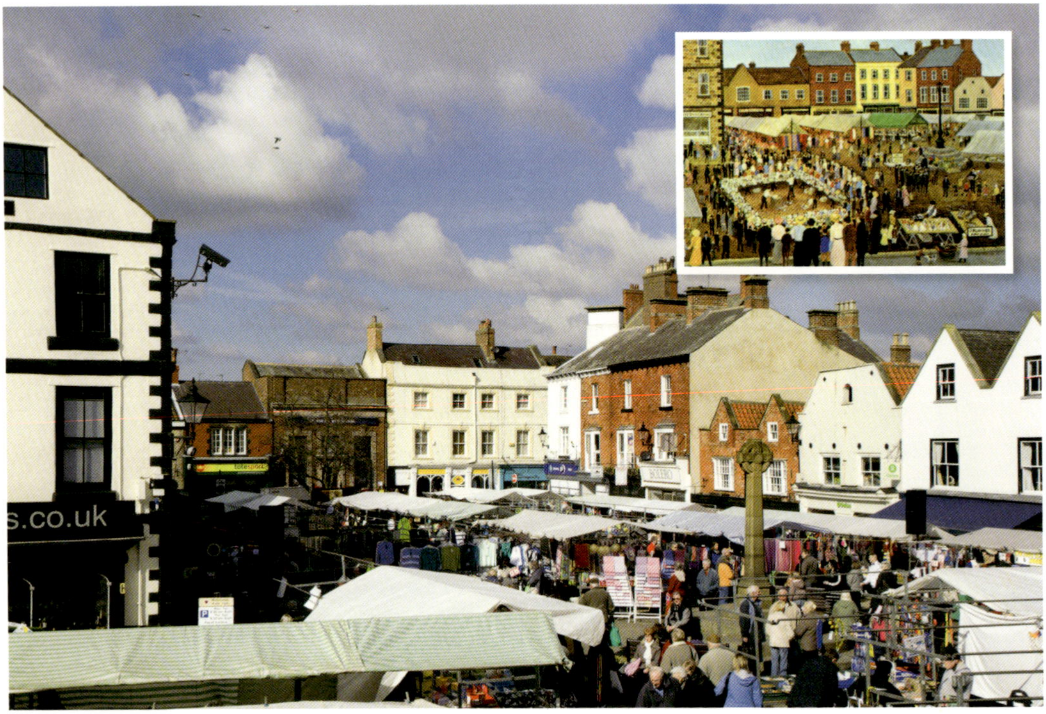

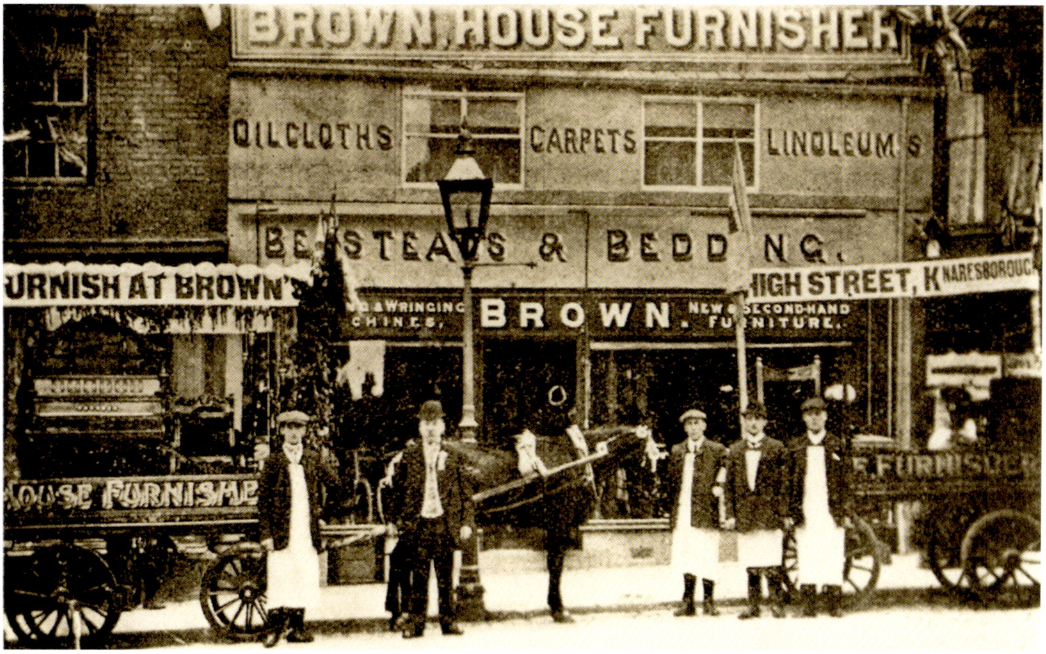

Browns, House Furnishers

Say 'furniture' in Knaresborough and you automatically think 'Browns'; Browns started trading in the High Street in 1903 when Ben Brown set up the first shop opposite Finkle Street. The photograph shows (l-r) Alf Brown (one of Ben's sons), Ben Brown, Billy the horse and three employees; Mrs Brown is in the door way. Their warehouse was on the first floor of the building on the corner of Butter Lane which is now the Scope charity shop and goods had to be lifted up there by a crane in Butter Lane. In 1949 Fred Brown sold the business and eventually set up on his own initially in Jockey Lane then in Kirkgate and finally in their present premises back in the High Street in what was Clapham's bike shop.

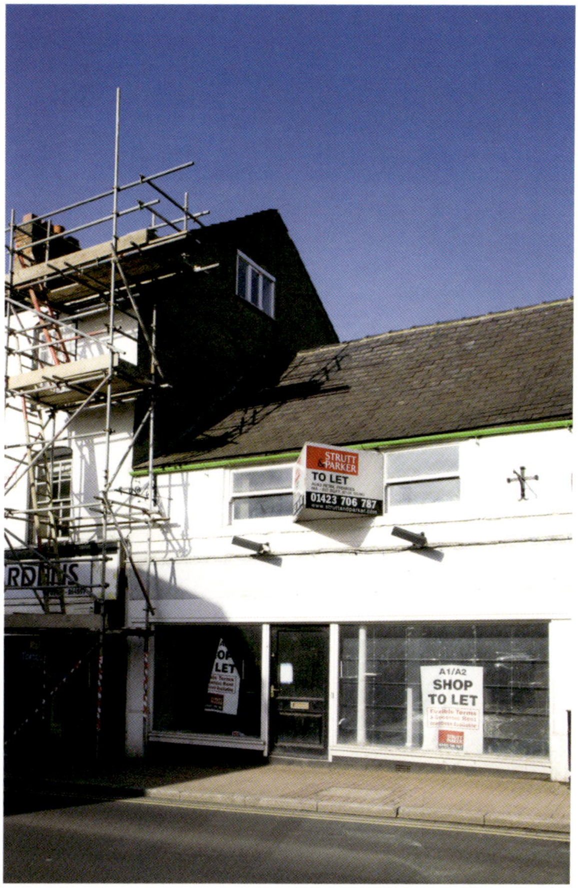

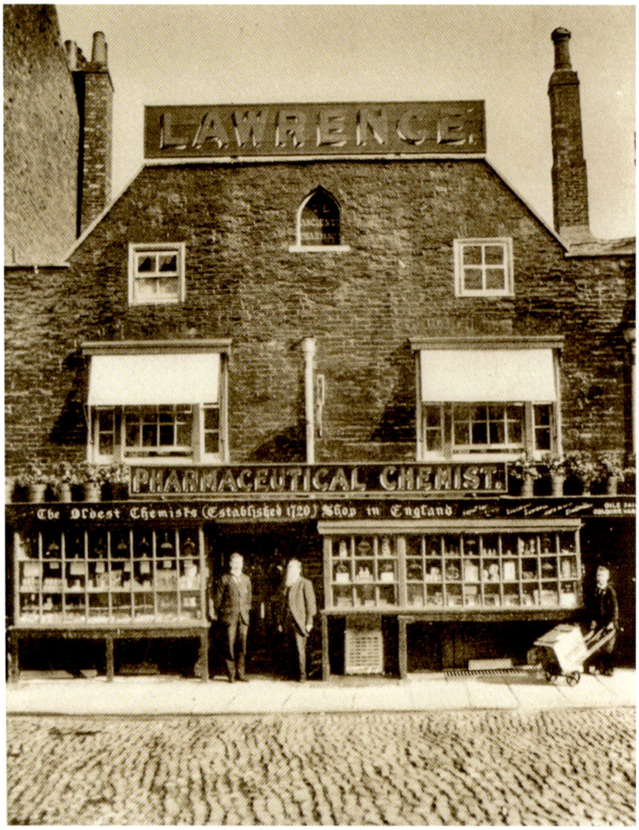

The Oldest Chymist Shoppe in England

Reputedly England's oldest chemist shop. Pictured just before the First World War are owner and son William Pierpoint and Edmund Lawrence, pharmaceutical and veterinary chemists who between them ran the business from 1884 to 1965. The shop was established in the 1720s (a John Beckwith was the apothecary) and the Chinese Chippendale style windows were added some forty years later. In 2001 the upstairs where Mrs Lawrence prepared 'Ye special old Englyshe Lavender Water' was converted into tearooms; the lavender water is still sold in the shop.

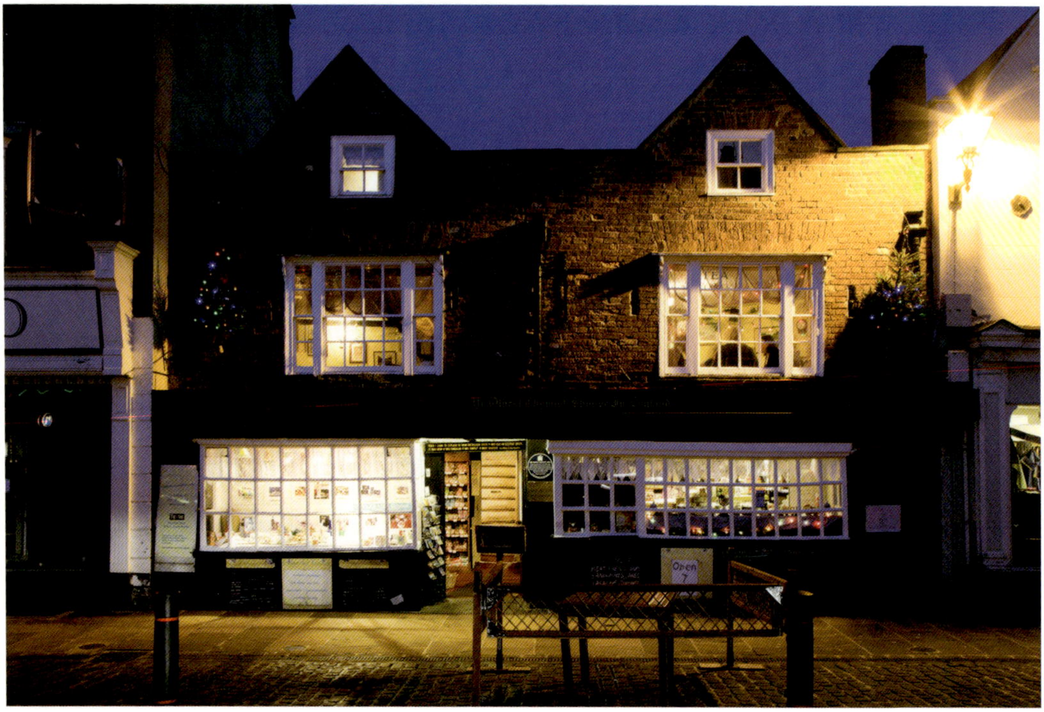

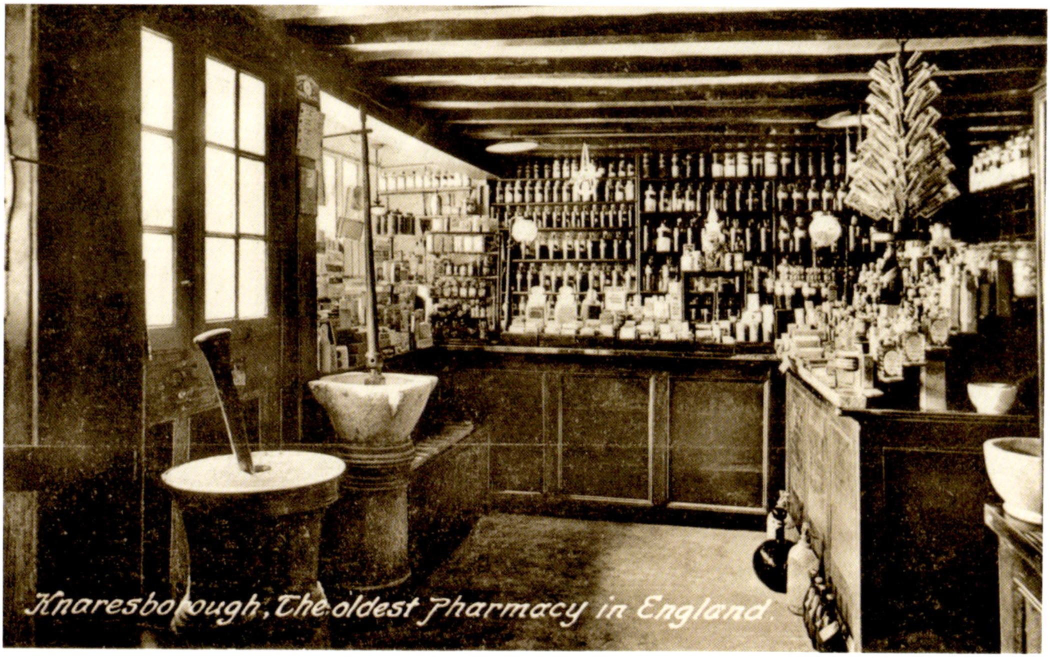

Bleeding with Leeches and Extractions

A fascinating glimpse into the past; this shows the huge mortar (mid left) used for grinding all manner of drugs and potions. Rows of medicine bottles (including one for leeches), a medicine cabinet, the couch where patients were bled and treated or had their teeth extracted can still be seen today. The shop today is a confectioners on the ground floor with the famous Lavender Rooms café and restaurant on the first floor.

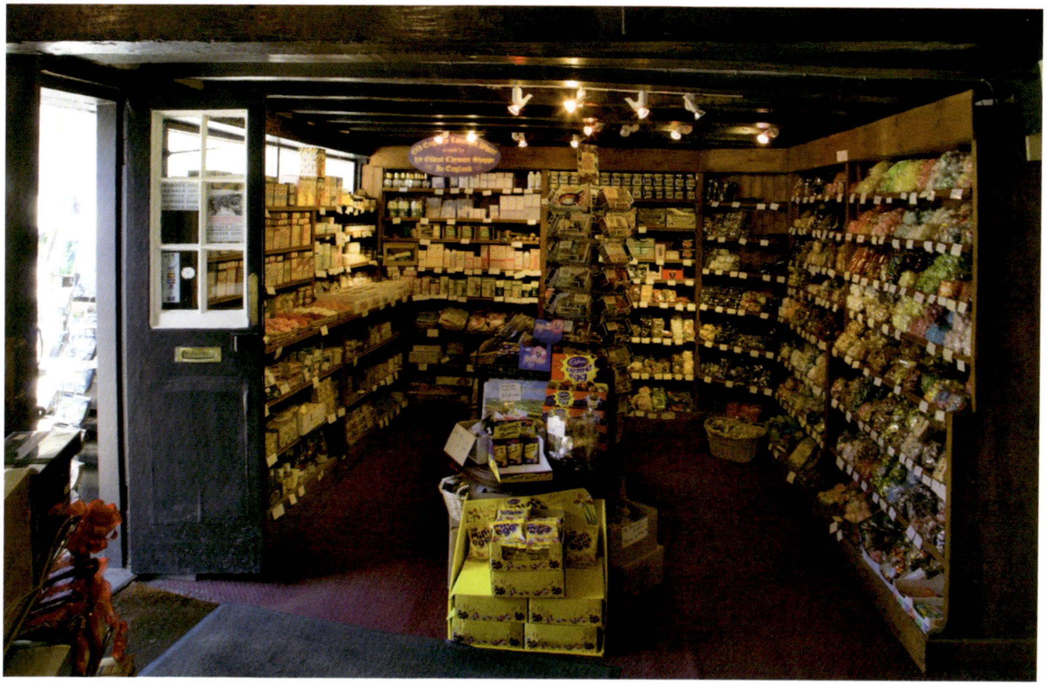

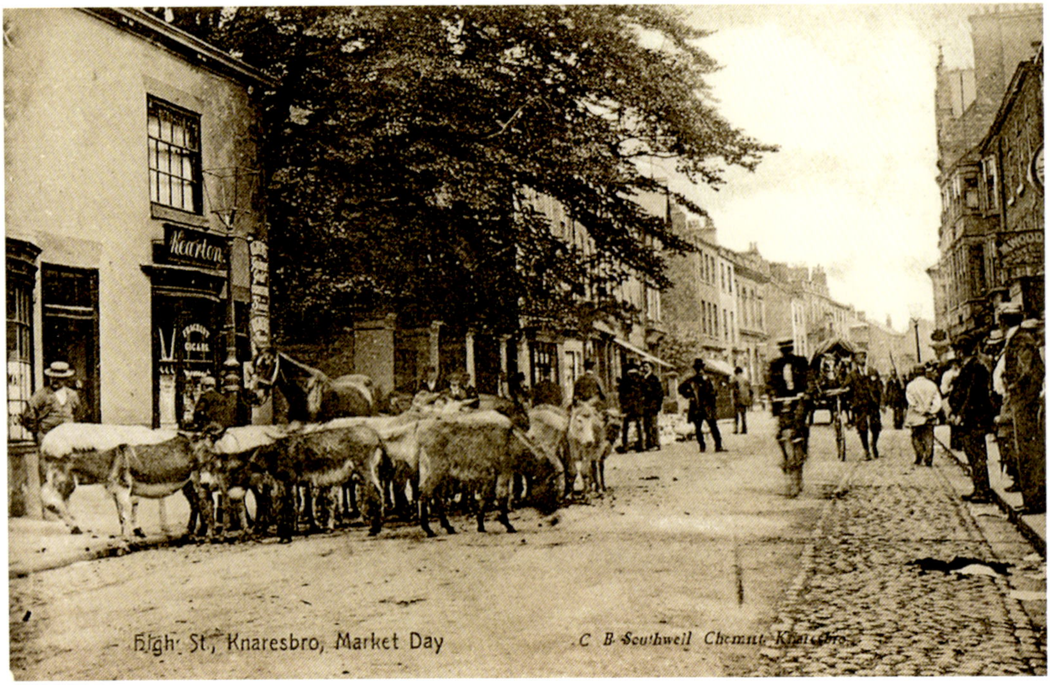

High Street Donkeys

Around 1905 when this photograph was taken it was not unusual to see livestock such as geese (shod as they came from afar), donkeys, cattle and sheep in the High Street on Wednesdays as part of the market. A purpose built livestock market opened in 1907. Knaresborough has a long association with donkeys thanks to Donkey Dave Allott – the Donkeyman – a familiar figure in the town for many years with his riverside donkey rides and charity donkey derbys.

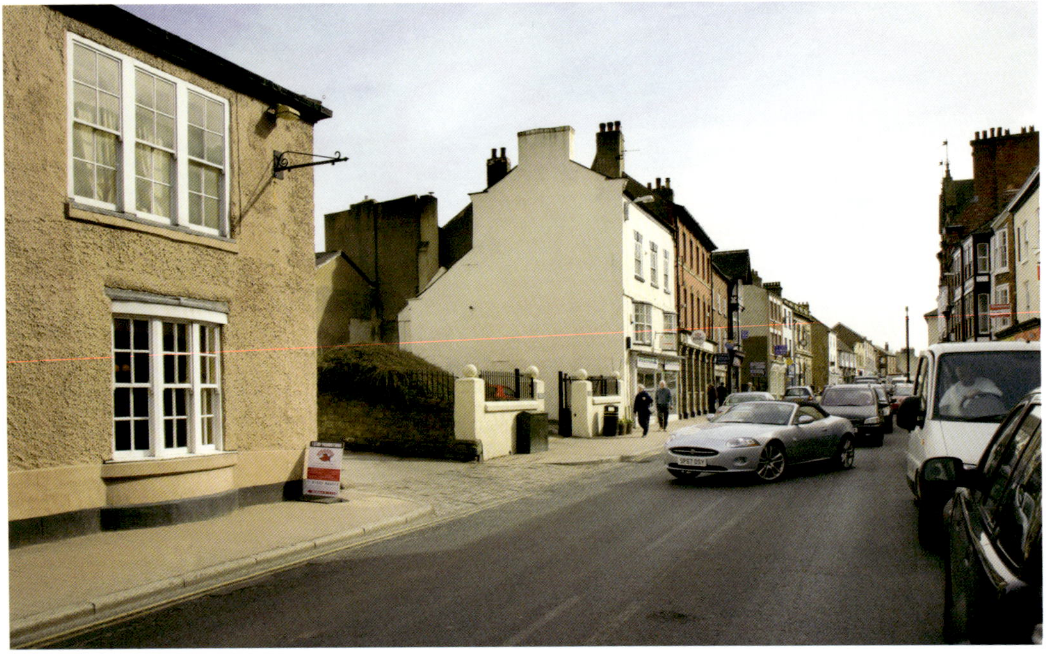

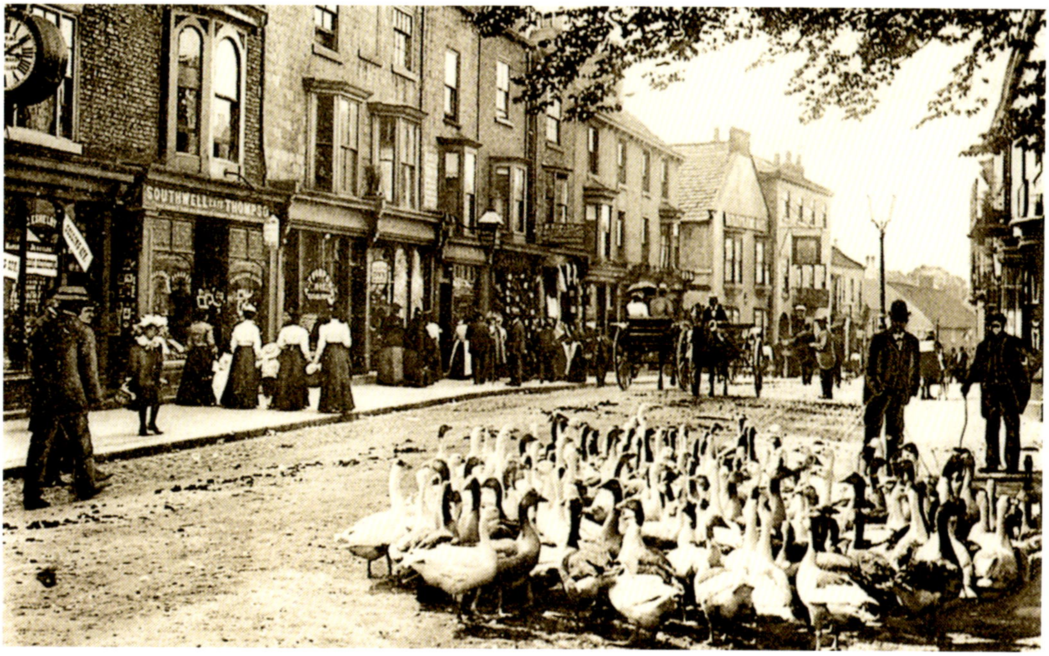

Geese Wearing Shoes and Perfume on the High Street

Southwells on the left (also known as Thompsons and now Naylors) was established in 1894 and famous nationally for their Knaresboro Bouquet: adverts from around 1890 tell us "Without exception the Sweetest most Refreshing and lasting Perfume". Its delicacy of odour surpasses many of the most expensive Perfumes. Endorsed by none other than Mrs Langtry: 'Fragrant and delicate' and Miss Ellen Terry: 'It is delicious.' Was she drinking it?

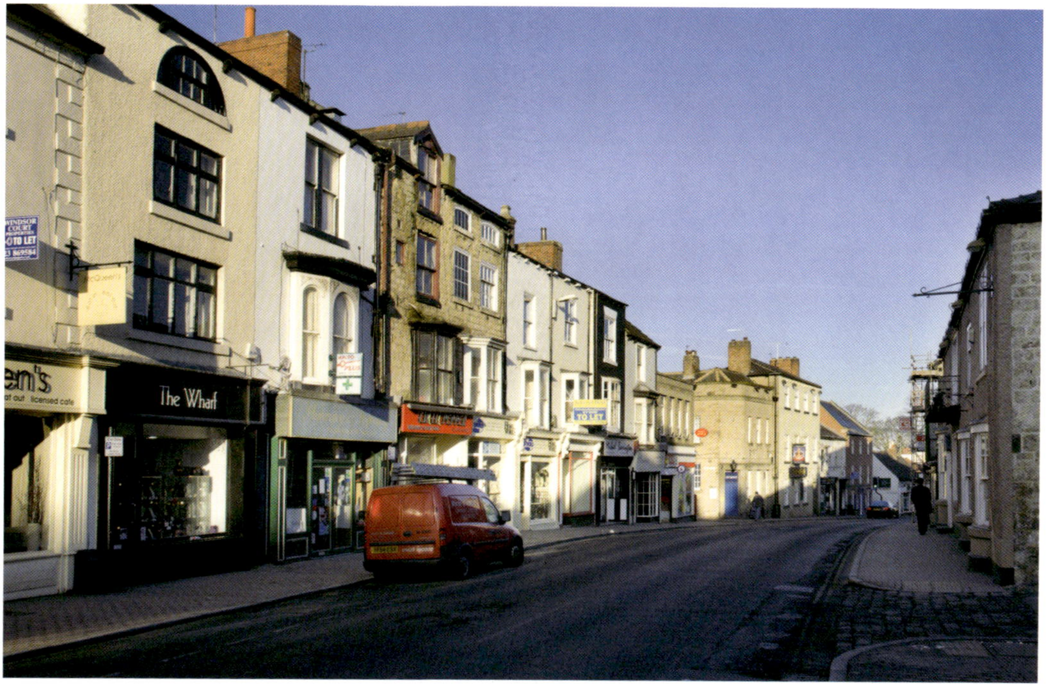

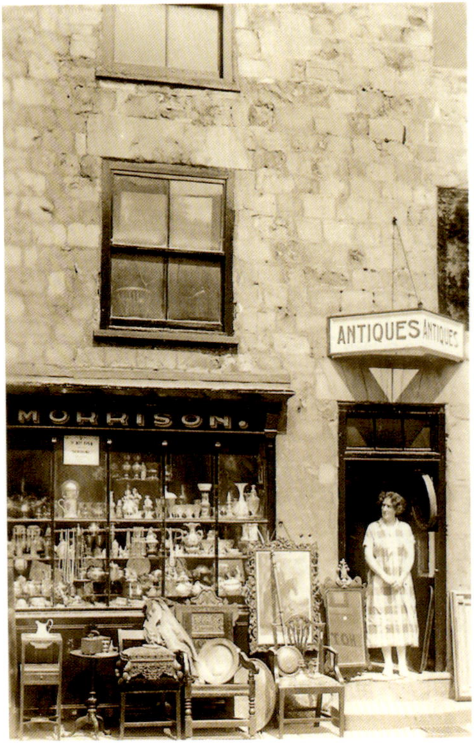

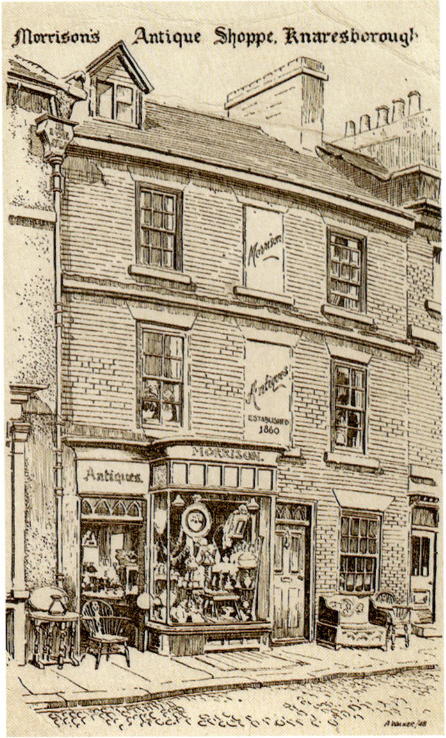

Morrison's Antiques

This photograph shows Miss Elizabeth Morrison outside her antiques shop established in the 1860s at 28 Cheapside. The drawing shows the original shop in Market Place in what is now the Blind Jack pub. In the 1960s Miss Morrison sold the business to Vollans the photographers, established 1949, who still trades from the premises.

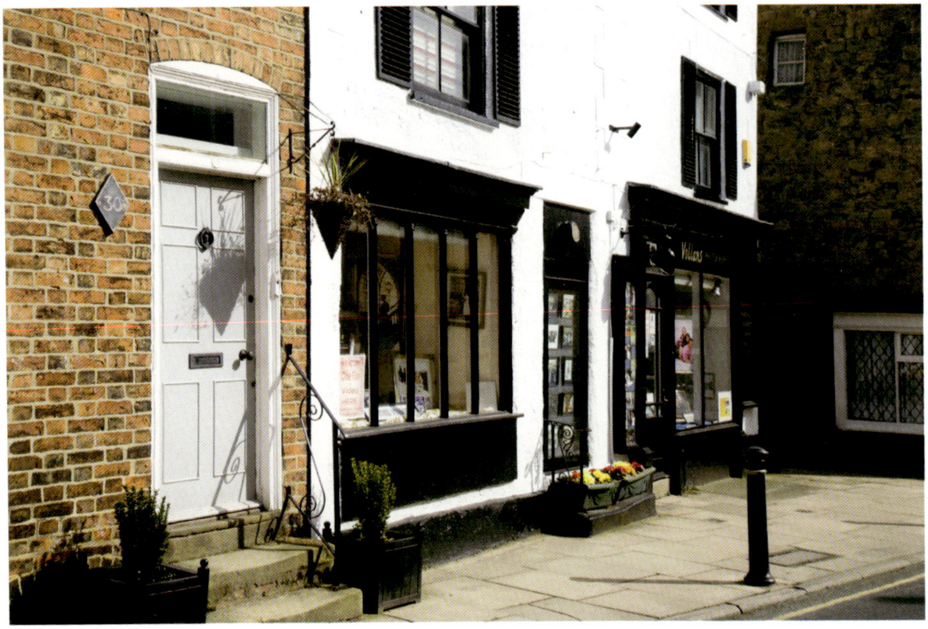

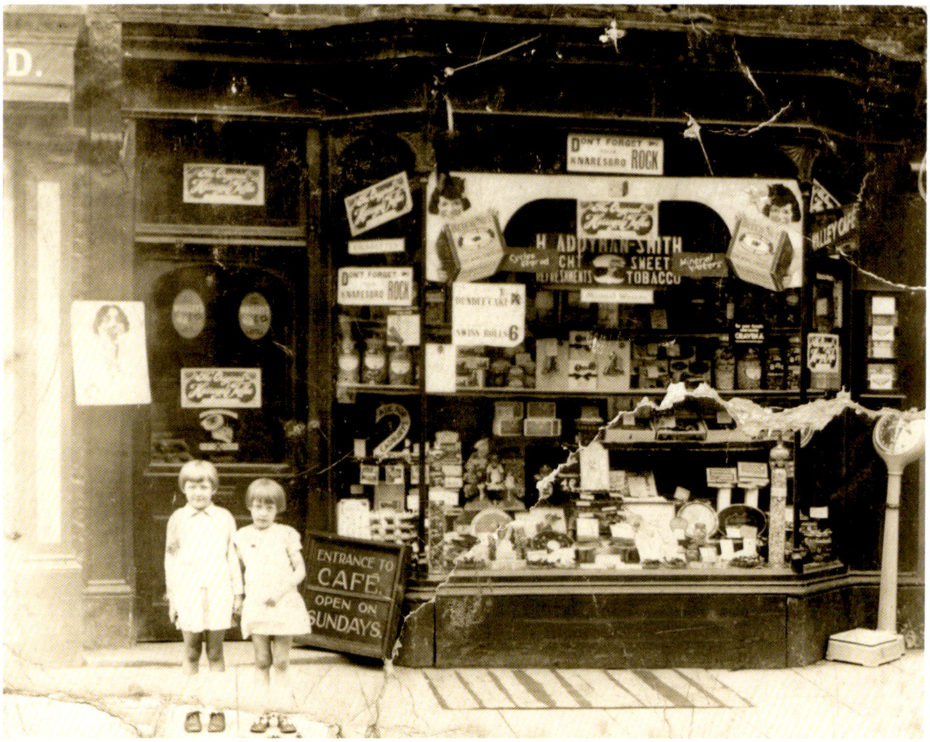

Knaresborough Rock Sold Here

Betty and Mary Fisher are shown here outside their sweetshop and café at 45 High Street. They had moved from London in 1931 and later moved to smaller premises at 25 Castlegate. One of their specialties was Knaresborough rock. The property has retained much of its original character and is now the toy and gift shop Indigo.

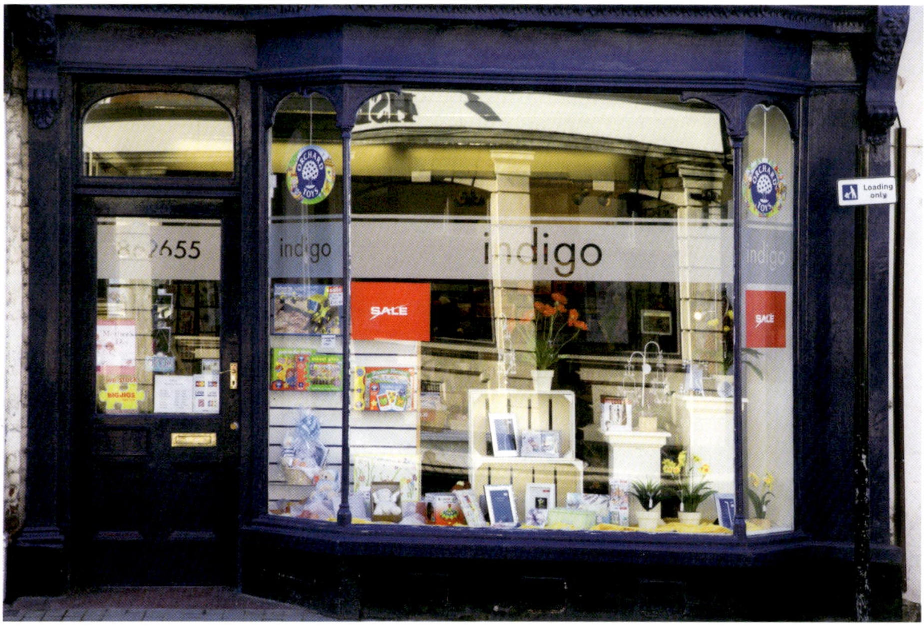

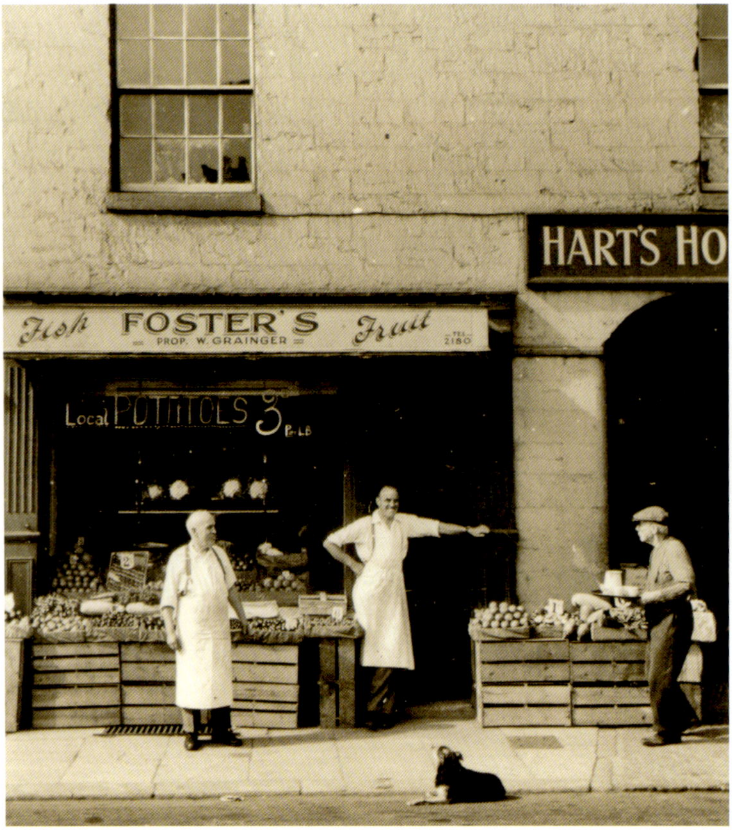

Chinese Alternative Remedies
Sellers of fresh fish and vegetables Fosters at High Street was run by W. Grainger at the time of this photograph. Herbal Land is there now next door to the Hart Hotel and characterises Knaresborough's new multiculturalism. Tea time for someone and the dog is lying on what are now double yellow lines.

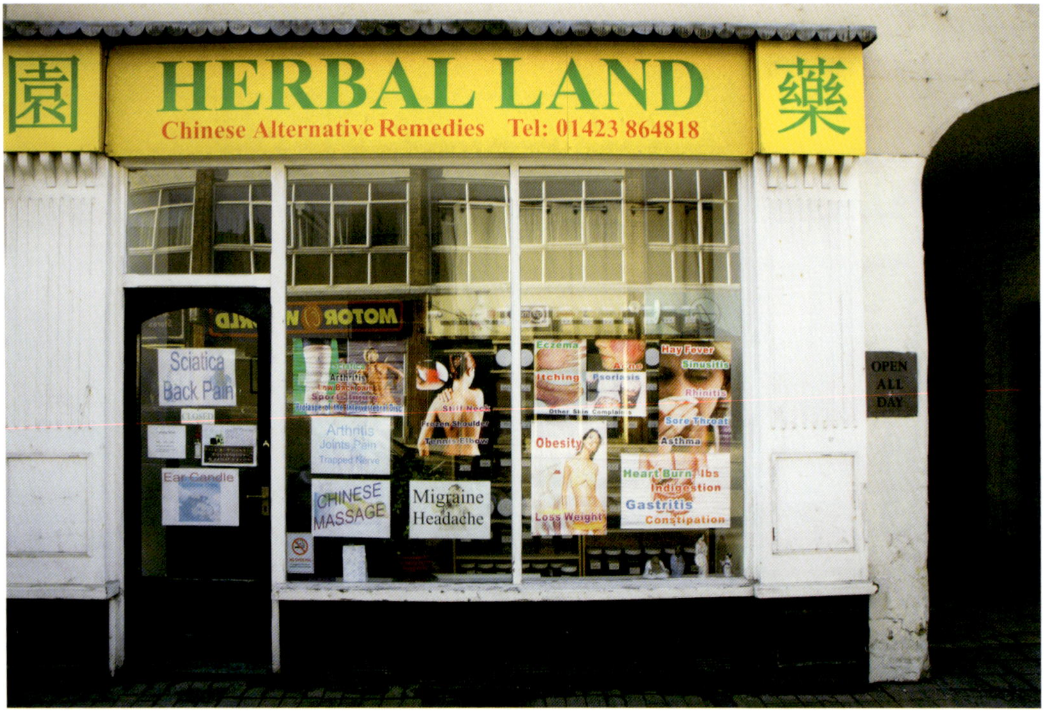

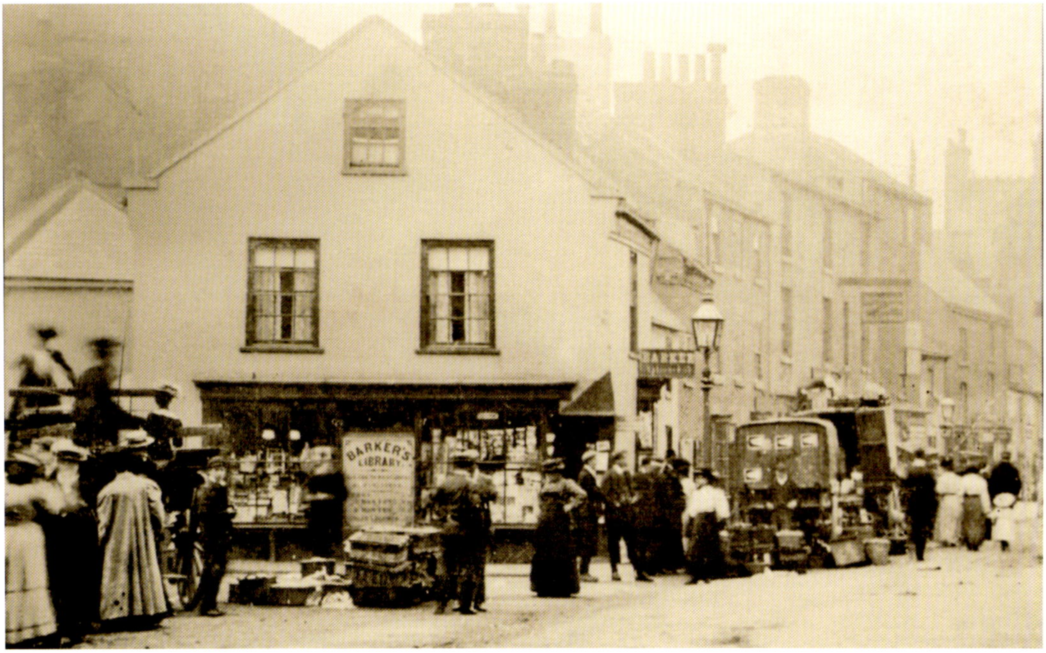

Barker's Library

Booksellers, library, post office, printers – Barkers at the junction of the High Street, Fisher Street and Silver Street served all these functions. The building is now occupied by Hirst the bakers, established 1973. The Knaresborough Bookshop further down the High Street now caters for the town's book-buying needs and regularly brings authors to the town for signings including Lucy Adlington, Gervase Phinn, Harry Gration, Roger McGough and Sophie Hannah in 2009.

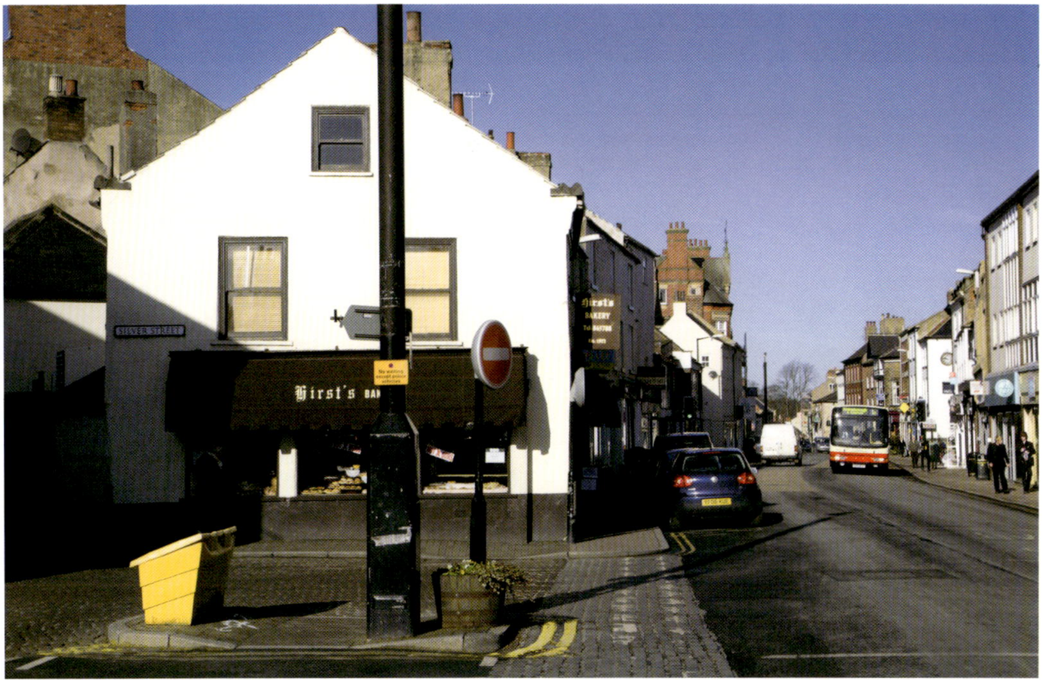

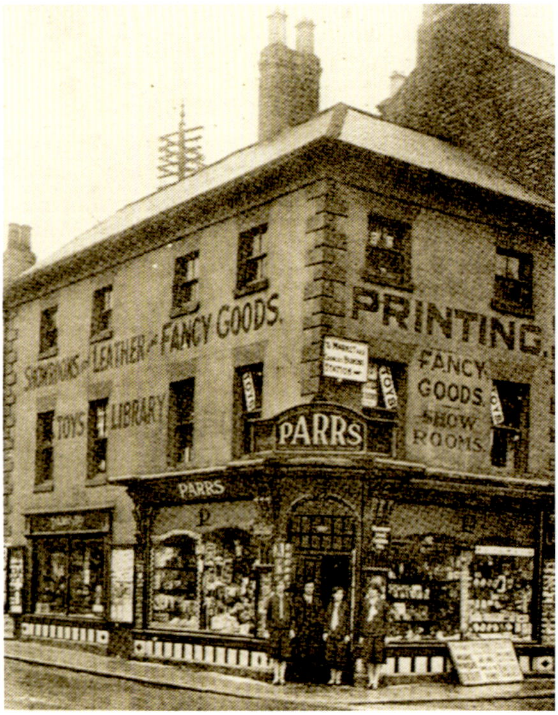

Parrs, High Street

Competition for Barkers came in the form of William Parr's on the corner of the High Street and Market Place. Parr's was also a lending library and sold newspapers, books and stationery as well as toys, leather goods, gifts, pens, wirelesses and cameras. They printed many of the local guidebooks although their most famous publication was the annual *Knaresborough Almanack*. This started life under A. W. Lowe well known for their "variety of useful & fancy articles" and photographs of Knaresborough : their 'stock of local views is the most complete in the district'. They also sold opals and medallions – all sizes (coloured and uncoloured) from 6*d* to 6*s*.

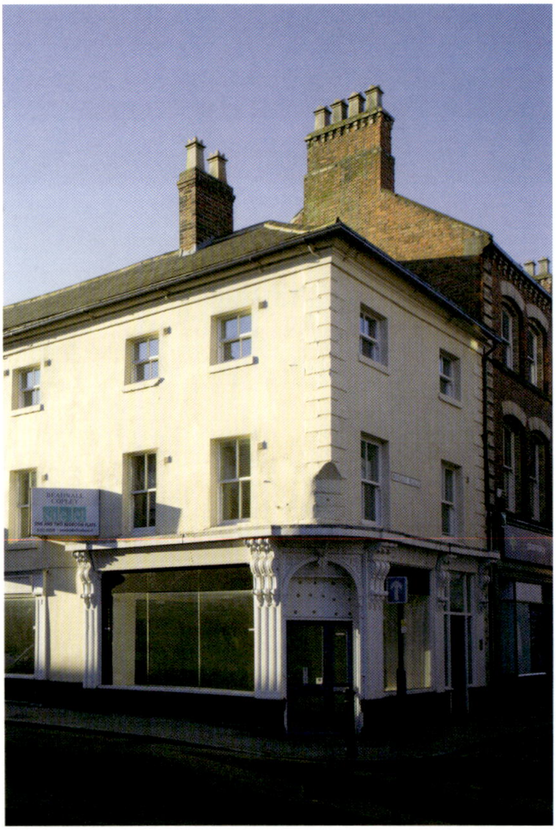

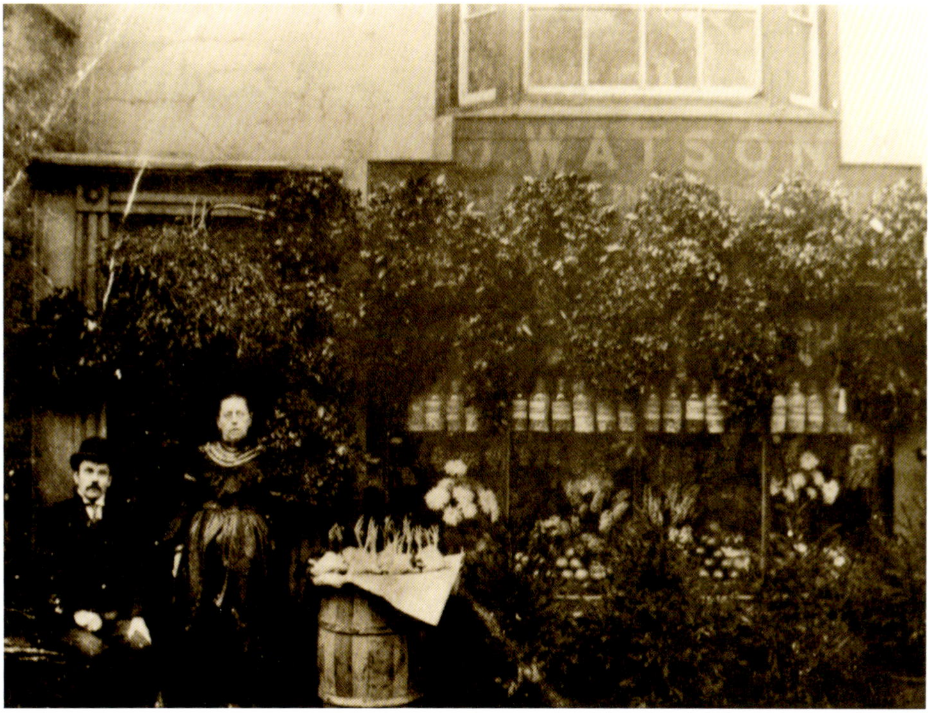

Watsons Fruit and Vegetables (and poultry)

This superb photograph from 1894 shows Mr James Watson and Mrs Mary Watson outside their fruit and vegetable shop in Castlegate where Mungo Deli now is. There is a wonderful sense of continuity here in that the Watsons' great grandchildren now run the fruit and vegetable stall every Wednesday outside Hi-Spirits on market day. Note the chickens. If you think Mr and Mrs Watson are looking a bit solemn, there's good reason: Mary was pregnant with her sixth child and James had recently hurt his back and had to remain seated.

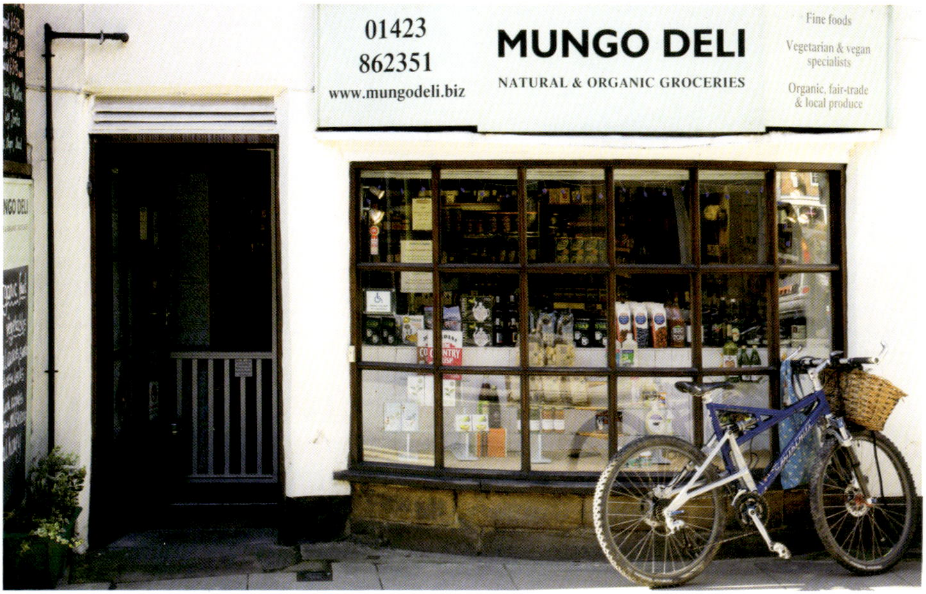

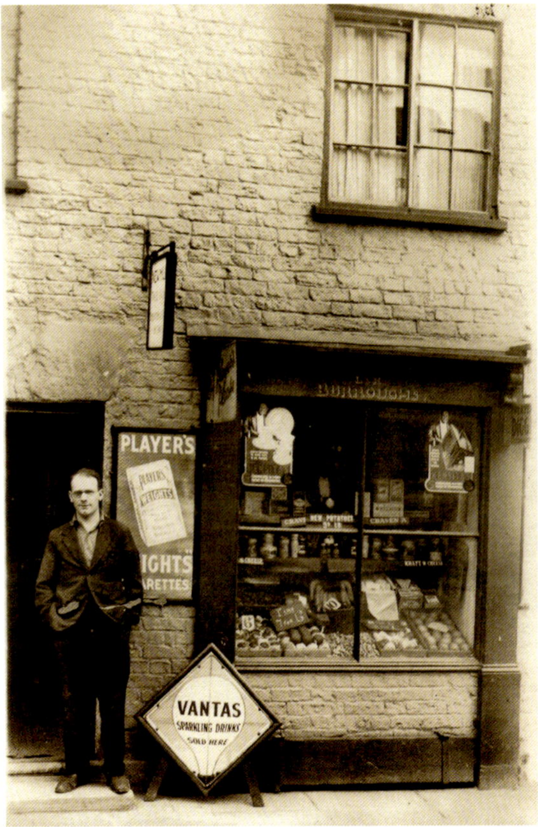

Leslie Burroughs/Florence Lowcock

The shop at 4 Briggate shows some interesting advertisements: Player's Lights, and Vantas, a soda. SodaStream dates back to 1903, when it was launched by Gilbey's, gin distillers. Gilbey sold the machines, which add sparkle to tap water via a pressurised carbon dioxide cylinder, to better off families including the royal household. In the 1920s flavour concentrates were introduced, such as Cherry Ciderette and Sasparilla. In the '30s Gilbey's launched its Vantas model, also known as 'The Penny Monster', which was sold to shopkeepers to make drinks for customers. Craven 'A' cigarettes, the advertising slogan for which was 'will not affect your throat', were also on sale.

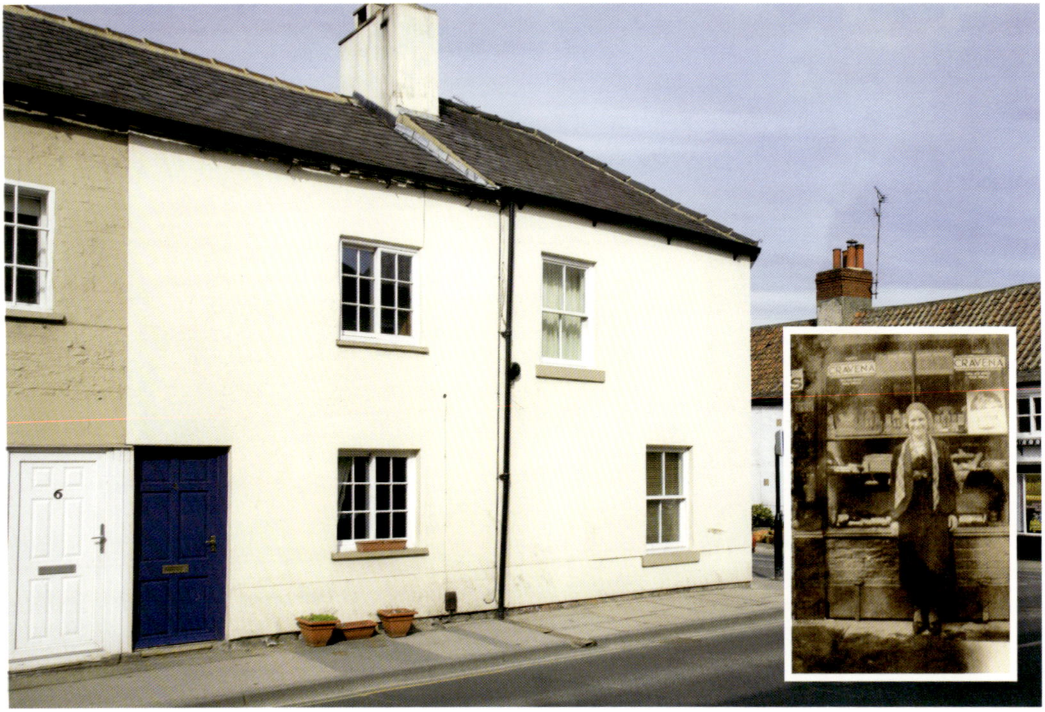

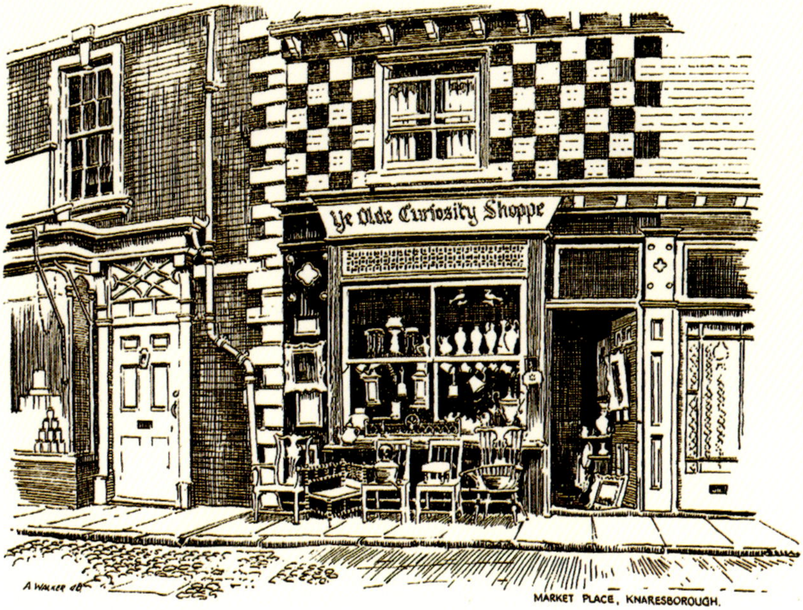

Ye Old Curiosity Shop

This pencil drawing shows the Aladdin's cave that was the Old Curiosity Shop at 4 Market Place to have been owned by a George Newstead at the time. Now a health food shop, nothing much has, thankfully, changed on the façade of this fine building.

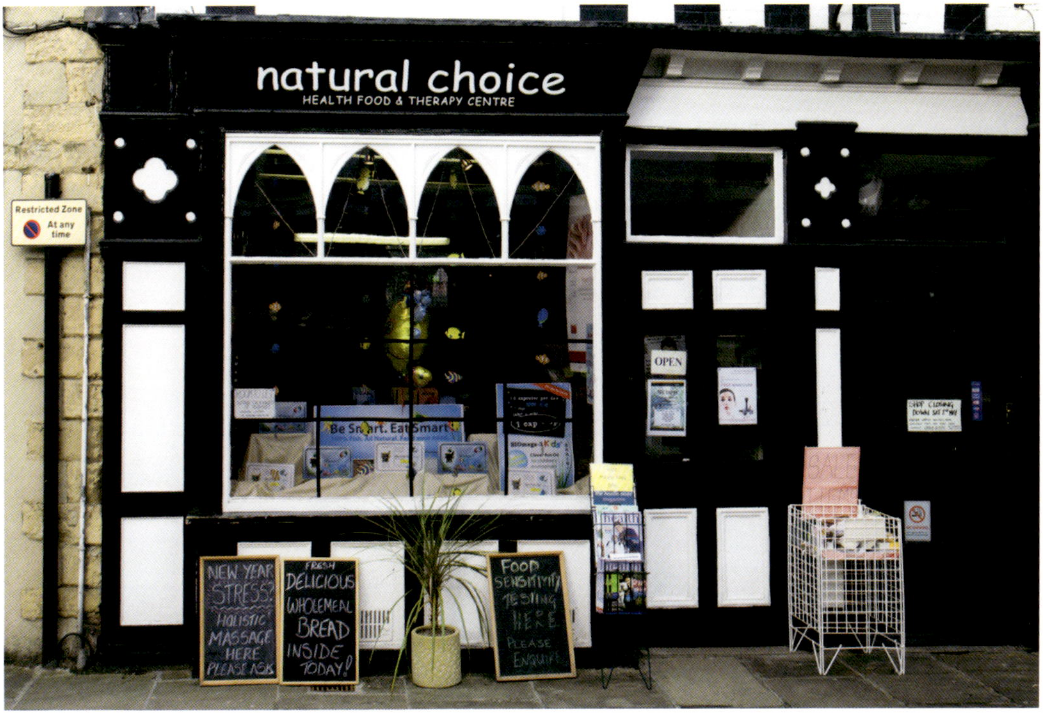

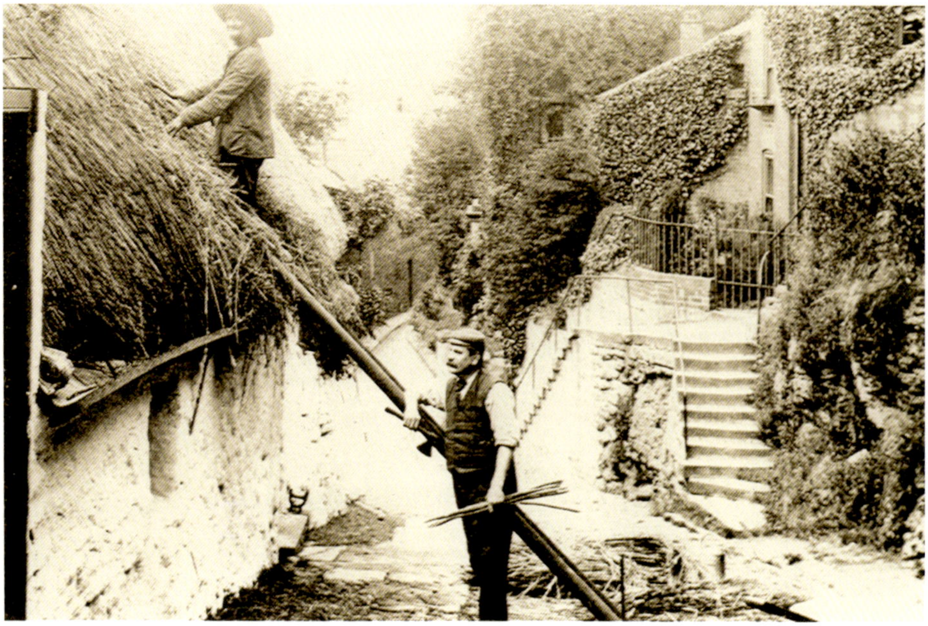

Manor Cottage Thatchers in Water Bag Bank

The only surviving thatched dwelling in Knaresborough is also one of its oldest, built as it was in Tudor times. Sadly the thatching and some of the sixteenth century beams were completely destroyed in an arson attack in April 2009 and £300,000 worth of damage was inflicted on the Grade I listed building, now being repaired. The cottage is at the foot of Water Bag Bank, named after the leather water bags carried up to the town full of water from the sewage filled Nidd on mules – to assist the women who did the job for a halfpenny a trip.

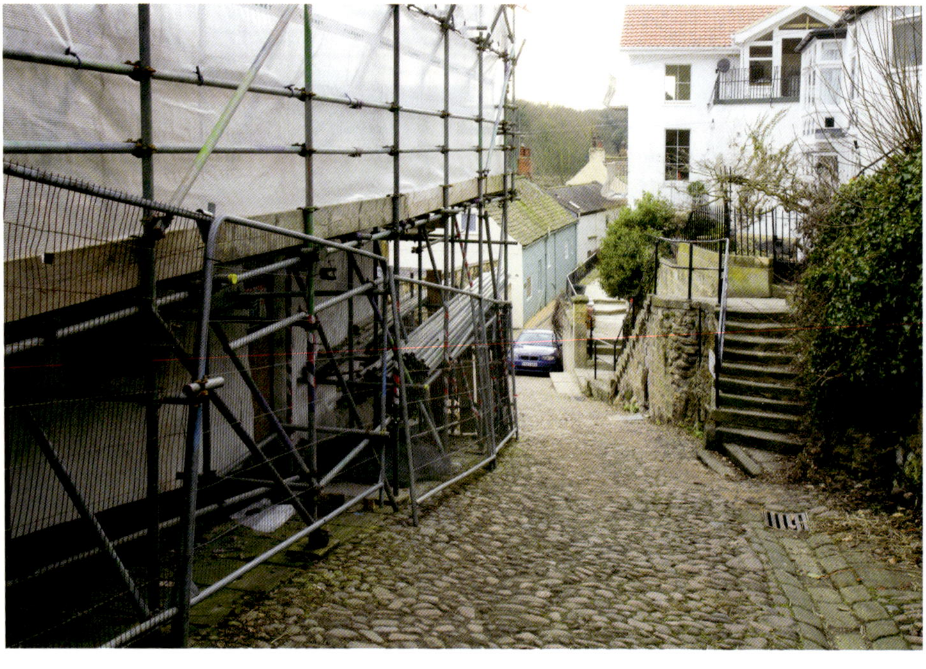

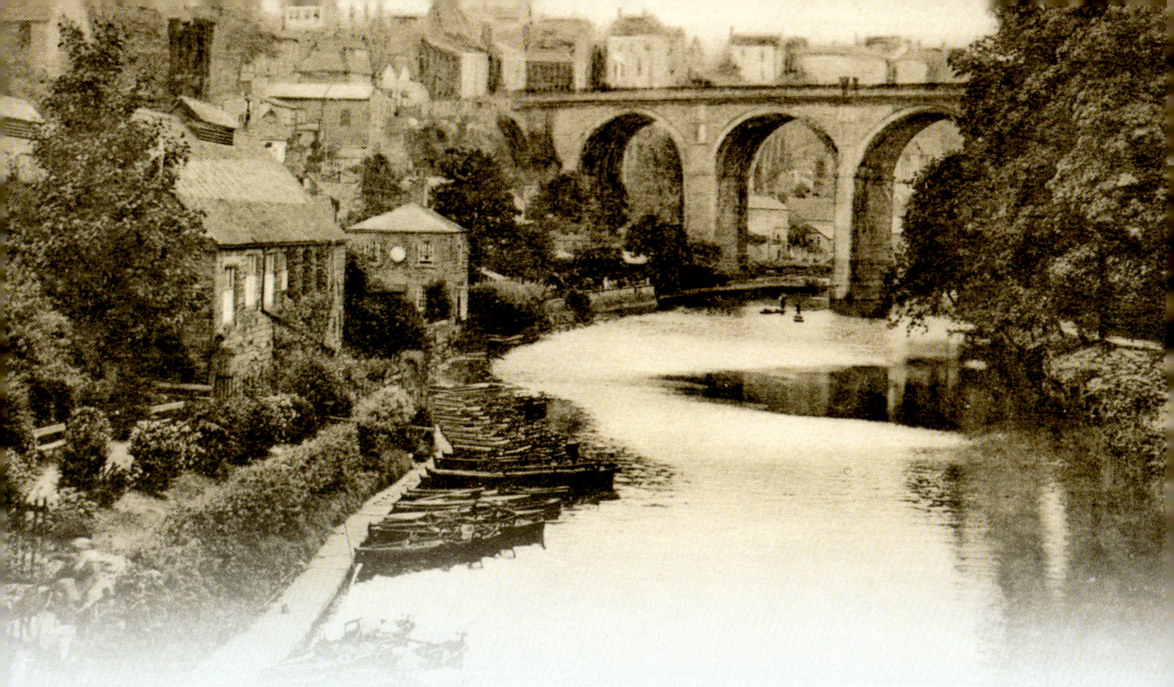

CHAPTER 6

A Tour Around Knaresborough

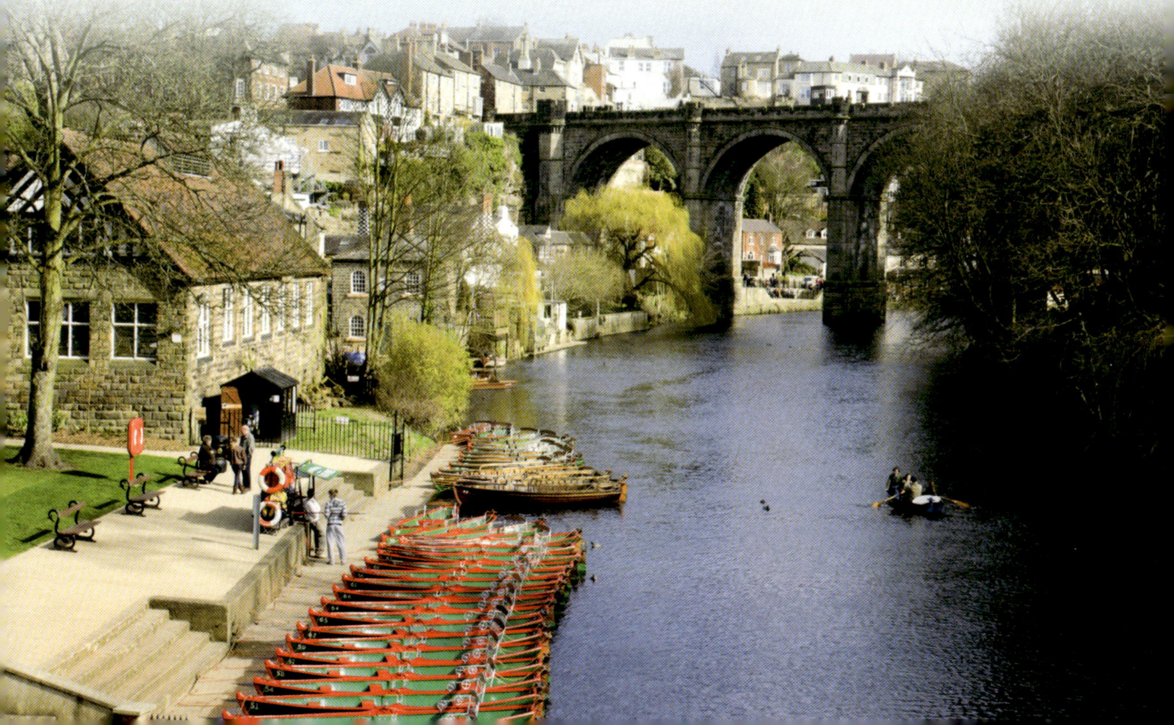

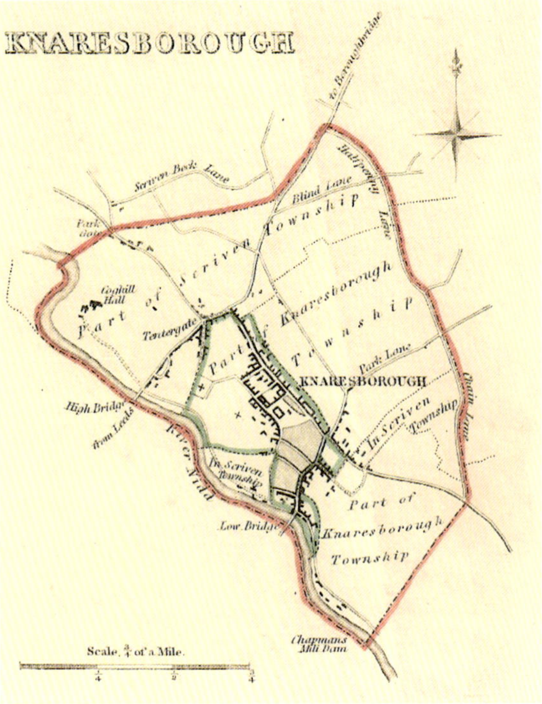

Knaresborough in Maps

The current OS map clearly shows the development of the town since this map dating from around 1800 was drawn. Note the absence, therefore, of the railway line and viaduct. The shape of the town has been roughly maintained and the High Street can be clearly seen on both maps.

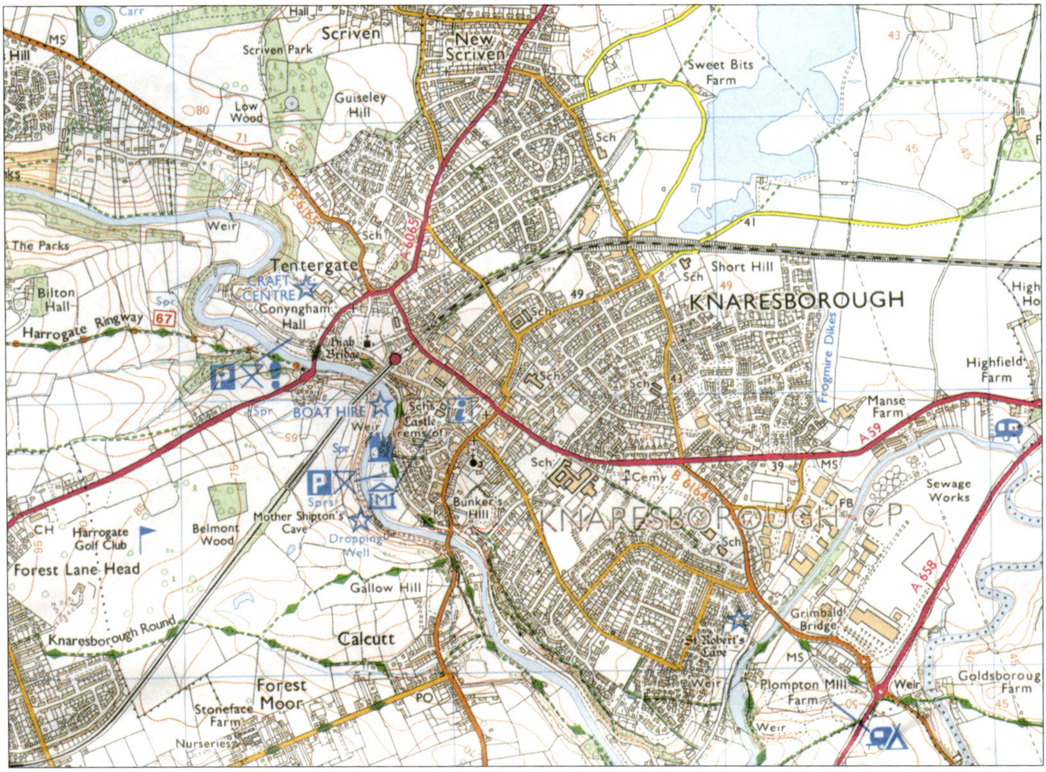

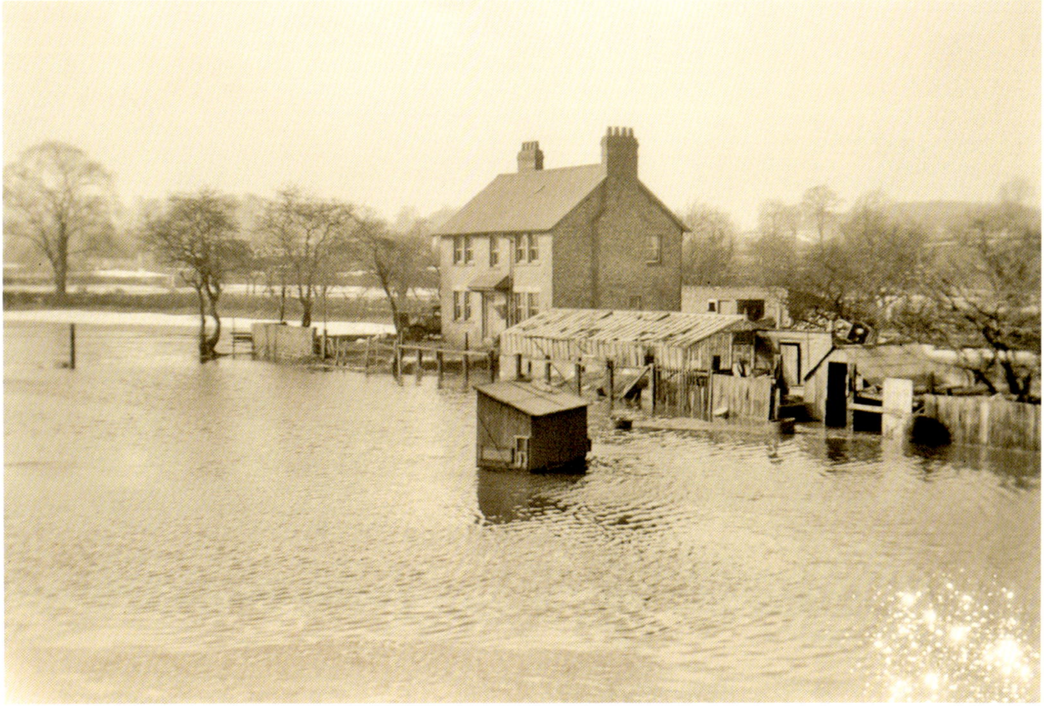

Water Lane under Water

The floods in 1947 were caused by snow melting after the great freeze and, according to residents at the time, were an unusual event. Thankfully the snow shown here in the new photograph in the winter of 2010 melted away without causing much trouble.

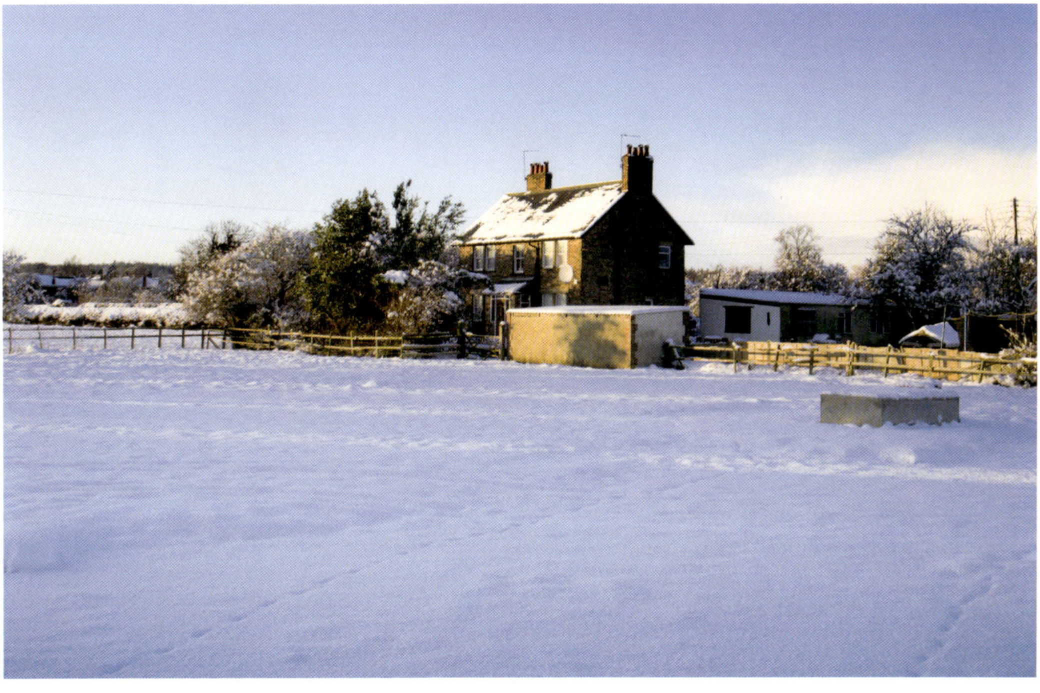

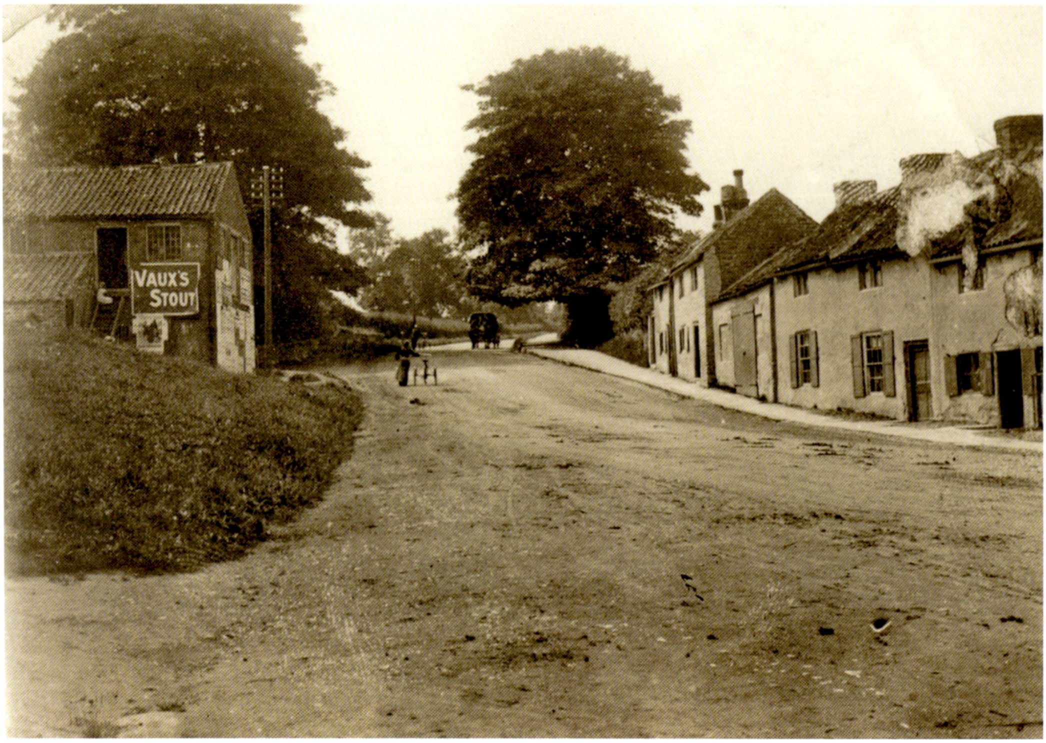

Harrogate Hill

The Vaux 'pub ' on the left of the road (pictured about 1910) has been replaced by the Yorkshire Lass pub on the right of the road – which in turn has replaced the cottages.

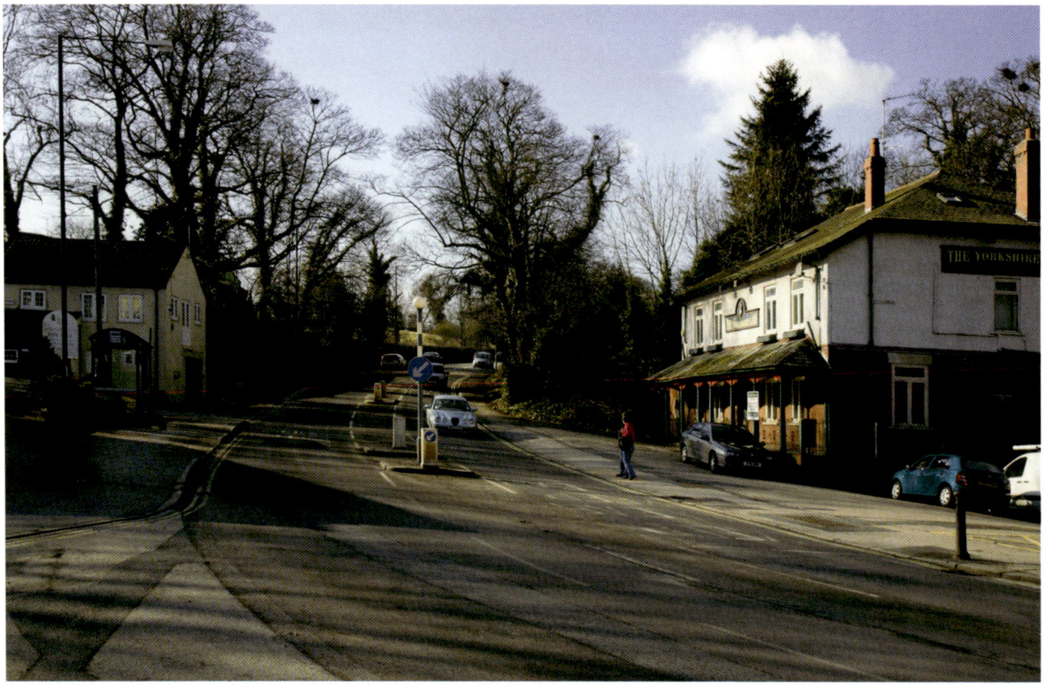

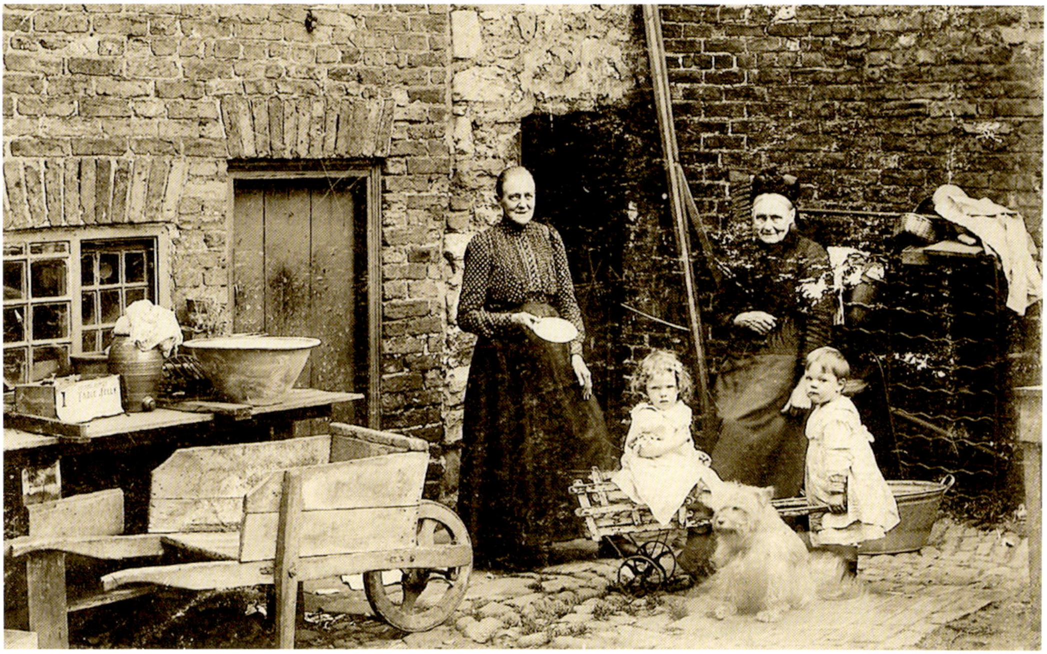

Bond End

A family scene from the end of the nineteenth century in cottages at Bond End near the World's End pub; through various slum clearance programmes these and similar dwellings are long gone; they are now replaced by some attractive landscaping as the new photograph shows. The box on the left contained table jelly.

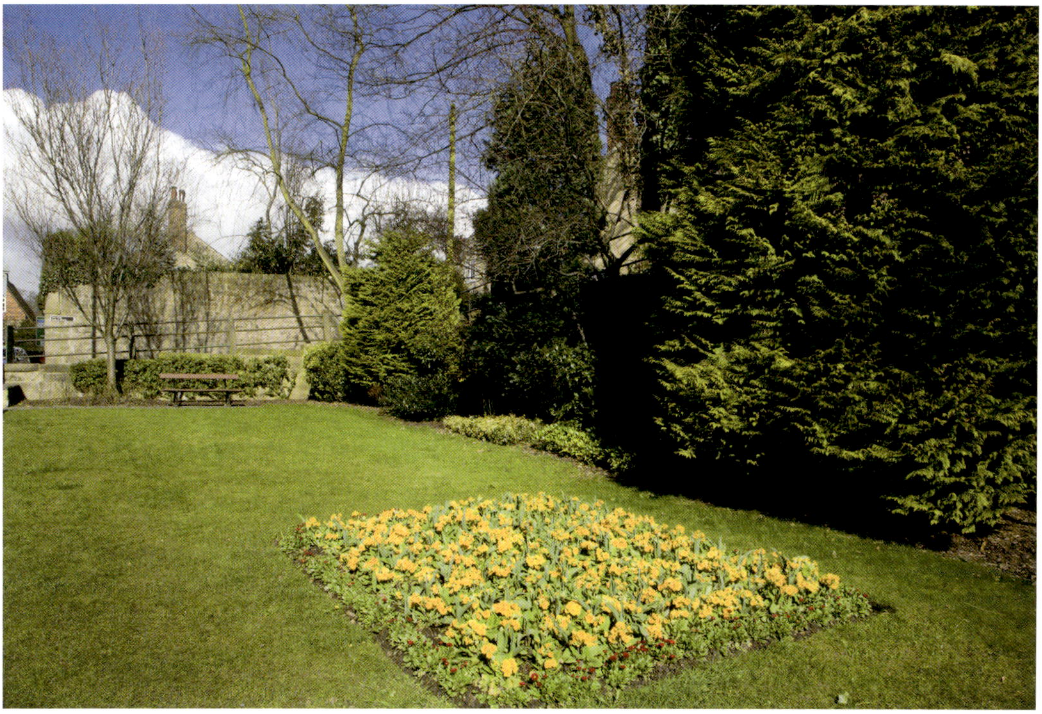

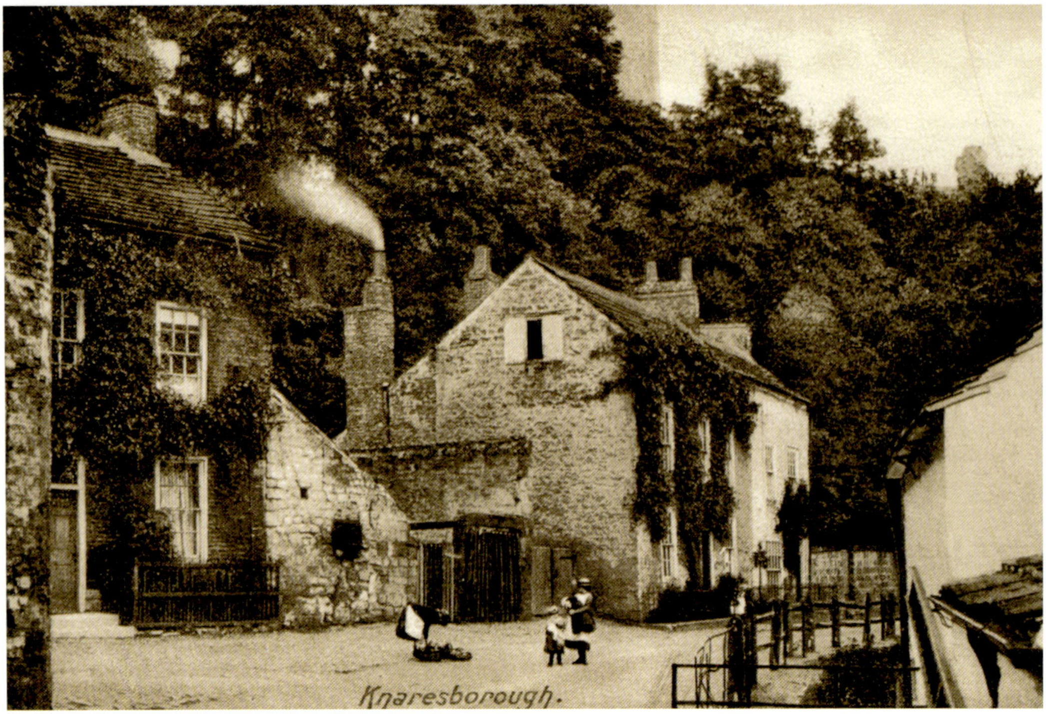

Riverside Cottages
Taken around 1909 with the castle towering in the background, this scene, maid apart, remains much the same one hundred or so years later.

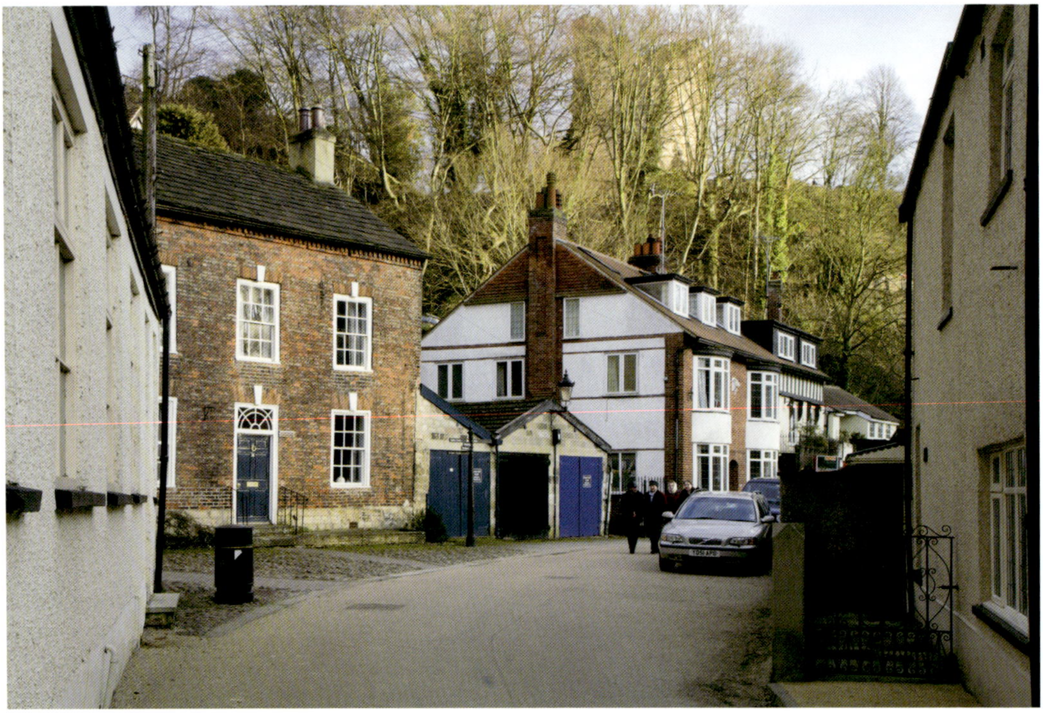

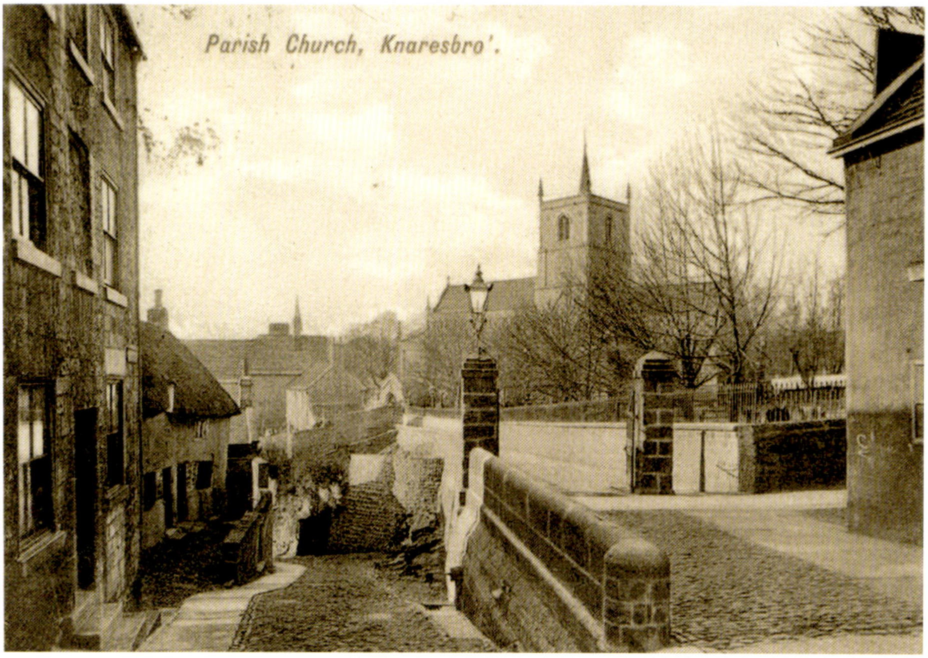

The Parish Church of St John the Baptist

Today the view of the church from where the old photograph was taken is largely obscured by trees. Built largely on Norman foundations it was heightened in the fourteenth century and acquired its unique miniature spire around 1520. Landscaping in 1973 was responsible for the removal of many gravestones. The 1890 *Illustrated Handbook to Knaresborough* tells us that it is 23' long, 67' wide and the tower 81' high with the unusual spire adding a further 27' with seating for 800. The eight bells cost £544 15*s*. 5*d* although this cost was defrayed by selling off the four old bells for £226 10*s*, and voluntary subscriptions of £102. 13*s*. 6*d*.

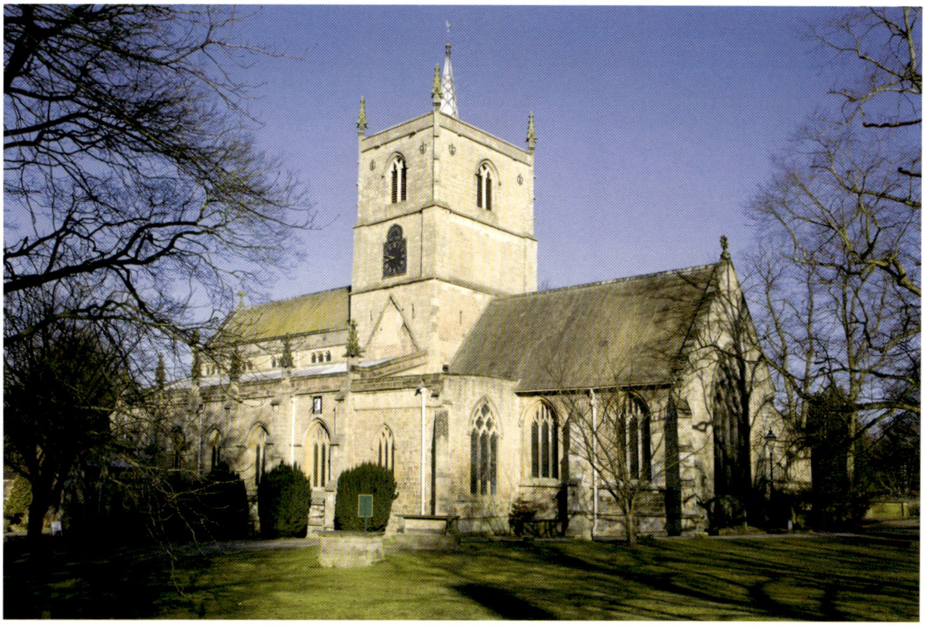

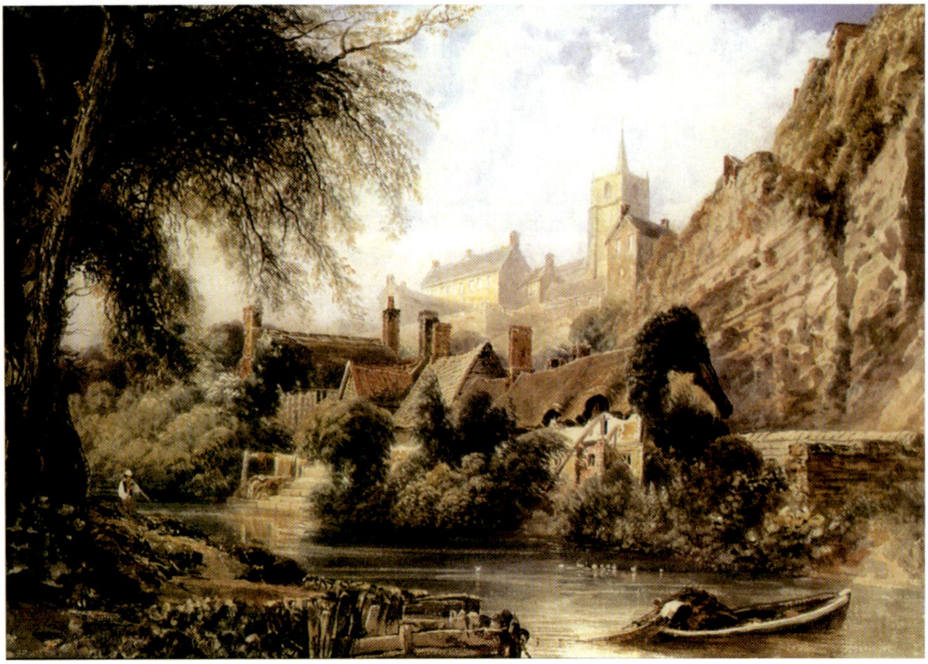

Peter de Wint's Knaresborough

A fine pencil and watercolour (21" x 31")which captures the drama of the scene perfectly with the parish church dominating. By Peter de Wint (1784-1849), English landscape painter. The painting of course predates the viaduct which now neatly frames the church in the 2010 photograph. The parish register begins in 1561 when there were 41 baptisms, 12 marriages and 21 burials. In 1807 there were 156 baptisms, 63 marriages and 129 burials (which means a population of roughly 4000).

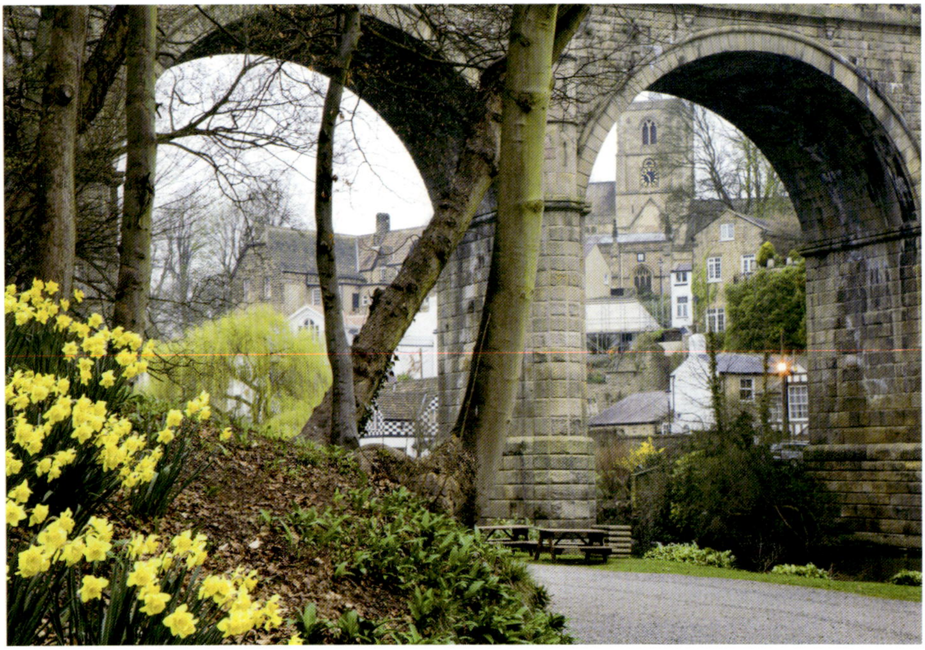

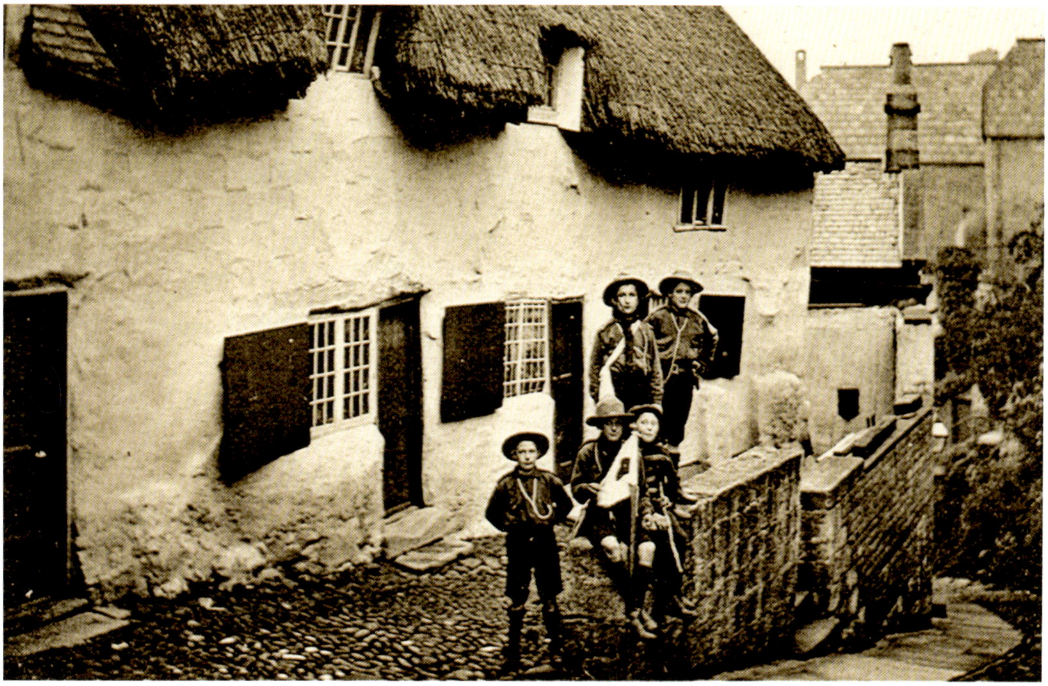

Philip Inman's Thatched Cottage

The scouts (pictured here not long after the movement was formed in 1907) are standing outside the house in Water Bag Bank where Philip, later Lord, Inman of Knaresborough was born in 1892. Inman founded the Tourist Board, was chairman of the BBC and ran British Railways catering – but we can forgive him for that: his life work was at Charing Cross Hospital where over sixty-six years he was Secretary, Chairman and finally Life President. The modern picture shows how the building has been superbly maintained.

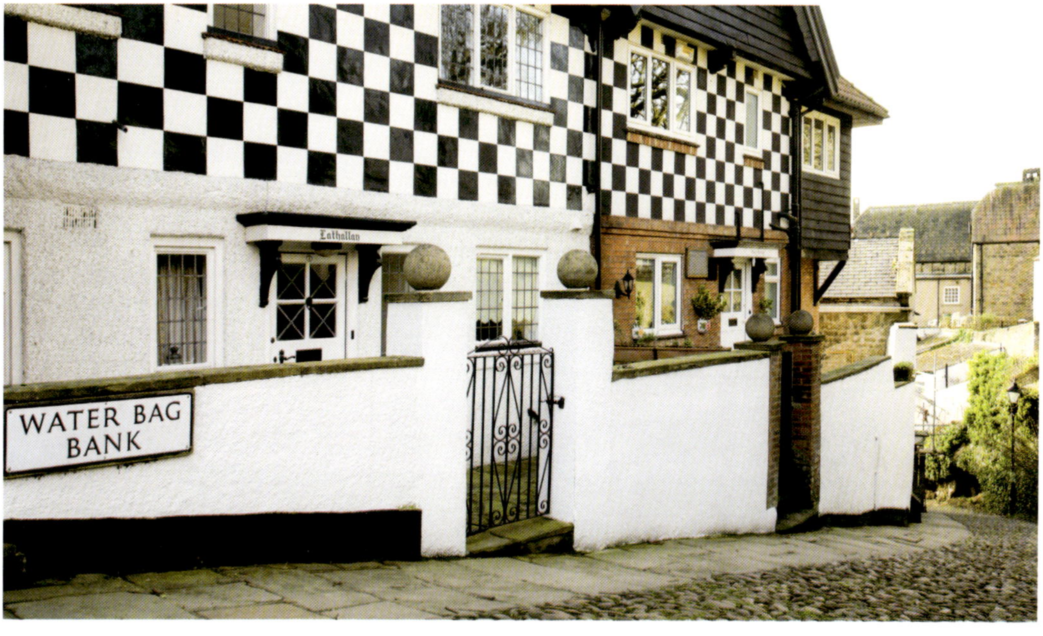

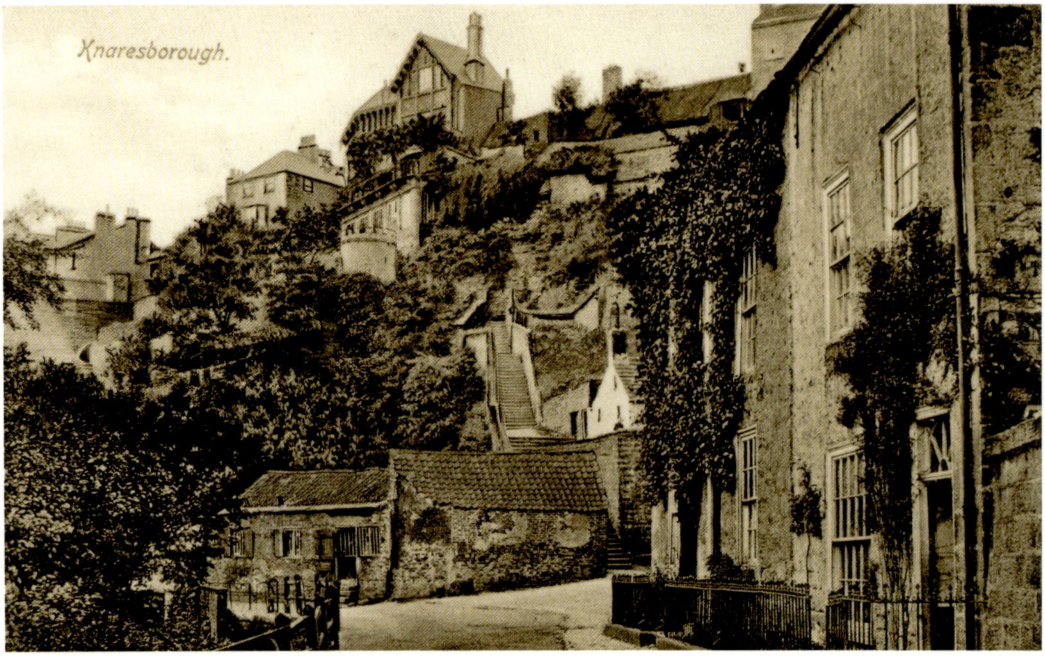

Gallon Steps

The ninety-six steps connecting Kirkgate with Waterside and named after a Mr R. N. Gallon who had a house at the top. This photograph was taken about 1926. You can just see the circular sally port in the middle of the old picture and the two cottages next to the Gallon House Hotel which were demolished to make way for the flat roofed house there now; the kitchen was hollowed out of the rock and provide a good cool room in which to store the ice cream and butter that was made there.

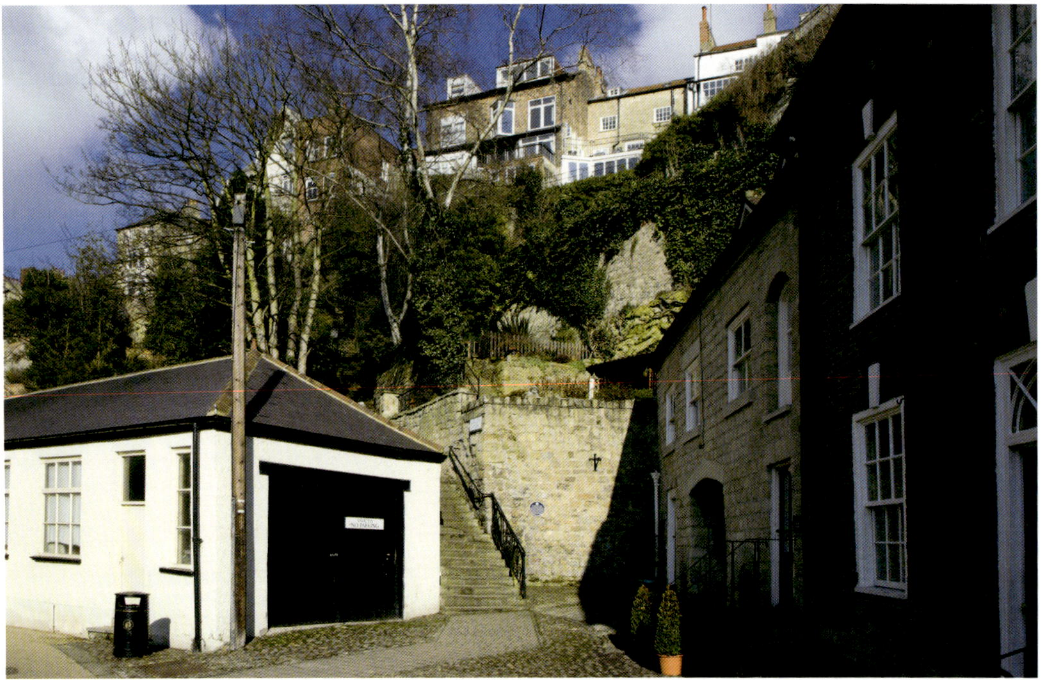

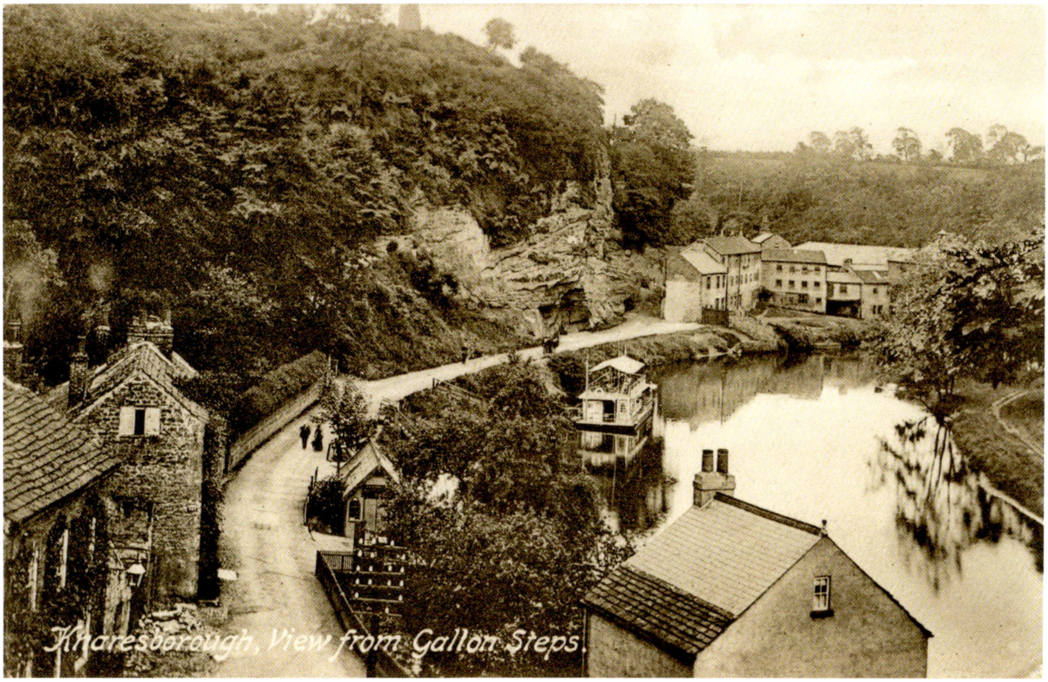

...the view from Gallon Steps

The view from the top of the steps (the new photograph was taken from the Gallon House Hotel, formerly Munich Villas) still affords another of Knaresborough's iconic views today. The *Marigold* can be seen on the river in the 1910 shot moored along Waterside; her memory lives on in the contemporary café of the same name.

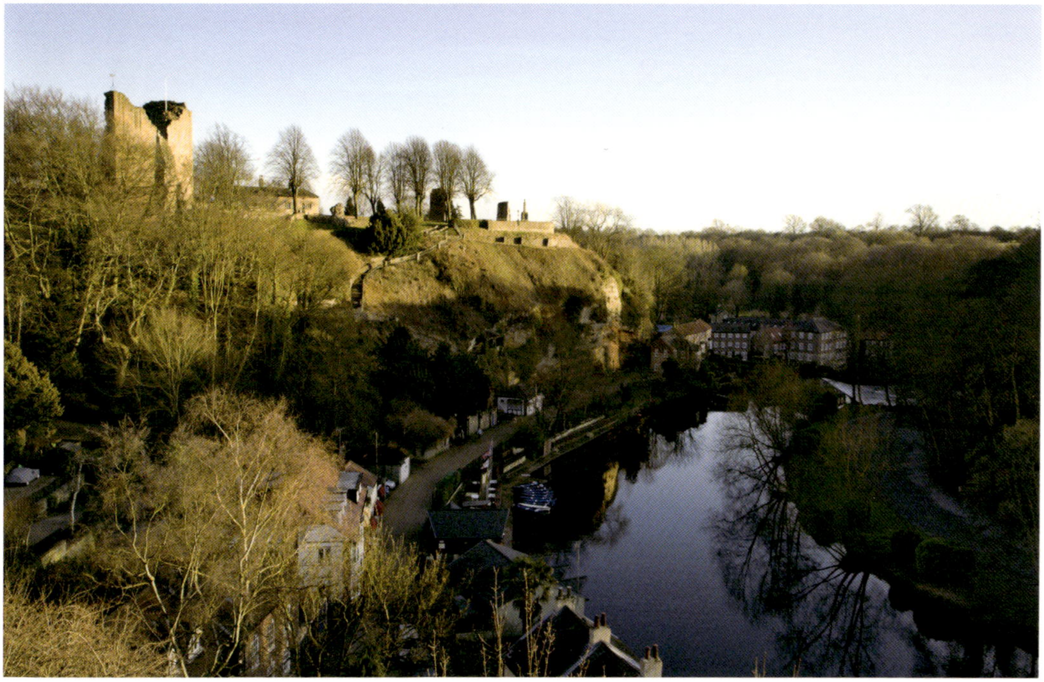

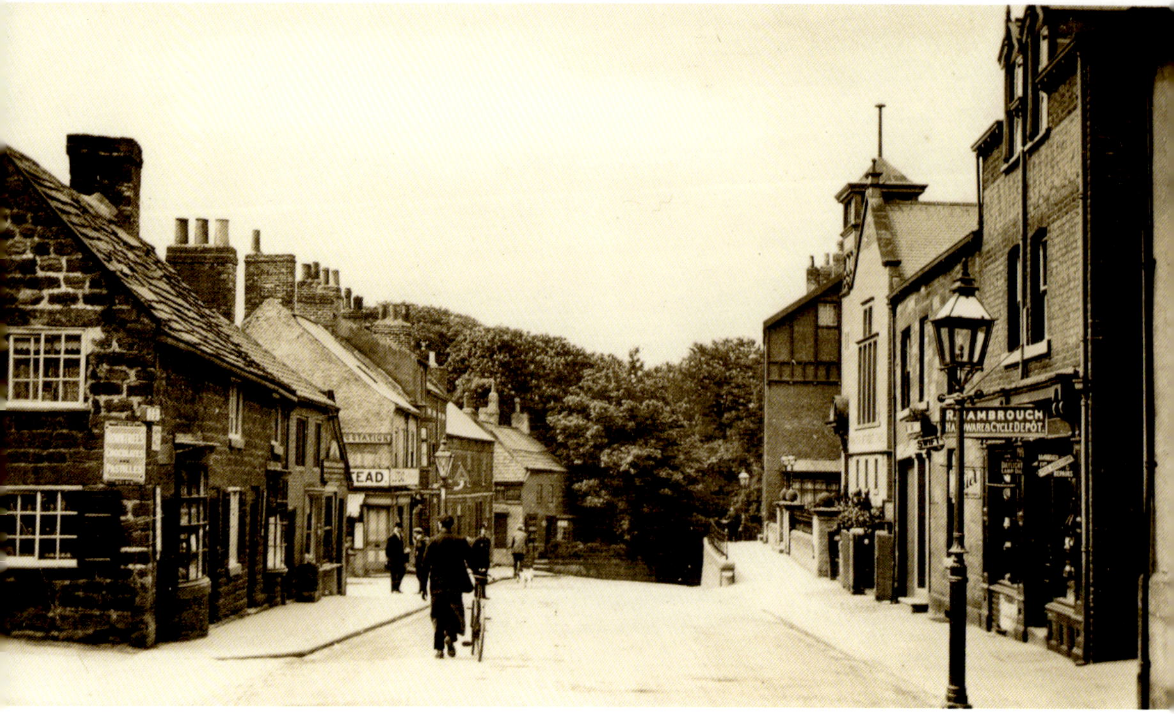

High Street at Hilton Lane

Taken around 1910 in the days when you could take a leisurely stroll down a traffic free High Street this shows one of the town's three Methodist chapels – now a bed shop.

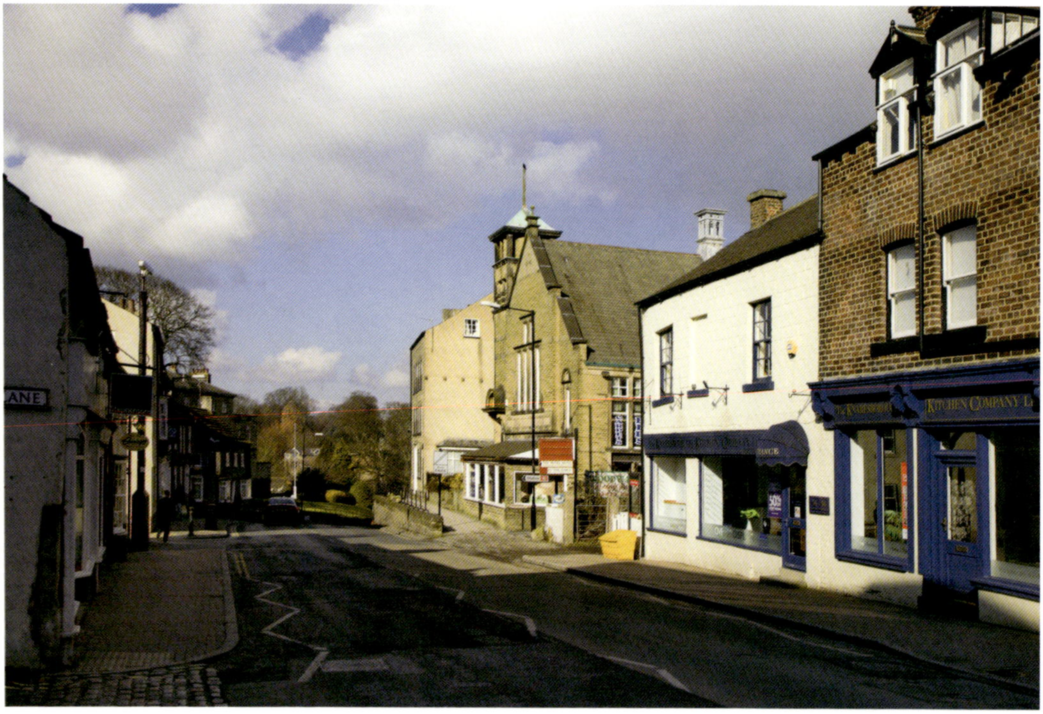

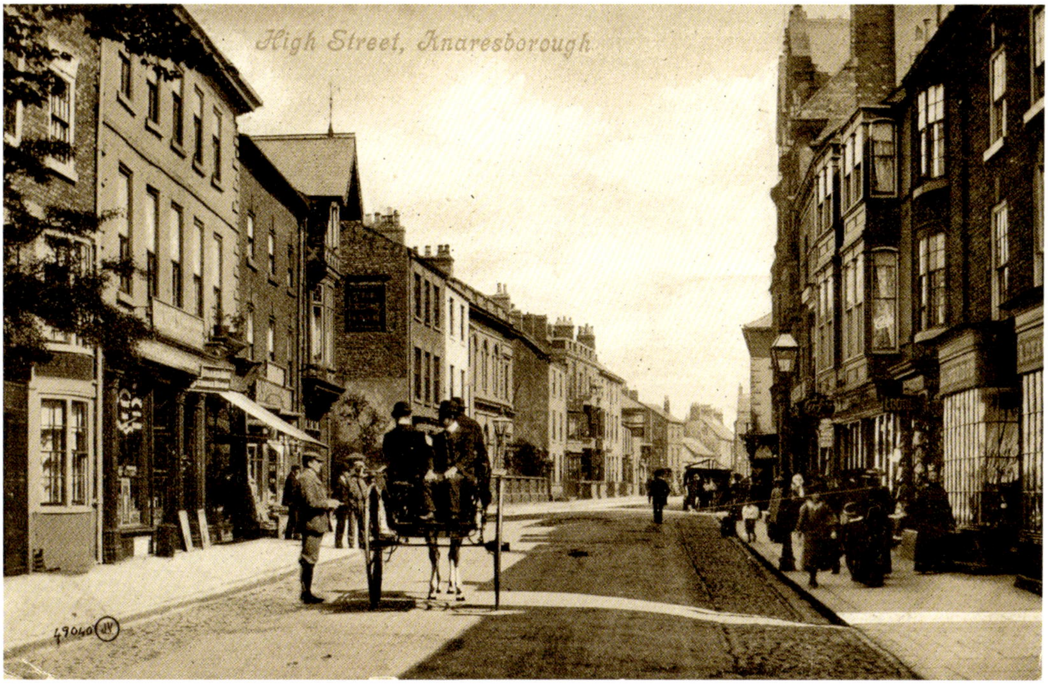

High Street Horse and Carriage

Further up the part-cobbled High Street you can see on the near right Bainbridge & Dearlove the drapers; contemporary adverts tell us 'funerals completely furnished'; stock comes from 'Selections from the Best Warehouses in London & Manchester...at prices within the reach of all'. Next door is Wood's – painters and sign writers. The gable-roofed pub on the left is the Eugene Aram cornering on White Horse Yard (now Park Square) where Aram had his school. Aram was a fraudster eventually found guilty of the murder of Daniel Clark, one of his accomplices (in St Robert's cave where the remains were buried) and hanged at York; his body was then displayed on the gibbet at Knaresborough near the Mother Shipton Inn in 1759, part of which can still be seen today (the gibbet that is).

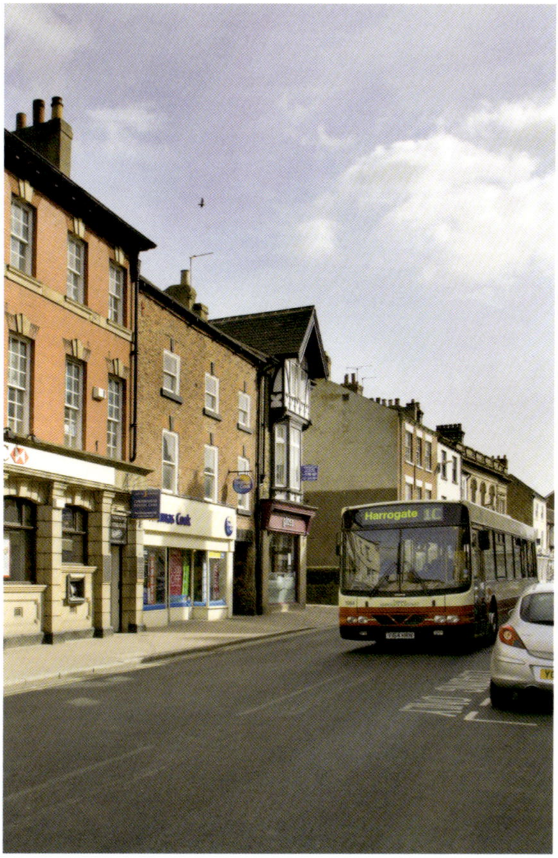

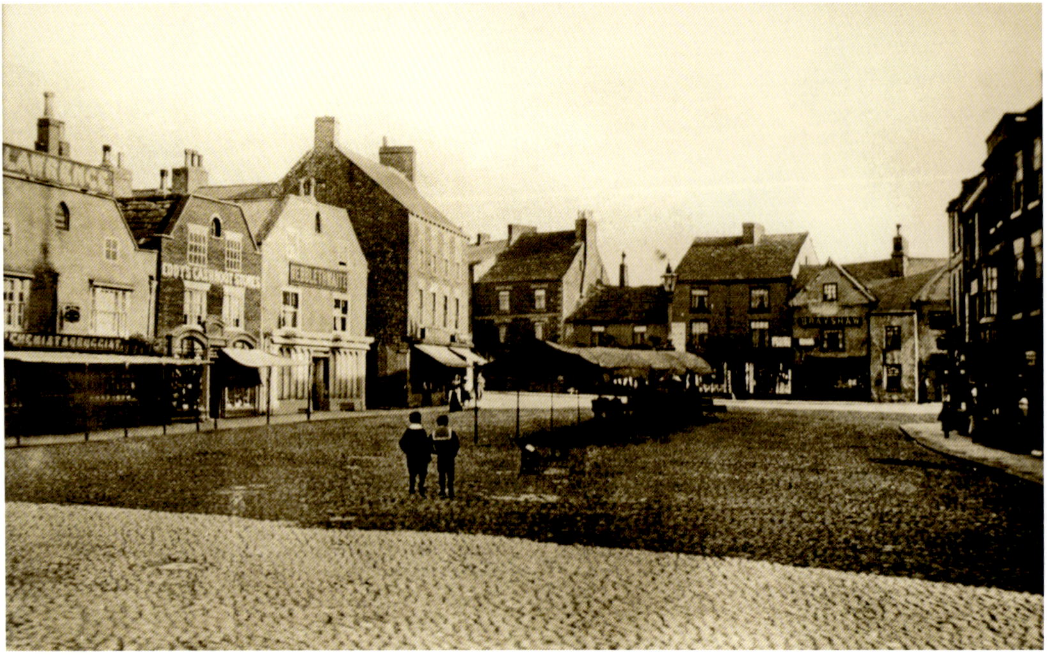

Market Place

A view of an uncharacteristically deserted market place from 1907 repeated in 2010 at the early morning market stall set up. It once boasted a bull ring and stocks (now in the Courthouse Museum) and was one of the venues for the Status Hiring Fair where servants and farm labourers were taken on (pre First World War rates: boys up to £15 per annum, girls and women £20 pa and men £30 pa with board and lodging).

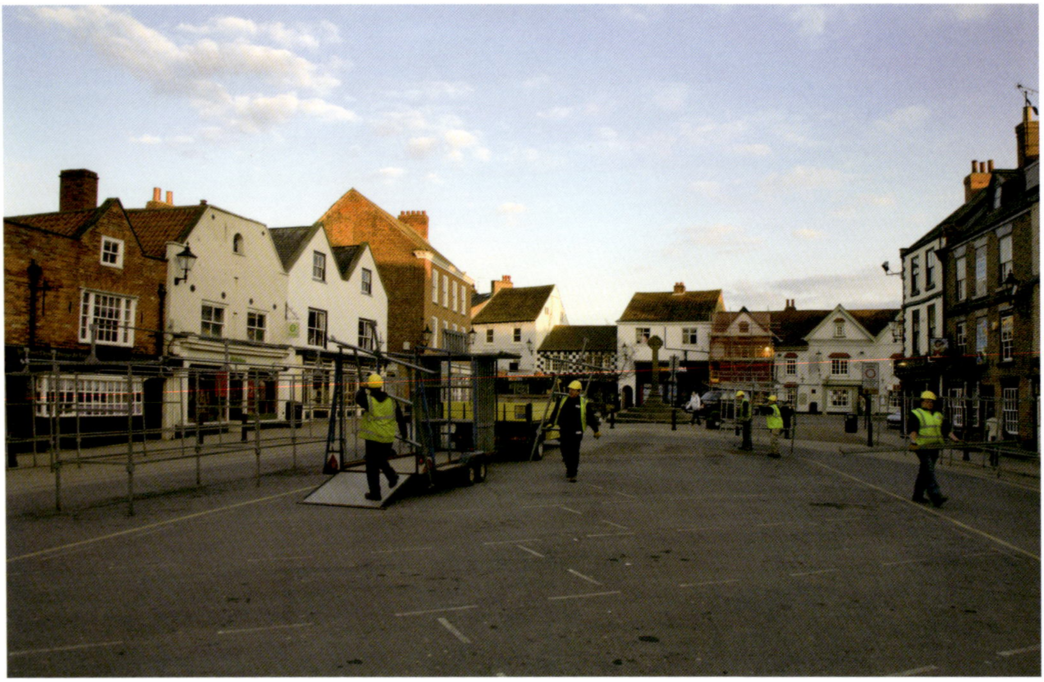

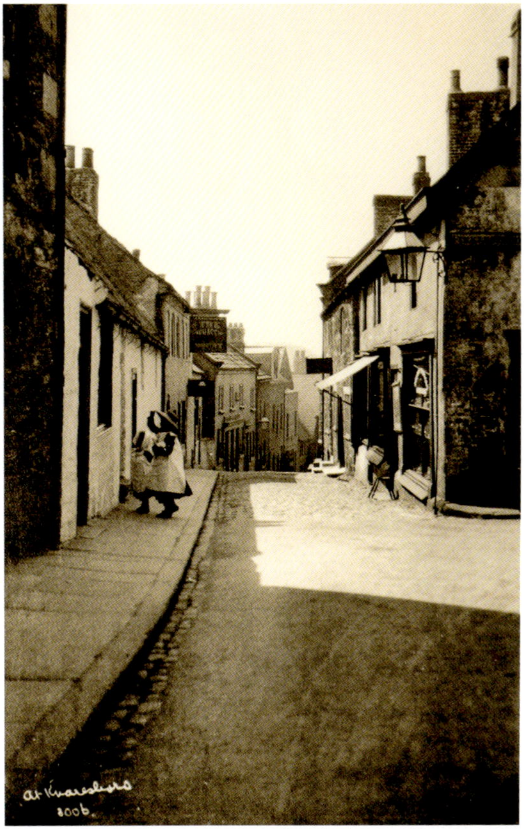

Kirkgate at Finkle Street

Two streets whose names are derived from the Norse for 'church street' and vinkle which means 'corner'. It earned that name because the street follows the line of the old rampart and ends at the north west corner. Finkle Street was originally called Swine Market after the pigs that were traded there. The cottages on the left date from 1721.

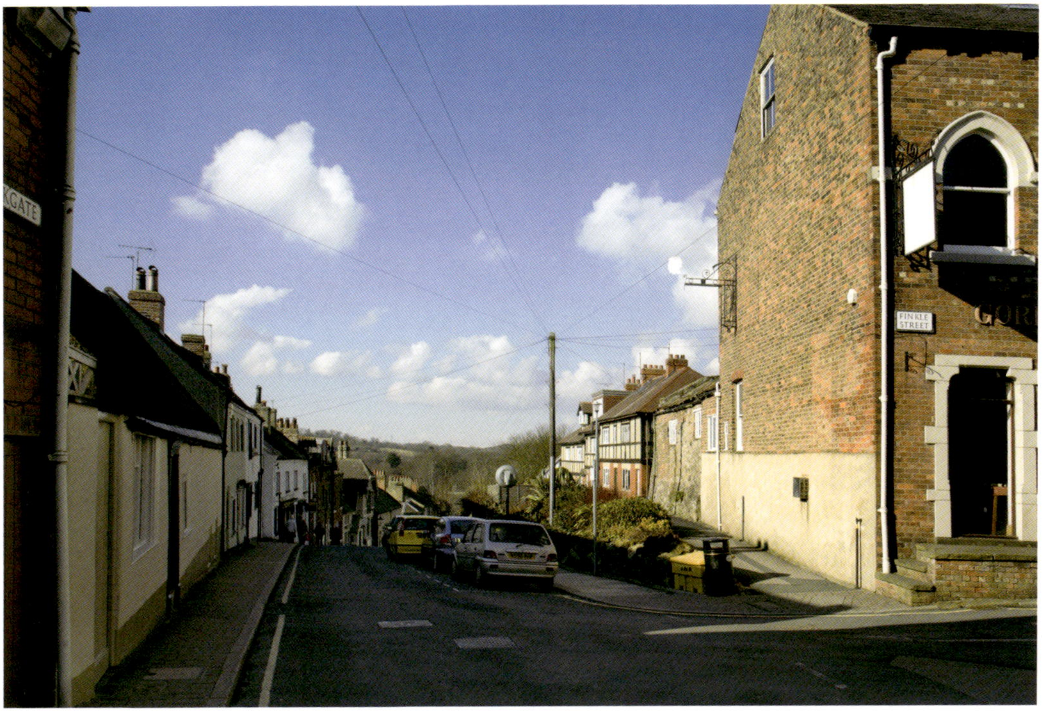

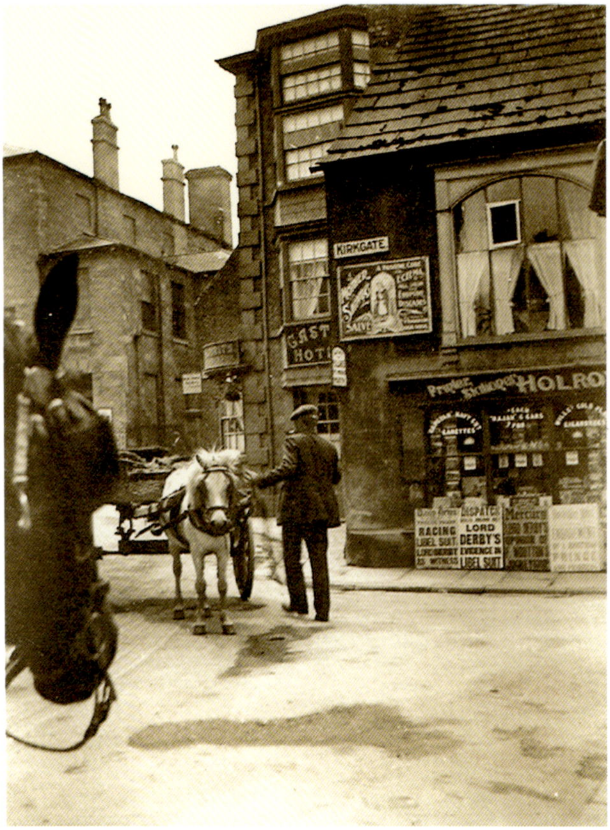

Kirkgate Horse, Carriage and Traction Engine

Holroyd's was a newsagents, printers and stationers as the boards outside show; it later became Herrington's the newsagents; now the site is occupied by the Bella Sicilia restaurant. The old police station is in the building on the left replaced now by its modern equivalent bristling with aerials; the pub in between is the Castle Vaults. The traction engine, though not typical of today's traffic, makes an interesting change.

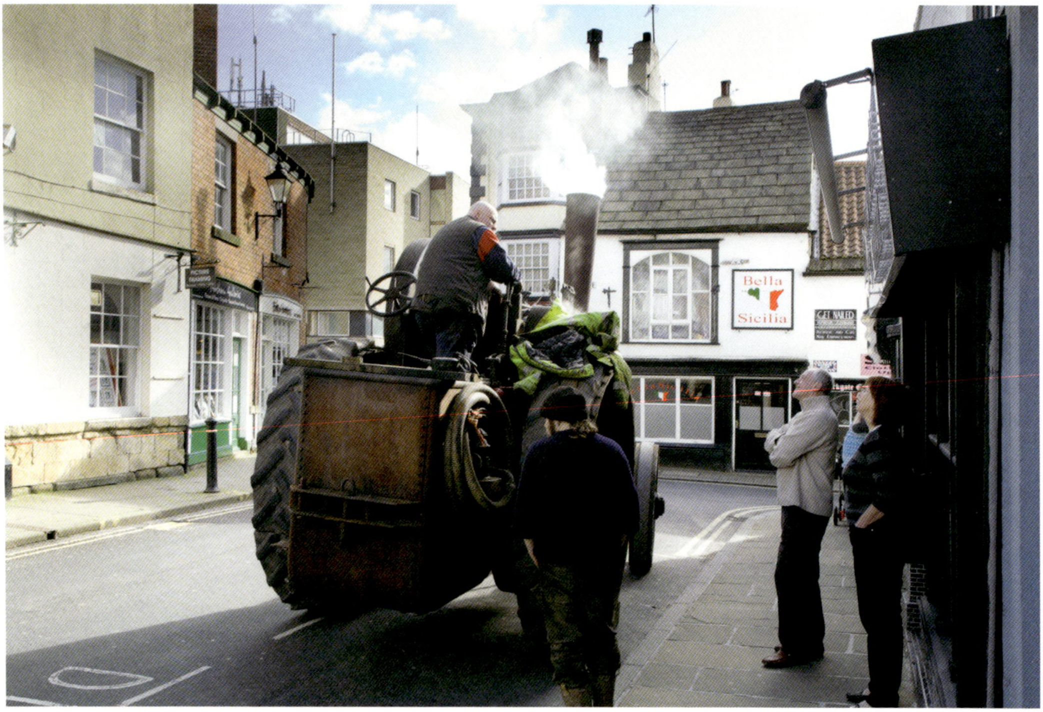

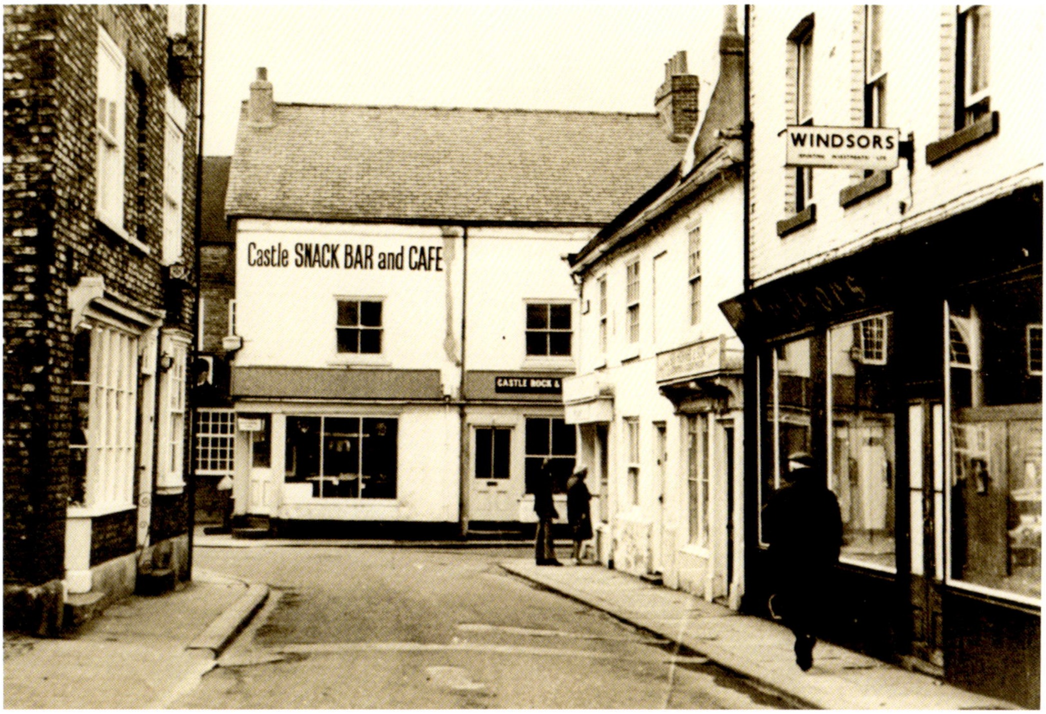

Castlegate

This shot of the street leading us to the castle clearly shows the old café in a building now occupied by a barbers and a dentist.

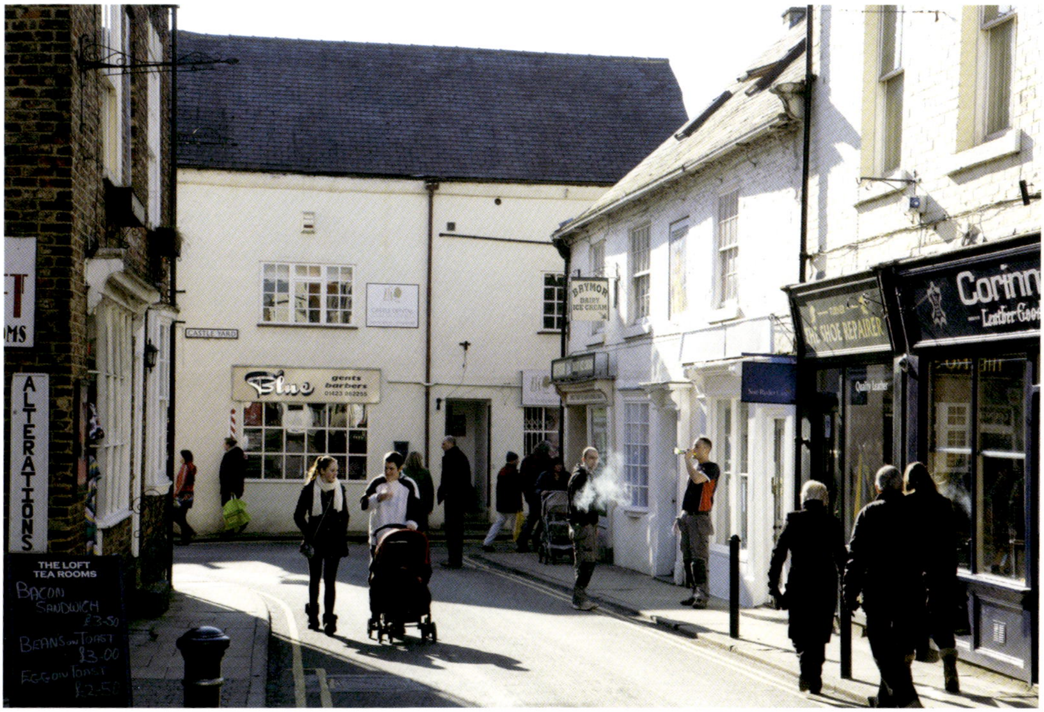

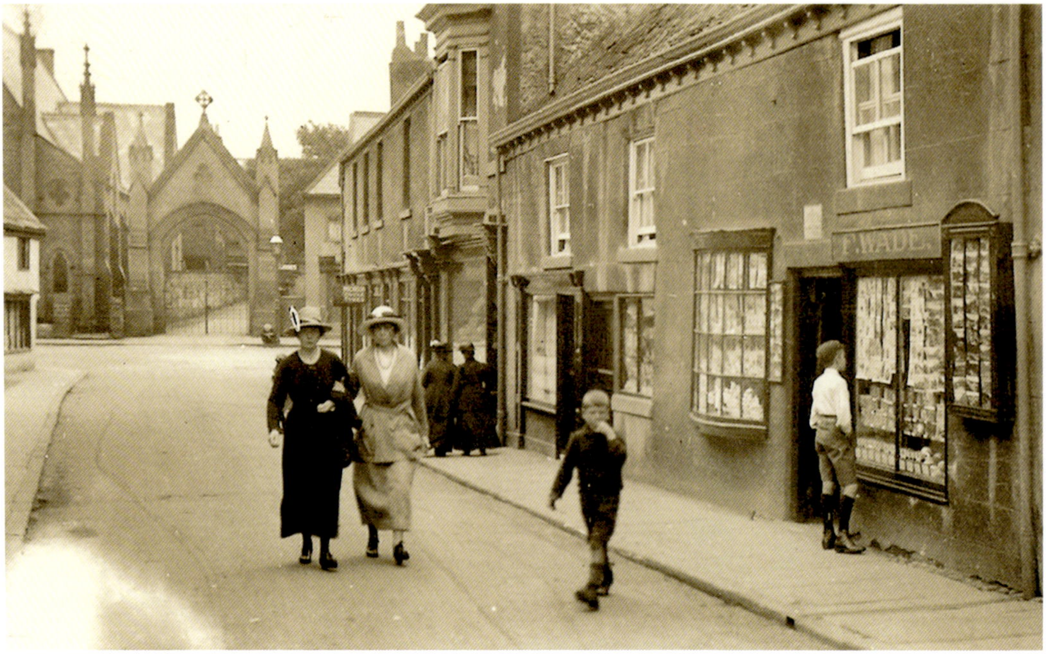

Cheapside

Cheap means market and signifies that this street bordered onto the market. The shop on the near right is F. Wade with the boy avidly looking at postcards in the window. Further down on the right the sign tells us that the shop there sells cycle tyres. Neat cottages have replaced the shops. The entrance to Holy Trinity Church is at the end of the road on Gracious Street.

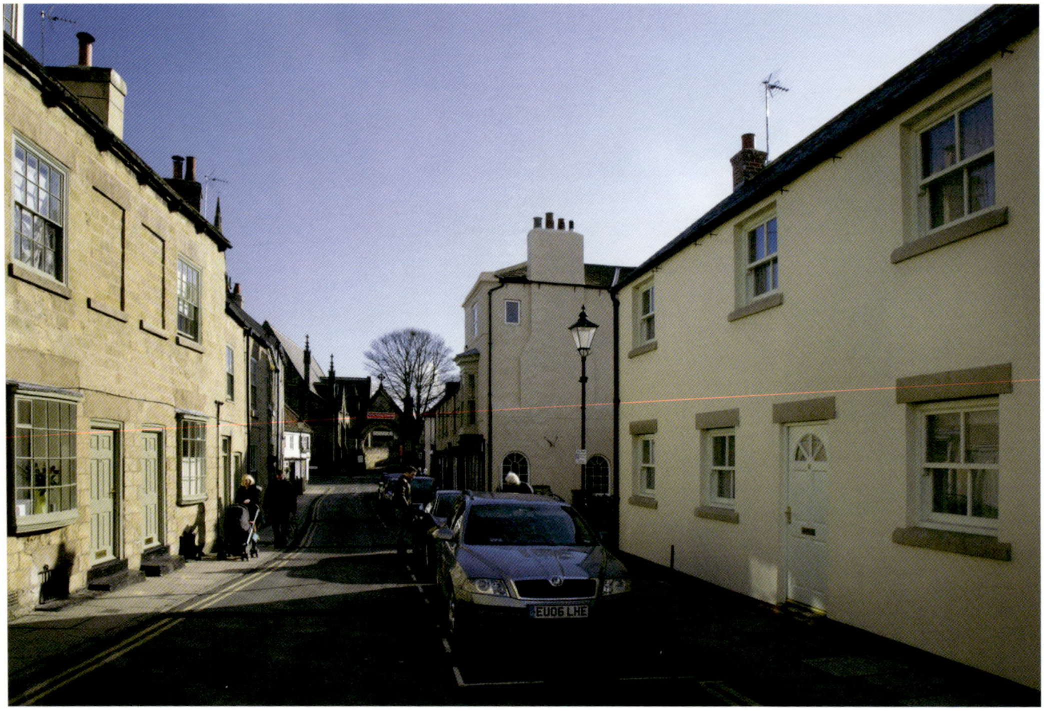

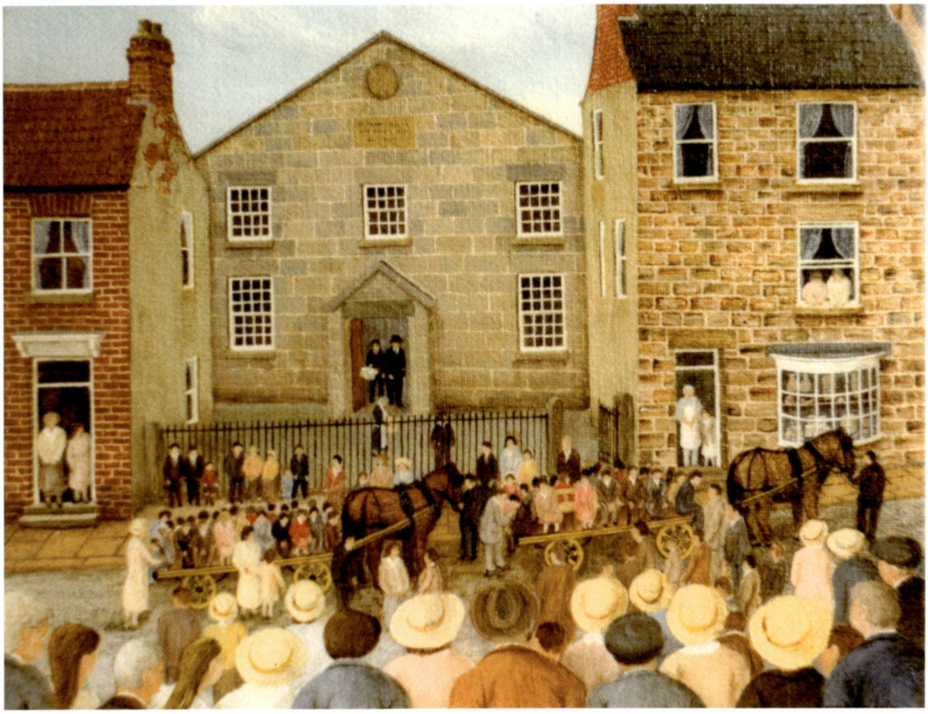

Town Mission Hall

This shows a Sunday School outing setting off in about 1919 from the 1854 Primitive Methodist Chapel at the top of Briggate and later called the Town Mission. The main Methodist chapel was built in Gracious Street; opened in 1815 it was also known as the Waterloo Chapel (after the battle in the same year) and held 800 worshippers; the third chapel was in the High Street.

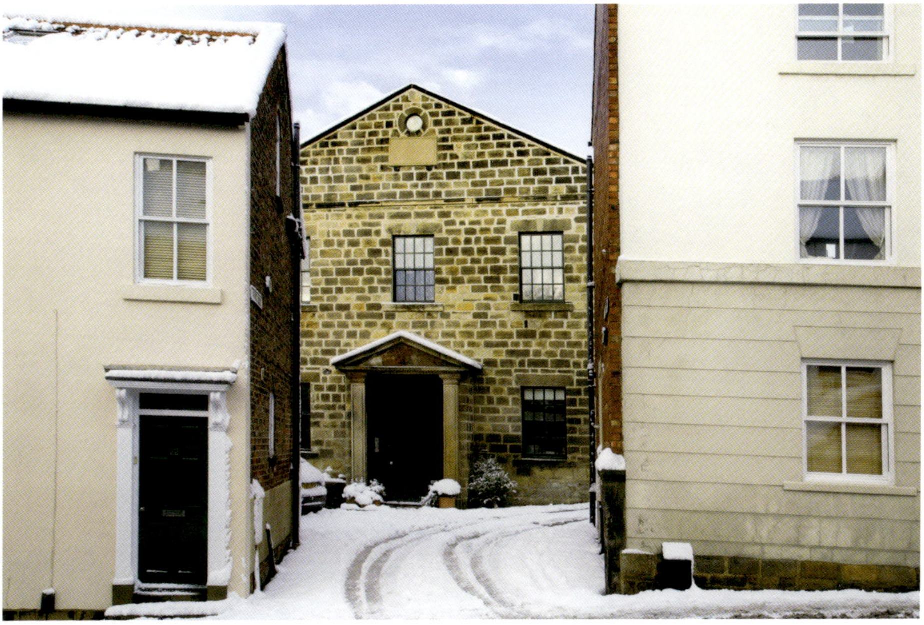

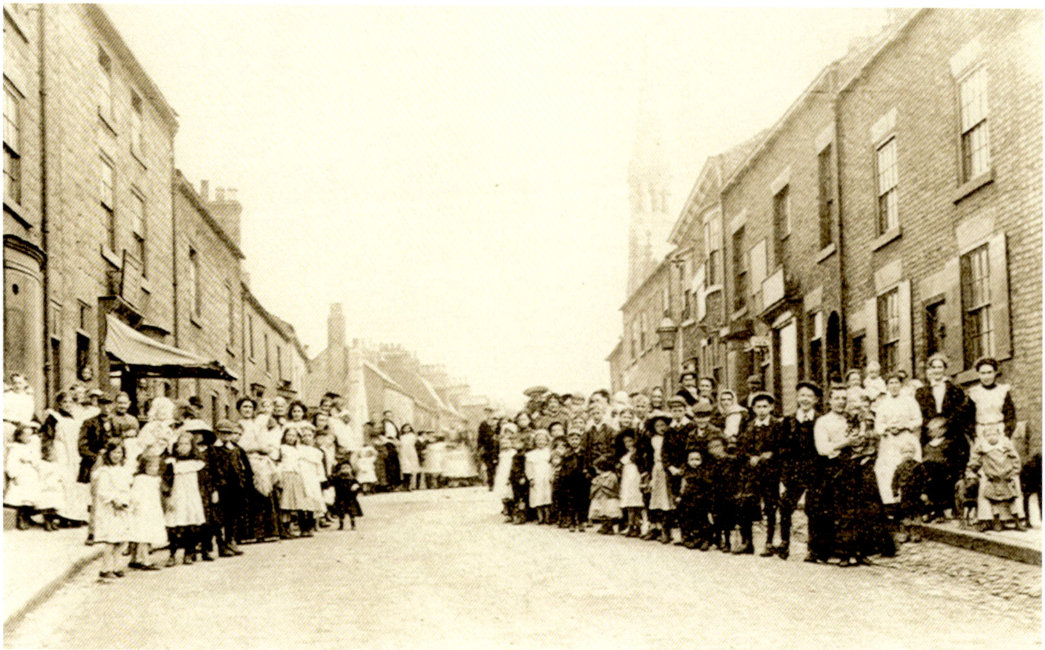

Briggate

Meaning bridge gate and, in this case, leading to Low Bridge. These Methodists posing at the top of Briggate were from the Town Mission Hall a building which later became a raincoat factory. The United Reformed Church is on the right renamed from the Knaresborough Congregationalist Church built in 1865 for £2200. An 1851 census counted the religions of the Knaresborough residents as follows: 2047 Anglicans, 843 Methodists, 227 Congregationalists, 105 Baptists and 250 Roman Catholics.

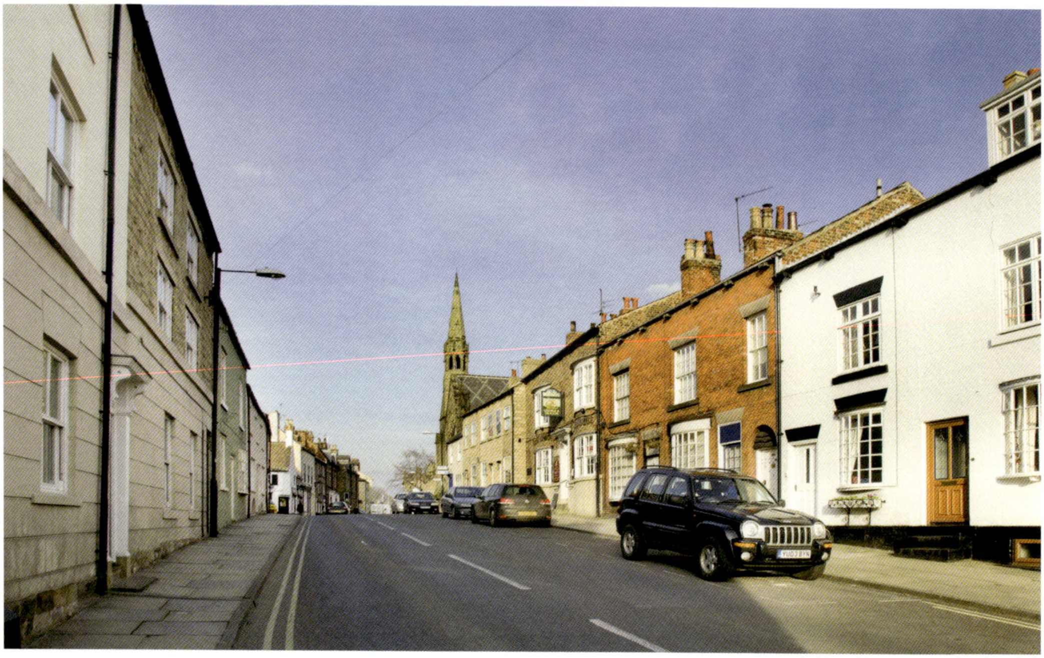

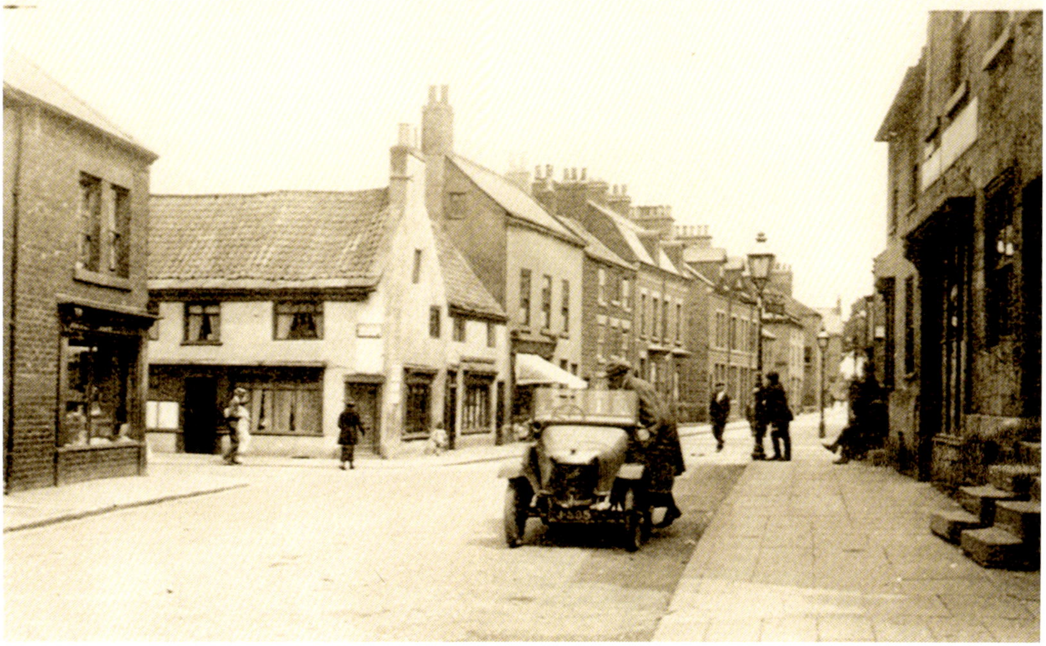

Gracious Street

A far cry from the traffic which now fills this street. The name derives from the Saxon word *grachthuys* for 'near the ditch' and may signify the former presence of the town's open sewer along here. The building on the corner of Cheapside dates from around 1644 and now accommodates a launderette.

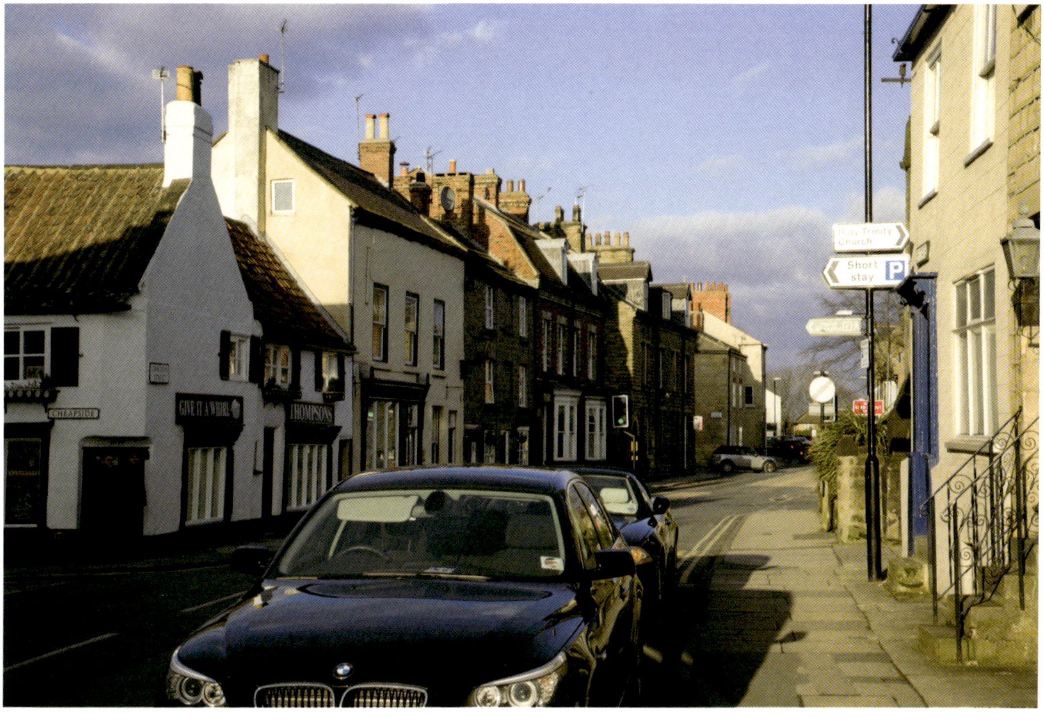

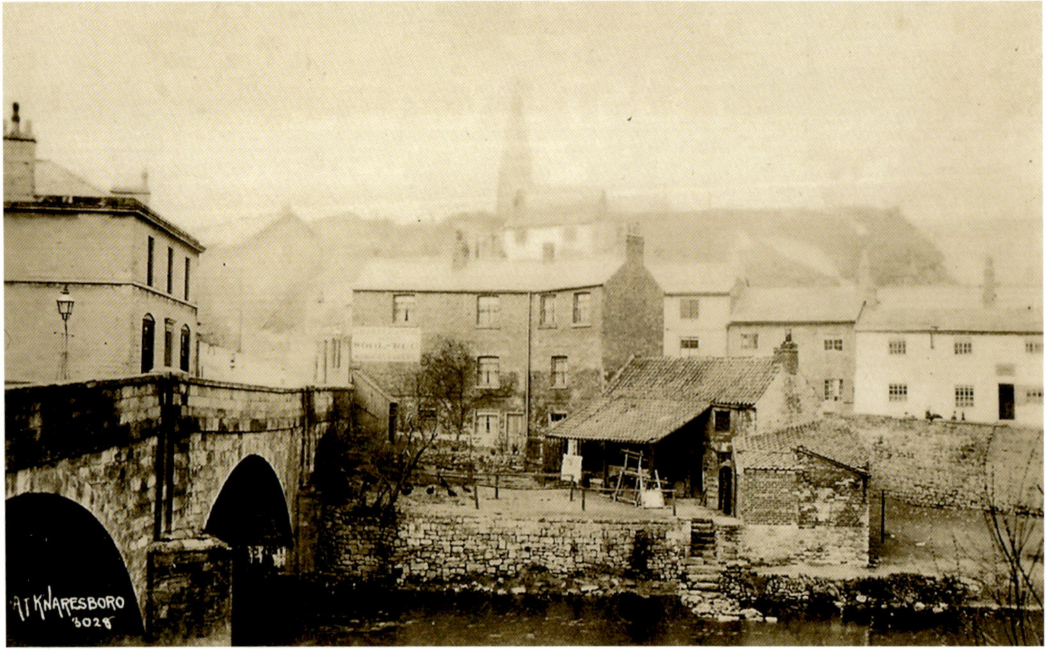

Low Bridge

Formerly known as March Bridge (which means a boundary) Low bridge was widened in 1779. The 1856 Holy Trinity Church off Gracious Street dominates the horizon with its 166 foot spire; designed by John Fawcett it cost £3, 800 to build. Harker's the rug manufacturers is at the far end of the bridge; it is now long gone although the other buildings over the road in Abbey Road largely survive, one of which is a shop selling doll's houses, models and second-hand books.

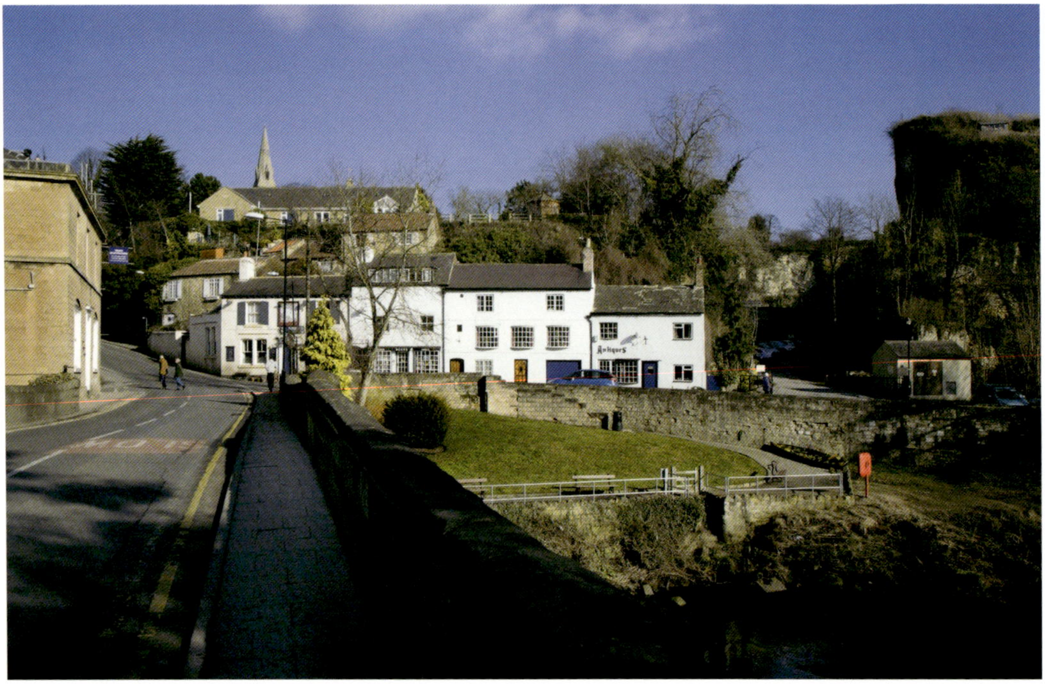

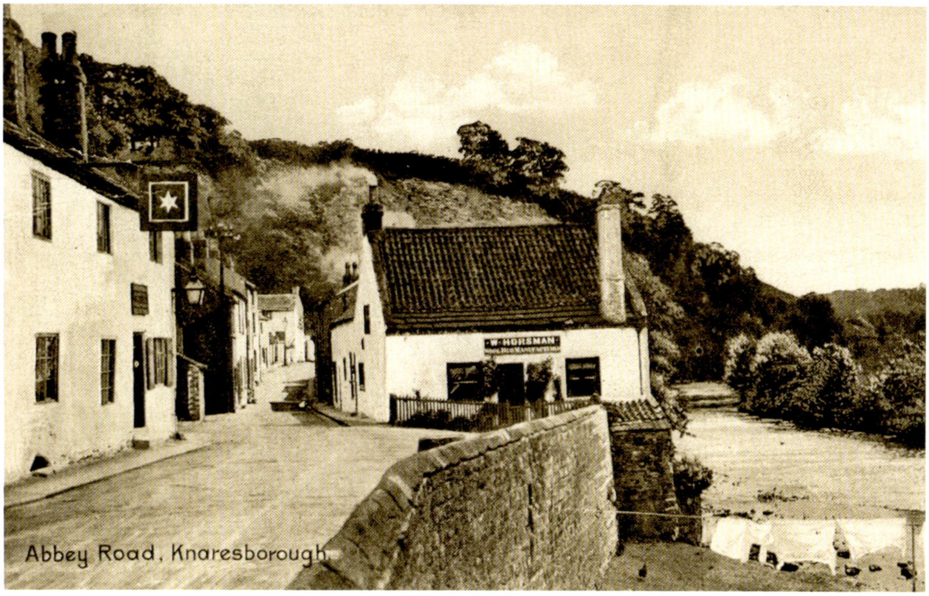

Abbey Road with Washing

The Star Inn on the left and Horsman's the rug maker on the right of Abbey Road. This once led to the friary (the Trinitarian House of St Robert) which stood just below the Chapel of our Lady of the Crag. The original priory had been destroyed in 1318 by the armies of Robert Bruce but rebuilt by Edward III. In 1366 Archbishop Thoresby decreed 'that in future the cloister and dormitory should be kept free from the invasion of secular persons, and especially women of doubtful character, both day and night.' Robert Ashton, one of the organisers of the Pilgrimage of Grace was a friar here in the 1530s. The washing, part of the pub and Horsman's are no more but much else remains the same.

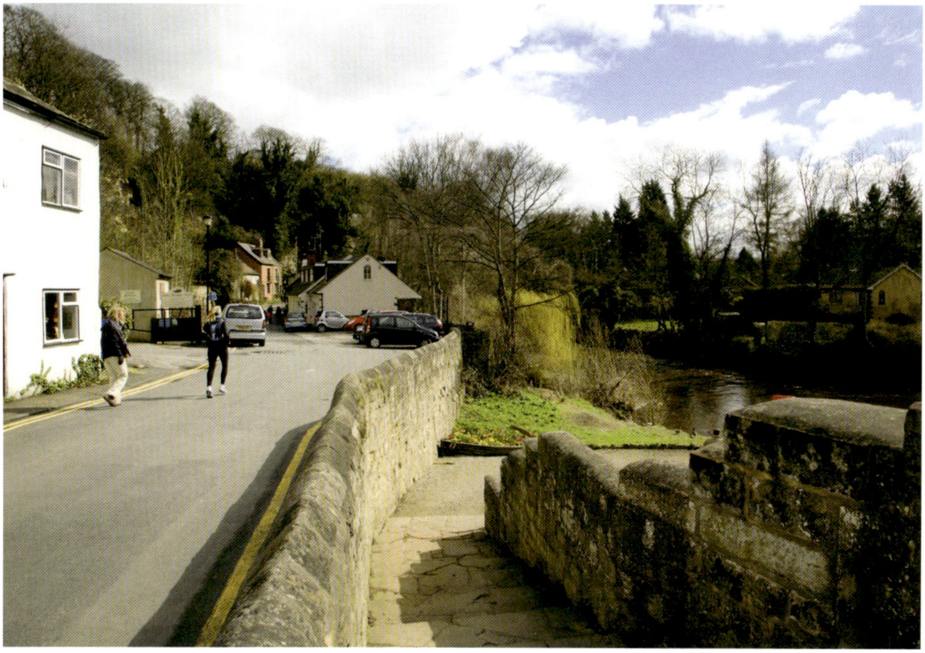

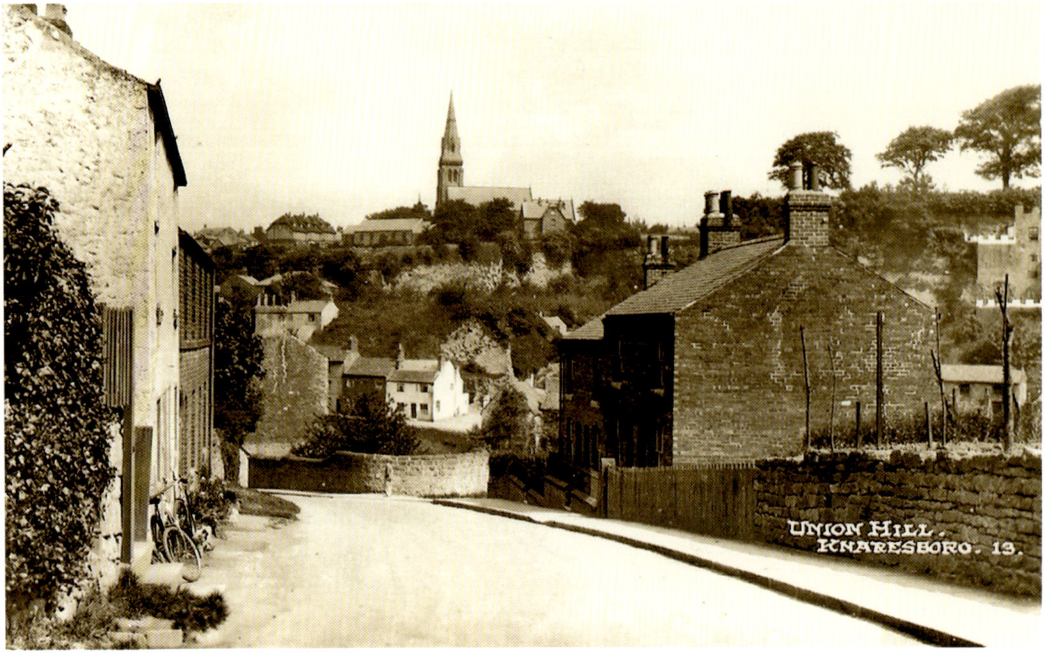

Union Hill

Leaving Knaresborough on what is now Blands Hill, if you pause to take one last look at the town, Holy Trinity Church again dominates the horizon. On the left is Birkham's View comprising Hoy Towers and Granddad Cottage. Originally there was a café here popular with cyclists. To the left was a blacksmith's forge. Middleton's Cottages are on the right. What was the Star Inn in Abbey Road is the white building which can be seen in the distance in the older photograph.

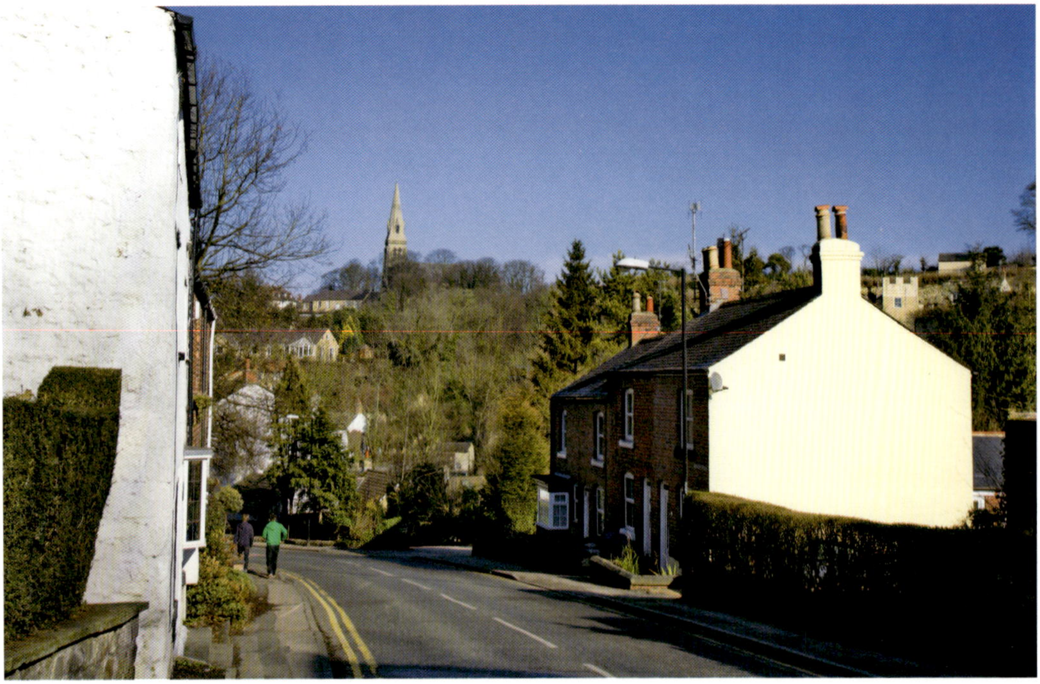